ULTIMATE
GOLF
TECHNIQUES

ULTIMATE
GOLF
TECHNIQUES

MALCOLM CAMPBELL

SPECIALIST CONTRIBUTOR
STEVE NEWELL

SPECIAL PHOTOGRAPHY
DAVE CANNON

DORLING KINDERSLEY
LONDON · NEW YORK · STUTTGART · MOSCOW

A DORLING KINDERSLEY BOOK

For my father and for Janey and in memory of my dear mother who played the last so bravely… and Bill McCandlish who played sadly fewer than he should.

PRODUCED FOR DORLING KINDERSLEY BY
COOLING BROWN
9-11 HIGH STREET, HAMPTON, TW12 2SA

PROJECT EDITOR David Preston
ART EDITOR Alistair Plumb
ASSOCIATE EDITOR James Harrison
ASSISTANT EDITOR Tim Barnett
PICTURE RESEARCH Phil O'Connor

Dorling Kindersley Limited
EDITOR Sharon Lucas
MANAGING EDITOR Francis Ritter
MANAGING ART EDITOR Derek Coombes

Copyright © 1996
Dorling Kindersley Limited, London
Text copyright © 1996
Malcolm Campbell

FIRST PUBLISHED IN GREAT BRITAIN IN 1996 BY DORLING KINDERSLEY LIMITED, 9 HENRIETTA STREET, LONDON WC2E 8PS

A CIP CATALOGUE RECORD FOR THIS BOOK IS AVAILABLE FROM THE BRITISH LIBRARY

ISBN 0-7513-02570

COLOUR REPRODUCTION BY SCANNER SERVICES SRL, ITALY
PRINTED AND BOUND IN ITALY BY A. MONDADORI EDITORE, VERONA

Title (page 2) *The legendary Jack Nicklaus.*

CONTENTS

INTRODUCTION

EVER SINCE MAN first put club to ball in the name of the game we call golf, he has been obsessed with finding a better way to play it. The very nature of the game guarantees it. In golf there are clear winners and just as clear losers, and no-one wants to be on the wrong side of that equation. Success, in golf, is not a matter of opinion. There is no panel of judges to award marks for content or artistic impression; there are no team-mates upon whom to divert the blame for defeat. The scorecard indelibly exposes the outcome, and this damning evidence of record is there for all to see. In golf, there is simply nowhere to hide.

Walter Hagen
Winner of 11 major championships, Walter Hagen was not only an inspiration to those who followed him, but he also brought great style to the game.

ROAD TO IMPROVEMENT

From the earliest days on the east coast of Scotland, where the game laid its roots five centuries ago, those who have persevered in this insidious triangular conflict between nature, the elements, and fellow human being have been in search of improvement. They have sought a road to advancement to take them through the metamorphosis that turns a mere player *at* golf into a player *of* golf, and with it acceptance by the fraternity. No game in the history of organized sport has been so obsessed by the techniques for this accomplishment. A whole industry, almost as big as the game itself, has evolved to encourage the golfing pilgrim to find the promised land. Millions of words have been written by learned men and perhaps even more by others not so erudite –

Bobby Jones (right)
Bobby Jones learned to play by mimicking the rhythmical swing of his local professional.

The Home of Golf (left)
The unmistakable links of St Andrews.

Sam Snead
Nicknamed 'Slammin' Sam' because he hit the ball immense distances, Sam Snead might just as easily have been named 'Swingin' Sam', for he has long been renowned for having one of the best and smoothest golf swings around.

on the subject of how to improve at the game. Golfing gurus, whether self-appointed or sanctified have, in their droves, led followers onwards and upwards in dedicated search of golf's eternal truth.

Nevertheless, the trail of ongoing failure continues to stretch through the average golfer's life. Occasionally they might stumble upon that most winsome of suitors, 'the cure', which for a while eases their burden. It can be something very simple; a swing thought, a new takeaway, a repositioning at address or, at its most extreme and financially penal, a complete new set of golf clubs.

THE QUICK FIX

The outcome is that euphoric state recognized by all golfers in which they believe they have at last found the ultimate truth. Suddenly drives are longer and straighter, iron shots crisper, even the putts begin to drop. They start to figure in the monthly medal. There is a new sprightliness of step, a bonhomie rekindled. But for most this is little more than a false dawn; illumination has been no more than

hallucination and soon despair looms again. The quest resumes for another quick 'cure', but the cycle of elation followed by failure becomes a process that repeats itself with considerably more

Ben Hogan
There is no better example of what can be achieved in golf through dedication and practice than the legendary Ben Hogan, one of the greatest players of all time.

consistency than that enjoyed by most golf swings. The beguiling 'quick fix' with the promise of lavish rewards is no more than fool's gold.

The object of this book is not, therefore, to offer false hope or the promise of an instant cure for every golfing malady. Neither is it to reveal some long-hidden 'secret' kept locked away and jealously guarded for generations. For in truth the only 'secret' to playing better golf is that there is no secret at all. There is no short cut to sustained improvement, only a well-trodden track along which everyone who enjoys genuine success has had to pass at some stage.

This law of golf applies as much to the professional as it does to the amateur. It is only the scale of achievement that is different. Teachers of golf are, broadly speaking, either professional golfers or enthusiastic amateurs. Professional golfers know how to play but not necessarily how to teach, while enthusiastic amateurs, it must be said, rarely know how to play nor how to teach. This volume is the response, therefore, to a long-held conviction that, ultimately, we can all be our own best teachers.

Arnold Palmer
Such was the popularity of the swashbuckling Arnold Palmer that when he putted with a knock-kneed style in his early career, millions of golfers around the world immediately followed suit.

Gary Player
South African Gary Player is a classic inspiration to all golfers lacking in physical stature. By dint of intense hard work and dedication, Player turned himself into one of the strongest golfers in history.

Jack Nicklaus
Jack Nicklaus has the finest record of any player in the history of golf. His capacity for intense concentration and always selecting the right shot to play is a model for any players who wish to improve their game.

We know our capabilities better than anyone, providing we are honest in our self-evaluation. Teaching ourselves, a unique opportunity exists to use the received wisdom of generations who have pioneered the way before us, for real and meaningful progress. We can all learn from the great players, both past and present, providing we know what to look for and how to apply it.

Byron Nelson
Byron Nelson is recognized as having one of the best swings in the history of the game. He has spent his latter years as the mastermind behind the phenomenal success of Tom Watson.

David Leadbetter
One of the top teaching gurus of the present day, David Leadbetter's expertise has been sought by many of the game's leading players, including Nick Faldo and Nick Price.

WATCHING AND LEARNING

The success of the great players of the modern era, from Ben Hogan and Sam Snead through to Jack Nicklaus and Arnold Palmer, and on still further to Nick Faldo, Ernie Els, and John Daly, owes virtually everything to the development of the techniques of the game by the great players of the previous generation such as Walter Hagen, Bobby Jones, and Sir Henry Cotton. Yet this trio, in their turn, had already taken the game forwards as a direct result of what was learned from those who came before them, such as Old Tom Morris, Allan Robertson, and the Great Triumvirate.

And just as all these great players learned by careful study of their forebears, so too can we learn from those who have mastered the game. Everyone who plays golf has the capacity to improve. In the case of the low handicap player the extent of any possible improvement is obviously restricted much more than for the

Bob Toski
Like Gary Player, Bob Toski was not gifted with great physical stature, but he nonetheless became a top golfer and, later on, one of the world's foremost teachers of the game.

higher handicap player who has greater room for manoeuvre. For the less skilled player, the emphasis is most likely to be on technique, while for the better player, strategy and management of the overall game may well hold the key. The clues to finding the way forwards lie with those who have found the answers that work.

Ernie Els
South African Ernie Els is the classic example of the modern player, combining exceptional strength and power with a delicate touch.

ULTIMATE AIM

In assembling this volume it has been my determination not to promote my view, nor anyone else's for that matter, of the right or wrong way to play the game of golf. Rather it has been to distil a golfing elixir from the knowledge, teachings, and experience of generations of the world's greatest players, from which we can all take a sip in the eternal quest for improvement. This book is proffered solely with that objective in view and if I have succeeded in any part I will rest well content.

Nick Faldo
In his determination to become the best player in the world, Nick Faldo took two years to 'remodel' his swing under the guidance of his teaching mentor, David Leadbetter.

MALCOLM CAMPBELL
Lower Largo, Fife, Scotland.

John Daly
Although John Daly is renowned as a player who can send the golf ball phenomenal distances, his touch around and on the greens is also an object lesson for those who think that power alone is the key to successful golf.

Robt Jones Jr.
June 25, 1930.

CHAPTER ONE

The PLAYERS and the TEACHERS

Golf instruction via a cigarette card in the early 1920s

IT IS A FUNDAMENTAL *truth that there are as many different swings as there are golfers playing the game, all aimed at developing the predictable, repeating action – the foundation of the modern golf swing. However, it has not always been so. Much of the way golf is taught* today has been influenced by changes in equipment and the rule book. Just as important has been the example set by the top players down the generations.

Golf tuition has developed into an industry worth multi-millions and this chapter looks at the players, equipment, and teachers who have influenced its development.

Master of all trades
The greatest amateur player of all time, Bobby Jones retired in 1930 but has continued to inspire generations of players through his teachings in print and on film.

Golf magazines have always been a major source of tuition for golfers keen to improve their technique

Learning by example

MANY PRESENT-DAY professionals would shrink from the swings of their 19th-century predecessors. Even more would be amazed at the equipment of the time. Yet from the earliest days, golf has been about watching, learning, and refining. Whether it has been through invention, deed, or even inspiration, the great players of every era have played their part in formulating and influencing the way the game is now played and taught.

Old tutor
The legendary Tom Morris Snr learned his early golf at St Andrews as an apprentice to Allan Robertson in his ball-making shop alongside the Old Course.

Gentleman players
The cost of playing golf up until the mid-19th century meant that it was strictly a pastime for the gentry, as this scene from the North Berwick club in Scotland illustrates. The less wealthy were restricted to playing the role of caddie.

For most of us, our ideas of how to play golf are conditioned by what we observe and learn from others, be they top-flight professionals, recognized teachers, or simply our partners in a Sunday morning fourball. But up until the middle of the 19th century it was only a handful of privileged people who had any idea about how to play golf at all.

Golf was little more than a pastime with virtually no organization and restricted to a relatively limited number of players. They consisted mostly of the gentry, who could afford the cost of clubmaking and more particularly the very high cost of the feather balls of the time.

"Stand as you do at fencing. Hold the muscles of your legs and back and armes…

fixt or stiffe, and not at all slackening them in the time you are bringing down the stroak. Your armes most move but very little; all the motion most be performed with the turning of your body about." And so, in the 1687 diary of Thomas Kincaid, continues one of the earliest insights into how to play golf. Though alien to those who play the game today, these methods continued to be the benchmark until the middle of the 19th century.

Men such as Tom Alexander and Tom Geddes, from Musselburgh, near Edinburgh, together with the brothers Tom and Alexander Pirie, of St Andrews, were foremost among the game's early masters with the feathery ball. But it was Allan Robertson, widely regarded as the finest player of his day, who is now generally

recognized as the first golf professional. He made feather balls in his shop alongside the famous Old Course at St Andrews, assisted by Tom Morris Snr – later to become known as Old Tom and one of the game's most legendary figures.

THE END OF THE FEATHERY

These early exponents had techniques developed from play with the feather ball, a fragile leather pouch filled with boiled goose feathers. Of little relevance to the game we now play, these techniques were as much addressed to preventing damage to the ball as to the outcome of the stroke itself. However, the arrival of the gutta percha ball in 1848 signalled the end of the feathery, and the effective end of Robertson's business. The new ball was made from a rubber-like substance obtained from the tropical percha tree. It was recyclable and much less expensive to produce, thereby allowing golf to spread among the masses.

The evolution of the grip
The old-style 'baseball grip' (left) was the only recognized way to hold a club until the arrival of the overlapping grip (above) at the turn of the century.

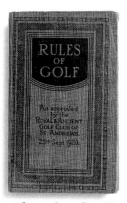

The Rules of Golf
Drawn up in 1764, the rule book now places strict restrictions on the type of equipment used.

Social background was never a bar to anyone interested in playing 'the gowf' in Scotland; it was just the cost that made it prohibitive. However, the *guttie* ball brought an increased stream of new players who wanted to learn to play. But there was no real framework for teaching them. Many introduced themselves to the game by becoming caddies and took the opportunity to play whenever it presented itself; they learned by copying their employers on the links when they had a free moment.

With the added durability of the gutta percha ball, players could hit as hard as they liked and new techniques inevitably followed. With hard hitting, though, came the necessity to cushion the shock of the blow, for the guttie ball was stone hard. Padded grips of chamois leather protected the hands while leather inserts in clubheads helped absorb the shock, as well as helping to protect the soft beechwood heads.

THE BASEBALL GRIP

The thick grips made it necessary to hold the club in the palms of both hands, with the thumbs outside the grip (similar to the way a baseball bat is held). The hands were then allowed to slide on the shaft during the swing. All the top players of the period made their reputations by holding the club in this way. Robertson and Morris were two who used this method and their example was followed by great amateurs of the latter part of the 19th century such as John Ball Jnr, Edward Blackwell, Harold Hilton, Horace Hutchinson, and J.L. Low.

Though the grip undoubtedly served them well, the baseball style seems slightly incongruous when compared to the fingers-and-hands grip used by the majority of modern-day players. Indeed, the great British champion Henry Cotton was once moved to question how any of these great players "could win such fame" with such loose grips.

As the century drew to a close, a new breed of players emerged, one that recognized the benefits of both hands working together on the grip. Among them were the Great

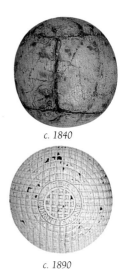

c. 1840

c. 1890

Old balls
The feathery ball (top) was not only expensive to produce but was also extremely fragile. It was killed off by the arrival of the rubber guttie (bottom).

Early swinger
An early swing sequence of James Braid dating back to 1903. Notice that, while the left foot is pointing at 90° (left), the rest of the address and backswing have changed relatively little (right).

Gripping yarn
A member of the Great Triumvirate, J.H. Taylor was one of the earliest exponents of the overlapping grip.

Triumvirate of James Braid, Harry Vardon, and John H. Taylor, together with Leslie Balfour Melville and John Graham Jnr. All employed the kind of grips that would not look out of place on a course today.

THE TWO-HANDED GRIP

It was at about this time that the overlapping grip, or *Vardon grip* as it would later become known (see page 69), began to gain in popularity. Although Harry Vardon is widely credited with the invention of the grip, which involves overlapping the last finger of the right hand (for a right-handed player) over the index finger of the left hand, both Melville and Taylor had scored major successes with it in earlier years.

Even in the 1880s, the advantages of keeping the hands as close together as possible on the grip had already been recognized. Indeed, Sir Walter Simpson, in his famous 1887 book *The Art of Golf*, warned readers that every inch (2.5cm) the hands were apart on the grip could knock as much as 30 feet (9m) off the length of a shot. A long, free-flowing swing, which encouraged considerable body movement, became the vogue, thanks greatly to the Vardon grip and guttie ball combination.

The influence of the guttie was certainly considerable, and its introduction undoubtedly played a large part in laying the foundations for the golf swing as we know it today.

However, the arrival of the wound rubber-core Haskell ball from the United States in 1902 had even greater significance in the history of golf. It had implications far beyond simple technical improvement in golf-ball production. The Haskell ushered in the modern age of the game and brought with it a major change in the way golf was played.

The rubber-core 'wonder ball' was invented by a wealthy American amateur golfer, Coburn Haskell, in collaboration with Bertram Work, an engineer from Akron, Ohio. It proved to be an instant success. The new ball was livelier and flew considerably further than the guttie, and when Sandy Herd won the British Open Championship with a Haskell ball at Hoylake in 1902 – with a winning score that equalled the championship record – the guttie ball was rendered virtually redundant.

POPULAR INNOVATION

The new ball also brought with it a huge leap in the popularity of the game. Even the least gifted of players could obtain reasonably satisfactory results when they mis-hit it. But it had other effects, too. The long hitters became even longer hitters, though they were obliged to perfect the art of control, something far less critical with the dead guttie ball. The controlled and measured backswing for approach shots, and the introduction of iron clubs with more loft to provide increased backspin and better control, were other

Hickory follower
It is in the followthrough where James Braid's swing differs from that of modern-day players. Because of the torsion in the shaft, the hands have a pronounced 'roll-over' (left) and then run down the shaft to maintain control (right).

immediate benefits. The rubber-core ball also demanded careful thought about the shot to be played. The new ball presented a choice of action where there had been none before. Strategy now became an extremely crucial element of the game.

EXPERIMENTAL PERIOD

There was extensive experimentation with the new ball to help the player to realize his true potential on the links. With no limit to the size or weight of the ball at that time, all sorts of extreme combinations were tried. There were players who favoured a small, heavy ball, while others preferred a larger and lighter ball to the point where it would actually float if it landed in water. Combinations between the two extremes were tried and tested: small and heavy balls for driving into the wind; larger, lighter balls for play downwind.

Between 1902 and 1921, when the standardized ball was introduced, the tactical input by the player was every bit as important as his dexterity with the club, and the most successful were those who best married the two elements together. The period also saw considerable experimentation with golf clubs, and shafts in particular.

Club shafts had always been made of wood, usually hickory, and, by paring down the wood, different characteristics could be introduced into every club in the set. The shafts also had a considerable amount of

torsion, or twisting, in them, requiring players to learn the characteristics of every club before developing a repertoire of shots to play with each. Touch and feel and that elusive element known as 'timing' were the keys to success. The hands, still the most important element in the golf swing, became even more important. They had to be trained to a far greater extent than is considered necessary by today's players.

Contemporary images of the great players of the early 20th century clearly reveal the existence of the torsion in the shafts. The very pronounced turning over of the wrists, forearms, and shoulders for the pitch-and-run shot is one example. Another is the dragging of the hands away as the first movement of the swing on the full shots while the head of the club lags behind. This was a technique common to all the great players of the period and was employed to take some of the torsion out of the shaft.

SKILL OVER POWER

The ability to play a wide range of different shots was the premium. None of the Great Triumvirate was by any means lacking in strength, but sheer power was not the name of the game at the turn of the century. Skill in conceiving the shots and skill in their execution reaped their own rewards.

Wood, of course, was the standard material at that time, but metal-headed drivers

Jersey giant
Channel Islander Harry Vardon dominated the game at the turn of the century, as well as giving his name to the overlapping grip.

appeared in 1890, around the same time that a blacksmith, Thomas Horsburgh, together with leading professional, Willie Dunn Jnr, had begun experimenting with steel shafts. Horsburgh had even gone so far as to patent the idea, though sadly he allowed it to lapse. By 1912 the first seamless steel shafts were being made in Britain, although it was the American manufacturers who fully exploited their potential.

THE STANDARD BALL

The standardization of the golf ball in 1921, followed by the arrival of the steel shaft on a wide scale at the end of the decade, marked a significant shift in the way the game was played. The decision to introduce a standard ball, which measured 1.62in (42.67mm) in diameter and had a maximum weight of 1.62oz (45.93g), was not a universally popular move. Its arrival was viewed by some as a further sacrifice of individual skill in favour of conformity. Now there was no need to select a ball according to strategy or conditions: a standard ball for any situation would suffice. All that was needed was a new technique to cope with this latest innovation.

This was made considerably easier with the arrival, from the United States, of the matched set of steel-shafted golf clubs. The matched set was a major step towards a more mechanical approach to technique. The theory that came with the matched set (progressively lofted irons, usually numbered one to nine) was that the game could be reduced to one standard swing, using a different club to take care of any variations in distance and trajectory.

The legendary Bobby Jones from Atlanta, Georgia, was the first real master of this mechanical though long and free-flowing

Hickory house
Hickory-shaft manufacturers such as Scotsman Robert Forgan helped develop clubmaking into an art, taking immense care over the exact choice of materials used.

Cotton drive
There can have been few keener students of the game than Britain's only golfing knight, Sir Henry Cotton.

swing. But there was a lot more to Jones' game than that. Once described by Harry Vardon as "the finest judge of distance I have ever seen", Jones was equally at home with hickory or steel in his bag, and his example was copied by students all over the USA. Known as the 'American swing', its appeal quickly spread across the Atlantic to Britain.

NO FRILLS

When the leading British player Henry Cotton went to the United States in 1928 to find out just why the Americans had started to dominate the game, he quickly found the answer. He discovered a young American by the name of Horton Smith cleaning up on the winter circuit, thanks in no small measure to his set of steel-shafted clubs. As Cotton recalled: "Smith was only 20 years old and he had hardly known golf with anything but steel shafts. He knocked all the fancy shot-making frills off low scoring. He used a slow and deliberate three-quarter swing, which he repeated mechanically for every shot

Fairway club by Willie Park Snr, c. 1870

Long spoon by Peter McEwan, c. 1890

and he never took three putts." An example that remains just as pertinent today.

Cotton was quick to take in the ramifications of his discovery, and to follow the example of Smith (who would go on to become the first US Masters champion). In *A History of Golf in Britain*, Cotton commented: "Seeing Horton Smith play was quite a revelation. I saw straight away that the day of learning to play all the shots was over – the steel shaft had made golf an easier game. The soft watered greens of the USA showed that one shot, if you could repeat it, was good enough to win any event.

"This fact did not really register at home until the steel shaft was legalized in Great Britain, and then we too all hunted for one swing to go with our new matched sets which had steel shafts in them. At last everyone could have the exact set of clubs used by his favourite champion."

BRITISH STEEL

Sir Henry was one of the great students of golf technique and, unlike many, had no difficulty in making the transition from hickory to steel. He was the last professional to win an important championship with hickory-shafted clubs playing against opponents using the steel equivalents. He won his three British Open Championships using steel-shafted clubs and was therefore well qualified to compare the methods of the two eras. Sir Henry always maintained that any study of the styles and methods of his era showed that the advice on offer was fundamentally the same as it had been 50 years before.

He further concluded that it would be advice just as valuable 50 years on and, save for equipment changes, there is little in the way golf is played today that was not known when Cotton, and the Great Triumvirate before him, held sway.

But while the great man's observations were certainly correct, a few of golf's big names struggled to

come to terms with steel, including George Duncan, British Open champion in 1920, and Abe Mitchell. It was 1929 before the Royal and Ancient Golf Club of St Andrews, the last bastion of opposition, finally sanctioned the use of steel shafts in Britain (supposedly to avoid the embarrassment of having to disqualify the Prince of Wales, who had turned up for a match proudly brandishing his new set of steel-shafted clubs). In doing so, the R & A had not just signed the death warrant of the hickory shaft, but had also effectively ended clubmaking as a craft.

LACK OF VARIETY

In the words of the eminent golf writer Bernard Darwin, "The making of shafts passed from the bench to the factory; from the individual craftsman to the Steel Cartel by whom shafts were mass-produced, leaving the clubmaker little to do but fit grips and heads to shafts and give the whole club its finish". And he added significantly: "Except in variety of model in head and grip, as favoured by different clubmakers and leading professionals, uniformity has ousted individuality in both the implements and play of the game." While a certain degree of uniformity was an undoubted

Dominant force
It didn't matter what type of shafts Bobby Jones employed. Despite the worldwide legalization of steel shafts, he used his hickory set to win the Amateur and Open Championships of both Britain and the USA in 1930.

First master
Horton Smith (left) was an early exponent of the matched set of steel clubs, scooping up a host of titles. He was a double US Masters champion, winning the inaugural tournament in 1934.

consequence, both players and manufacturers alike have done their best to cast doubt on Darwin's observations – be it through playing style or by experimentation with clubs.

NEW CLUBS

Perhaps the most significant breakthrough was the invention of the sand wedge in the 1930s, credited to the legendary American player Gene Sarazen, winner of seven major tournaments during the 1920s and 1930s. The production of a steep-faced club, with a broad flange on the bottom to help the club bounce through sand, rather than dig into it, removed much of the menace of bunkers as well as contributing to major improvements in short game play around the green.

Although the legalization of steel shafts was probably the last milestone to have significantly affected the way golf is played, it has not stopped manufacturers from coming up with a whole stream of supposed breakthroughs. The fact is that, because of all the strictures regarding what can and cannot be used, most ideas are little more than re-inventions. Steel still remains the most popular material for the construction of golf-club shafts. But the arrival and development of carbon fibre in shaft technology is now starting to threaten its dominance, in much the same way as steel did to that of wood in the 1920s.

Metal-headed 'woods' have now virtually taken over from persimmon or laminated wood, and when they became widely popular in the 1980s they were hailed as the most significant new invention in golf for years; conveniently forgetting the metal-headed drivers from some 90 years before.

A more significant modification was the development of perimeter weighting in clubhead design (both for woods and irons). This helps to spread the weight around the perimeter of the head, rather than evenly across, thereby helping to offset, to some extent at least, the effects of an off-centre shot.

But for all the developments in equipment,

Pro shops
Golf's leading performers have attempted to satisfy the public thirst for instruction for most of the 20th century – as J.H. Taylor (centre) amply demonstrates during a special 'teach-in' at Harrods in 1914.

The old school
Generally recognized as the best player never to win the British Open, Abe Mitchell suffered more than most by the introduction of steel shafts, which greatly reduced his ability to fade the ball.

the ever-increasing popularity of golf owes as much to the great players who have become international sporting heroes and given the game immense exposure through the medium of television. There are thousands of golfers who believe they can 'buy' a better game from the racks of clubs and equipment in their local professional shop, but there are at least as many more who, perhaps more sensibly, look to the great players for their inspiration.

POST-WAR BOOM

After the Second World War golf moved into a new phase. Television was a major influence in golf, just as it has been in many other walks of life. The game began to reach a much wider

Old and new woods
Metal-headed woods have been used for more than a century. While the basic design has changed little, the shafts are now made of steel or graphite, with steel replacing the aluminium heads.

Aluminium-headed hickory driver, 1890

Steel driver 1990

audience and golfers were suddenly able to study the world's best from the comfort of their own homes in a way that the masters of the early game could never have imagined. Televised tournaments were soon attracting big audiences in the United States, and as television gained in popularity so it highlighted the rise of three gifted Americans; three players who would go on to influence just about every aspect of the game.

HOGAN HERO

Although Ben Hogan turned professional as early as 1931, and started to dominate the US Tour money list from 1940, it was not until after the War that his influence on the game was truly felt. In 1948, Hogan, or 'The Hawk' as he was nicknamed because of his poker face and grimly determined attitude, was 36 years old and hardly in the first flush of youth, but he was indisputably the finest player in the world. Hogan practised for hour after hour underneath the white cap that became his trademark. He struck the ball with a timing and precision that made experienced commentators gasp in amazement.

Every shot Hogan hit made a sound that was distinctly and unmistakably Hogan. The Hawk became a national hero. Then fate struck a cruel blow. On February 2, 1949, Hogan was critically injured when his car was in a collision with a Greyhound bus in Texas. There were reports that he would not live, but Hogan, the dour battler, survived. He had to learn to walk again and he had to learn to play golf again. Incredibly, with a completely rebuilt

Practice makes perfect
There have been few more dedicated golfers on the practice ground than Ben Hogan.

technique, Hogan went on to dominate golf through the early 1950s. The undoubted highlight was in 1953 when he won all three of the Majors that he entered. The victory at Carnoustie was his first and only tilt at the British Open, and gave the home crowds a rare glimpse of his awesome powers; the sheer perfection of his play and determination to win were an inspiration.

THE PALMER PHENOMENON

The popularity of golf today, both as a spectator and participant sport, probably owes more to the influence of Arnold Palmer than to anyone else in the history of the game. His swashbuckling, go-for-everything approach to golf, coupled with a charismatic personality and the business acumen of an American lawyer named Mark McCormack, took professional golf into the big time, encouraging thousands of newcomers onto the golf course for the first time.

The Sunday morning fourball was never the same for millions of golfers after the arrival of Arnold Palmer. His distinctive early putting style, in which he locked both knees together, produced a generation of knock-kneed golfers with strange followthroughs – inspired by Palmer's flourishing finish developed as his own antidote to the hook.

The sand man
The winner of three Majors at 21, Gene Sarazen (centre) spent nine years in the doldrums before – with the aid of his newly-developed sand wedge – he won the British and US Open titles in 1932.

GENE SARAZEN AND THE WILSON TECHNICAL STAFF AT WORK IN THE GOLF CLUB FACTORY-WILSON-WESTERN SPORTING GOODS CO. CHICAGO

In the groove
Bob Charles confounded the many pundits who claimed a left-hander could never win a Major by taking the 1963 British Open title at Royal Lytham and St Annes. The New Zealander has continued to prove an inspiration to all 'wrong 'uns' by becoming one of the top money winners on the US Senior Tour.

The inspiration
It is a simple fact: no-one has done more to encourage people to play and watch golf than Arnold Palmer. It was also his enthusiasm for the British Open that helped to re-establish the championship as golf's premier tournament.

The 'Great Bear'
One of the all-time greats, Jack Nicklaus, at the 1970 British Open presentation ceremony, has been immensely influential both on and off the golf course.

But above all Palmer brought enjoyment to the game. He cast aside frills in favour of thrills. "If you can see it you can hole it" was the Palmer philosophy, and invariably he did. He was the golfing knight in shining armour, the commander of the legions they called 'Arnie's Army', and no-one before or since has had a deeper love of, or commitment to, playing the game of golf.

In his book *My Game and Yours*, Palmer avowed that "golf is easier than you think". He claimed that too many writers on golf, and golf teachers, had been lured into too many complexities. "We have forgotten," he said, "that the game began with the very elemental discovery, by a Scottish shepherd who had never had a lesson in his life, that he could knock a pebble an astounding distance with a good swift lick of his shepherd's crook."

WILL TO WIN

If it was Palmer who made golf popular with the masses, it was Jack Nicklaus who took the game on to another plane. The American dominated professional golf for a quarter of a century with a version of the game very much in marked contrast to that of Arnold Palmer. Nicklaus brought intense concentration, single-minded determination, the philosophy of playing the percentages rather than going for broke, and raw power to golf in measures never seen before.

A somewhat stern and overweight figure in his formative years, by the 1970s Jack Nicklaus had become the epitome of the relaxed player. More importantly, he had also become world number one, thanks in no small part to his immense physical strength and an intense desire to succeed.

PRACTICE MAKES PERFECT

Nicklaus spent countless hours away from the course perfecting his game, though the strong man did have to compensate for his unusually small fingers and hands. As a result, he is one of the very few great champions to have employed the interlocking grip (see page 69). But, for all the strength and talent that has made him the greatest player of the modern era, much of Nicklaus' success can be put down to a Florida professional, Jack Grout.

The only teacher Nicklaus has ever turned to, Grout helped to instill the values of fair play and sportsmanship that have always been at the heart of the game of golf. There was no better example than when Nicklaus conceded a 3ft (1m) putt to Tony Jacklin in the 1969 Ryder Cup at Royal Birkdale, thereby allowing his opponents to tie the overall match.

No-one, perhaps with the exception of Hogan and Cotton, practised more than Nicklaus in his formative years, and in doing so the American helped to dispel the feeling – for a long time prevalent in Europe – that practice was a dirty word. In the early years of the game, particularly in Britain, practice was frowned upon as unsporting and almost tantamount to cheating. That is why very few of the old, traditional championship courses in Britain have proper practice facilities. The practice ground and the practice culture are relatively modern

phenomena in golf, and their popularity owes a lot to the likes of Jack Nicklaus.

European, effectively British, golf lay for a long time in the doldrums after the heyday of Henry Cotton. Even when the cream of American talent chose not to cross the Atlantic, South African and Australian players eagerly filled the void by picking up a string of British Open titles.

More distressing still, for the traditionalists at least, was Bob Charles' British Open triumph of 1963 – the New Zealander becoming the first (and so far only) left-hander to win a Major championship. However, the first glimmers of a power shift emerged in 1969.

EUROPEAN RISE

Victory in the British Open at Royal Lytham and St Annes saw England's Tony Jacklin break the overseas dominance and promised much for a success-starved public. The point was underlined 11 months later when he became the first Briton in 50 years to win the US Open, at Hazeltine. Jacklin's success inspired many a youngster to take up the game, and though he failed to repeat his triumphs, he was still to play a major role in the development of European golf – albeit over a decade later, and with a little help from others. Seve Ballesteros and Bernhard Langer had already

shown that there was life in European golf outside the British Isles, but it was their exploits, under the guidance and influence of Jacklin, that did as much as anything to shift the power in golf.

BACK ON COURSE

With Jacklin as the inspirational non-playing captain, Ballesteros and Langer teamed up with Nick Faldo, Sandy Lyle, and Sam Torrance to wrest control of the Ryder Cup away from the United States in 1985 – a triumph repeated two years later on American soil. This success was the major factor in a massive upsurge in interest in golf in Britain and throughout Europe.

There is little doubt that Jacklin's contribution to the wider popularity of golf, allied with the plethora of major titles brought back home to Europe, has lured thousands of new players to the game. Ranging from the charismatic, cavalier approach of Ballesteros to the professionalism and dedication of Faldo, the inspiration to learn and to improve remains as strong as it has ever been.

Role models
Two men who, in contrasting ways, have helped to inspire a whole new generation. Spain's Severiano Ballesteros (inset), with his raw, explosive talent, was at the forefront of the European resurgence in the late 1970s, while Englishman Nick Faldo (right) proved that hard work and a single-minded dedication to improvement can turn high-class potential into reality.

Mould breaker
Few have done more to inspire and revitalize European golf than Tony Jacklin. British Open champion in 1969, he became the first Briton since Ted Ray in 1920 to win the US Open the following year, before re-emerging to captain Europe to Ryder Cup success in 1985.

Showing the way

FEW SPORTS ENCOURAGE such a passion for learning as golf. Since the early gentle writings of 19th-century gentleman players, the golf instructional market has flourished to a point today that leaves virtually no aspect untouched. Here, we examine some of the ways – good, bad, and indifferent – in which the instructional gospel of golf has been spread throughout the world.

Early variety
By 1910 there was a flood of golf tuition books for the would-be player to choose and learn from.

It was not until the arrival of the gutta percha ball around 1848 that golfers really began to require teachers, teaching aids, and instructional material. Suddenly there was a stream of new players anxious to learn but with no infrastructure for teaching. Newcomers to the game had to wait until nine years or so after the arrival of the guttie ball for a book solely devoted to golf and how to play the game. *The Golfers' Manual*, published in 1857 under the pen name of 'A Keen Hand', was written by a Scottish golfer named Henry B. Farnie. He divided players into two different categories based on physique and athleticism: 'Golfers Agile and Golfers Non-Agile'. How

Book clubs
The rights and wrongs of the swing have remained the same for more than 60 years, as this book of the 1930s illustrates.

well the book sold history does not reveal, but certainly Farnie's pioneering work was the start of an outflow of literature on the subject of golf and how to play it.

Significant golfing works of the late 19th century included: *Golf: A Royal and Ancient Game* by Robert Clark (published in 1875); *The Art of Golf* by Sir Walter Simpson (1877); *Reminiscences of Golf on St Andrews' Links* by James Balfour (1887); and Robert Chambers' *Golfing* (1887).

SPREADING THE WORD

Golf in printed form was beginning to catch on, and the first magazine solely devoted to the game appeared in 1899. *Golf Illustrated* was published in Britain and provided its readers with weekly news and hints on how to play. Still in publication today, under the title *Golf Weekly Illustrated*, the magazine was the staple diet for golfers looking for written golf instruction until the arrival of *Golf Monthly* in 1911.

In 1890 the first truly comprehensive book on golf was published in the Badminton Library sports series. The editor was Horatio

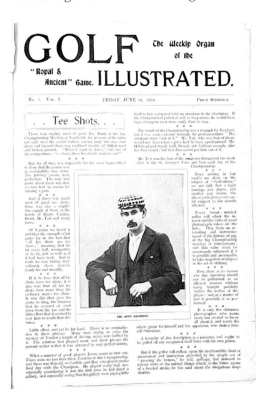

Star tips
Since 1889, magazines such as Golf Illustrated have recognized the club golfer's yearning for 'inside information' from the pros on how to improve.

(Horace) Gordon Hutchinson who, as well as being one of the great players of his era (he was twice English Amateur champion), went on to establish himself as one of the most prolific and authoritative writers on golf. Among his many titles were: *Famous Golf Links* (1890); *The Golfing Pilgrim* (1898); *The Book of Golf and Golfers* (1899); and *Fifty Years of Golf* (1919).

The Badminton Library volume, *Golf*, which he edited, was a remarkable publication by any standards. There were major contributions from such eminent players of the time as the Rt. Hon. A.J. Balfour, MP, Andrew Laing, and H.S.C. Everard, and the book even included a chapter written by Hutchinson himself entitled 'Hints to Cricketers Who Are Taking up Golf'!

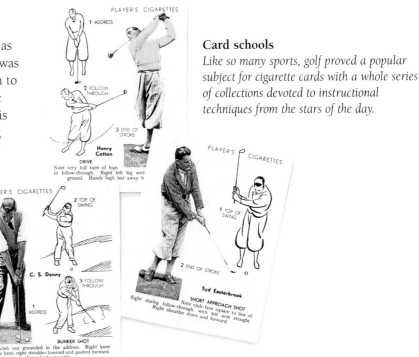

Card schools
Like so many sports, golf proved a popular subject for cigarette cards with a whole series of collections devoted to instructional techniques from the stars of the day.

THEORY INTO PRACTICE
Though some of golf's most famous books have been produced by top professionals, such as Tommy Armour and Bobby Jones, writing up until the turn of the century was very much the exclusive domain of the amateur players – literate, articulate gentlemen of some means in comparison to their professional counterparts. One of the first pros to break the mould was the twice British Open champion

Willie Park Jnr in his 1896 tome, *The Game of Golf*. Park, who once said "a man who can putt is a match for anyone" went on to exemplify the point with *The Art of Putting* in 1920.

The Great Triumvirate (see page 16) were not slow to take a lead from Park, with James Braid, J.H. Taylor, and Harry Vardon all supplying a steady stream of instructional publications in the early 1900s – for the professional, putting pen to paper was fast becoming a lucrative sideline. The fact that the leading players were now name sportsmen was further reflected by a series of instructional cigarette cards demonstrating various shots.

AMERICAN LAUNCH
In the United States, the first golf book appeared in 1895 – just seven years after the first club was founded, the St Andrews Club at Yonkers in New York. In his preface to *Golf in America: A Practical Guide*, the author, James P. Lee, said: "A new game has been added to the list of our outdoor sports." It was a book of the most elementary nature, a fact reflected in Lee's monitory: "There is no racing or any

Pros to prose
Winner of three major titles in the 1930s, Scottish-born Tommy Armour went on to write one of the game's most popular instructional guides, Play Your Best Golf All the Time.

Best seller
After he gave up the game in 1930, the legendary Bobby Jones wrote a series of best-selling golfing textbooks.

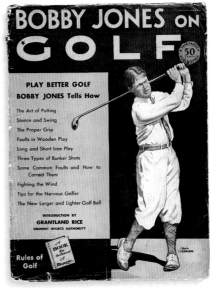

Getting into the swing of things
Following the invention of swing simulators, anyone could experience exactly what the correct swing should feel like, simply by guiding the club around a series of tubes.

effort to accomplish a hole in less time than your opponent." Elementary it may have been, but it didn't take the Americans long to take golf, and the yearning to play it, to the very heart of their sporting culture.

HITS AND MISSES ON CAMERA

As the professional game developed in the United States, and the popularity of golf spread across the continent, the demand for instruction books, and indeed any aid to improvement, spiralled. The potential for photography to play a major part in the instruction process was quickly recognized, even if its early limitations were not.

Just because fast golf swings were not compatible with very slow film was no bar to the use of the camera in golf instruction. In *Easier Golf*, published in 1924, the 1904 British Open champion, Jack White, used pictures to get his message across. White's posed images, necessary to accommodate the inadequacy of the camera, bordered on the comical, and even when the photographer did manage to capture the action for real, the club had invariably disappeared from the picture.

Perhaps not surprisingly, *Picture Analysis of Golf Strokes*, written by Jim Barnes – one of the few players to win the Open Championships of both Britain and the United States – is another example of early photography's limitations.

There were exceptions, however, such as Abe Mitchell's sadly rare *Essentials of Golf*. First published in 1927, the photography stands head and shoulders above other contemporary publications. Even as late as the 1940s, the problems were all too obvious, as Byron Nelson's otherwise excellent book *Winning Golf* amply demonstrates.

QUALITY RATHER THAN QUANTITY

Over the decades there have been countless hundreds of instruction books published. Unfortunately, many of them were inspired more by a desire to capitalize on a 'name' or a 'success' than to make a useful contribution to the spread of the tuitional word. There have, of course, been notable exceptions.

Tommy Armour's guide, *How to Play Your Best Golf All the Time*, first published in 1954, is still being reprinted some 40 years on. Ben Hogan's *The Modern Fundamentals of Golf* (1957) was one of the first books to use top-quality illustrations rather than photography, a format repeated countless times since.

Bobby Jones had taken up the writer's pen from almost the day he stopped playing, supplying syndicated columns and magazine articles throughout the United States. These were finally put together in *Bobby Jones on Golf*, a book that certainly gave some insight into

In-depth swingers
This swing-analysis example from the 1930s was one of the few early photographic guides to be of genuine use to would-be golfers.

the great man's genius. In more recent times, *Harvey Penick's Little Red Golf Book* stands out as one of the game's most famous and best-selling works – reflecting on more than half a century of top-class golf tuition.

OFF THE PAGE

Attempts to impart golfing prowess have never been confined to the written page. Running like an endless seam through the history of the way the game is played has been the search for 'the secret': that special move or key that unlocks the door to golfing success.

The quest to find it has resulted in the invention of some weird and wonderful apparatus. The 1930s saw the introduction of complicated machinery designed to simulate the perfect golf swing – and provide a benchmark from which the pupil could learn and develop. It was the signal for a whole range of weird gadgets to be produced. Unfortunately, although intended to help and improve performance, some have only helped to further confuse and befuddle the player's attempts to lower his handicap.

Where once upon a time Henry Cotton wound lead tape around an old driver to create a heavy club to use as an aid to loosening up, there is now a custom-made club with an extremely heavy head; a twisted shaft to produce a rotational force twenty times greater than a standard No 6 iron; and a shaped handle to encourage the perfect grip. As manufacturers started to realize the

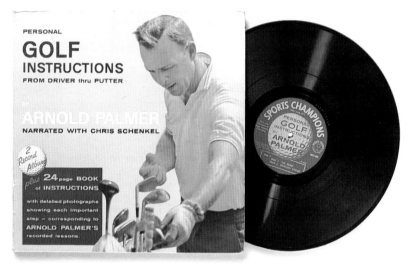

potential of teaching aids, so too did the film-makers and showbiz entrepreneurs. A year after Bobby Jones retired from championship golf following his famous 1930 Grand Slam, he was signed up by Warner Brothers to make a series of 18 short films on how to play golf.

The first 12, entitled *How I Play Golf*, followed by a further six, called *How to Break Ninety*, were all filmed at the Flintridge Country Club and the Lakeside Golf Club in Los Angeles, and featured stars from nearby Hollywood. The films proved to be hugely popular and helped to increase Jones' revered position in the eyes of the American golfing public.

Not to be outdone, in 1938 Britain's leading golfer Henry Cotton also revealed some of his tricks of the trade to the public – on stage. With the help of netting and a revolving stage, Cotton performed to full houses, many of whom had never seen a golf club swung before.

However, of more significance was the development of high-speed film. The ability to provide slow-motion analysis of the swings of the world's great players

Shooting shots
Those lucky enough to have access to a film projector could watch celluloid instructions from top players such as Tommy Armour and Bobby Jones.

Talk show
His immense popularity at the start of the 1960s saw Arnold Palmer attempt to transfer his genius on to vinyl in the shape of a double LP record.

Stage school
Golf instruction even made it into the music-halls in 1938 when Henry Cotton played to packed audiences with a show combining chat, swing sequences, and faults and their fixes.

brought an entirely new dimension to golf instruction. For the first time it was possible to see what actually happened during the swing rather than what was thought to happen. Common factors in the swings of the great champions could be looked at, and then applied to the teaching of the ordinary player. One of the masters of this form of instruction is veteran British teaching professional Bernard Cooke. Using his extensive library of archive film featuring, among others, Harry Vardon, Bobby Jones, Ben Hogan, Lee Trevino, Jack Nicklaus, and Seve Ballesteros, Cooke has been able to demonstrate, at first hand, a whole range of skills and techniques.

Father knows best
As well as being the father of Scottish Ryder Cup star Sam Torrance, Bob Torrance (kneeling) *also dispenses advice to some of Europe's top professionals, including Sandy Lyle and Ian Woosnam.*

WATCH, LISTEN, AND LEARN
Golf really has become a multi-media enterprise, with few areas left untouched in the name of instruction. Jack Nicklaus has committed his thoughts on the golf swing to cassette tape, and Arnold Palmer produced a double album record when he was at the height of his powers in the early 1960s.

However, neither medium really lent itself to tuition – something video could not be accused of.

If the introduction of film brought a new dimension to golf instruction, then the arrival of video totally revolutionized it. The video camera is the spy that cannot lie in the golf instructor's armoury. Videotape allows the instructor to show his pupil how it should be done and then compare that with the way his charge is doing it. Teaching sessions are easily monitored and the pupil has a reference to take away and work on, before heading out to the practice ground.

TAPES AND BEYOND
There are very few professional instructors today who do not utilize video in their teaching regime, and a whole new industry of instruction by video has developed. With it has come a vast library of 'how to' video tapes

fronted by leading players and teachers, while the Rules of Golf and the etiquette of the game are also explained in a series of tapes.

And video is only the start. The growth in the monitoring of sports performance now involves the most up-to-date computer technology. By connecting themselves to a series of light reflectors, players can now have their swings transferred onto computer. They can then watch a 3-D reconstruction of themselves from every angle – helping them to pinpoint any potential weak spots.

THE GOLF ACADEMY
Some of this technology has now become an integral part of the most recent approach to golf instruction, the golf academy. Where not so long ago the provision of a first-class practice ground was the mark of a new golf club's commitment to help improve the game of its members, a top-quality area is now considered the very minimum requirement. The move now is to the golf academy with the provision not only of extensive practice facilities, but also the very latest in teaching technology – and an instructional staff trained to make the very best use of both. It is very much a case of 'back to school' for newcomers to the game, who are steered through the theory and principles of the golf swing before

English teacher
As well as passing on his expertise to the top players, John Jacobs (left) *took instruction and practice to the masses by opening a string of driving ranges and schools in Britain.*

they even handle a golf club. Experienced players benefit from this back-to-basics approach too.

The golf academy is a natural successor to the long-established golf school concept pioneered by eminent teachers such as Englishman John Jacobs. A former Ryder Cup captain, Jacobs has been a highly respected teacher for many years and has helped amateur and professional players alike with their problems.

The demand for his schools continues to increase and, unlike the golf academy, a John Jacobs school can be held at any one of a number of golf-course locations. A former pupil of Jacobs, Scottish-born professional Peter Ballingall, based at Barnham Broom Golf and Country Club in Norfolk, England, is another teacher who has a base that might be described as an academy but who travels internationally to run golf schools for pupils of all abilities.

RISE OF THE GURUS

There is, however, another level of golf tuition. It is one to which only the chosen few are given access. Within its circle are the mysterious figures who have become known as golf's gurus. They are the teachers, the mentors, the soul-searchers, the fixers and, in some cases, the friends, without whom many

of the top players would apparently be unable to compete. Some have been great players in their own right, such as American veterans Bob Tosky and Byron Nelson, who have contributed so much to the success of Tom Watson. Jack Grout is the only teacher Jack Nicklaus has ever used, while Ben Crenshaw and Tom Kite have both been influenced by the theories of Harvey Penick.

Many of today's European stars argue the need for a tutor. Scotland's foremost tutor, Bob Torrance, has been an inspiration to many stars of the European Tour, not least Ian Woosnam. Even Seve Ballesteros has recognized the need for a regular mentor (former US pro Mac O'Grady) to help refine his wayward genius. However, it is Zimbabwean expert David Leadbetter, more than anyone else, who has created the image of the modern golf guru.

THE TOP LEVEL

Leadbetter's work over many years with his close friend Nick Faldo, during which time the Englishman rose to the very top of the world rankings, has made Leadbetter the most eminent of all golf teachers. In more recent times he has started to straddle the whole field of golf instruction. Academies on both sides of the Atlantic, a line of swing and putting aids, best-selling books and videos all bear the Leadbetter name – a name synonymous with success at the highest level.

Of course, few of us have the time or money to hone our game to the same levels of perfection as Faldo and his peers, but the very fact that the game's best players recognize the continual need to learn is a useful lesson in itself. Instruction, from the right people, can help us in our quest for perfection.

Head teacher
David Leadbetter (left) has helped to modify the games of many of today's stars, including Severiano Ballesteros (right). Coaching guru of two of the world's very best, Nick Faldo and Nick Price, the Zimbabwe-born teacher is just about the biggest name in golf tuition, passing on many of his secrets in a series of instructional videos.

Texan master
Harvey Penick (centre) advised some of the world's top players, including Tom Kite (left) and Ben Crenshaw (right). Crenshaw won the 1995 US Masters – sadly just a week after Penick's death.

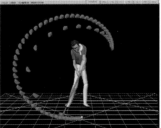

Computer golf
The hi-tech computer wizardry being developed and used by companies such as Biovision in the USA means that golfers – from the humblest to the greatest – can have their game dissected into the minutest parts.

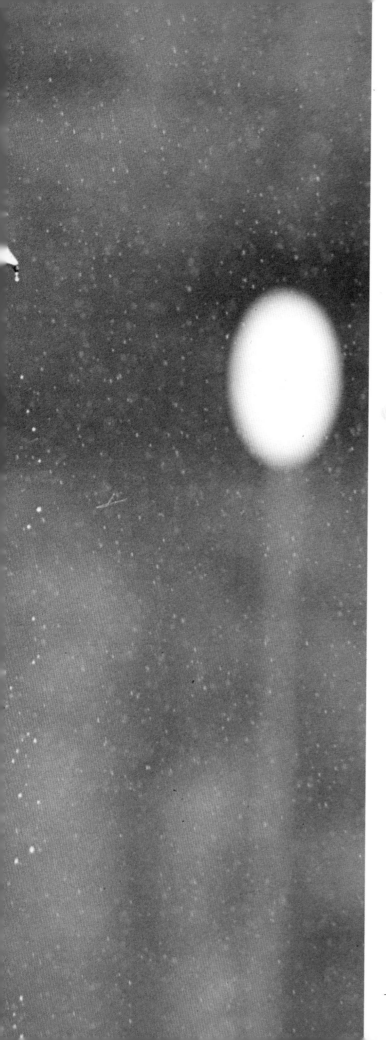

CHAPTER TWO

PREPARED
for the
GAME

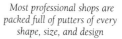

Every golfer needs to be properly kitted out before stepping onto the course

THE MODERN GOLF retail store is an Aladdin's cave of equipment and accessories. To journey through one is to be surrounded by hundreds of items of golfing goodies and paraphernalia – all designed to give the hopeful golfer that little bit of an edge, both in play and appearance. But selecting equipment is not just a matter of picking clubs or accessories off the shelf; there are several important factors to be considered. In this chapter we look at some of the criteria that should be borne in mind when buying and maintaining golf equipment.

In the wet (left)
The modern golfer needs to be prepared for every eventuality on the course as Ian Woosnam (right) and his caddie, Wobbly, quickly discovered on the rain-affected opening day of the 1995 US Masters at Augusta.

Most professional shops are packed full of putters of every shape, size, and design

Getting the best from your clubs

ACQUIRING AND MAINTAINING the right equipment is almost as vital an aspect of learning to play golf as the swing itself. Many players put themselves under an immediate handicap by playing with clubs ill-suited to their own particular needs. Follow these guidelines both for buying and getting the most out of equipment.

Swedish wood
Jarmo Sandelin's extra large 'all-in-one' wood means he can fill his bag with a variety of wedges.

Since the late 1930s, the Rules of Golf have limited the number of clubs a player can carry for a round to 14. Beyond that, it is up to the individual, but he will still be faced with plenty of choices in terms of both club selection and design.

The basic matching set of clubs comprises: three woods – usually driver, 3-wood, and 5-wood; along with nine irons – 3 through to 9, a pitching wedge, a sand wedge, plus a putter. That makes 13, which gives a little leeway to cover any potential weaknesses by adding an extra wood or wedge.

But these days it is not as straightforward as a driver off the tee, wood or iron from the fairway, and wedge around the green; golf has become a good deal more complicated. The production of different woods, irons, wedges,

The golfing tools of the trade
Golf clubs can generally be divided into four categories: woods, irons, wedges, and putters. While you have choices over the composition and design of shafts, no-one but you can decide whether a club 'feels' right or not. In a set of clubs, you may be happy with your long irons but not your wedge, so be prepared to shop around.

putters, shafts, and clubheads offers the possibility of all sorts of combinations to take out onto the course.

DRIVERS AND WOODS

Higher handicap players in vast numbers have taken to the concept of the utility wood, for example. These are lofted woods ideal for shots off the tee, fairway, or out of the rough, and they are a lot easier to hit than a long iron, traditionally the club with which the higher handicapper has most trouble.

With woods, the vogue has moved to oversize perimeter-weighted woods made from steel or graphite, and more recently, titanium. The traditional wooden-headed woods are fast becoming a rarity. The benefits of the oversize metal wood are all aimed at ease of play.

Numbers of woods
The standard set of woods usually comprises a driver, a 3-wood, and a 5-wood, although the lofted 7-wood is starting to grow in popularity, with more and more manufacturers supplying them as standard. 2-, 4-, and 6-woods have been made down the years, but the minor variations in loft mean that the modern-day set of four will cover just about every eventuality.

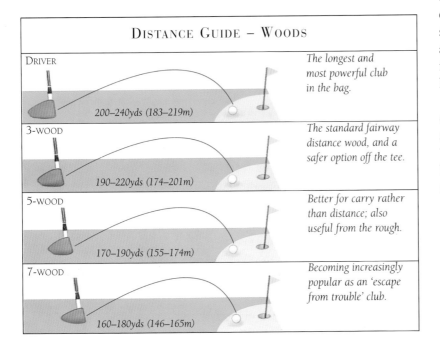

DISTANCE GUIDE – WOODS

DRIVER
200–240yds (183–219m)
The longest and most powerful club in the bag.

3-WOOD
190–220yds (174–201m)
The standard fairway distance wood, and a safer option off the tee.

5-WOOD
170–190yds (155–174m)
Better for carry rather than distance; also useful from the rough.

7-WOOD
160–180yds (146–165m)
Becoming increasingly popular as an 'escape from trouble' club.

BASIC GUIDELINES FOR MEASURING-UP

Much of club selection is down to personal taste. But there are some areas that can be 'measured up' to establish the best size of club for individual needs.

The most crucial factor is the lie of the clubhead. This is the angle formed between the sole of the clubhead and the shaft with the clubhead flat on the ground, and it must be correct for your natural stance and posture. If the lie is too upright, it creates a tendency to pull all shots to the left, due to the heel of the club hitting the ground first. Too flat a lie produces the opposite effect.

The length of the shaft never varies more than about 1in (2.5cm), according to height, and a golf pro should soon be able to spot the length requirements. For the correct grip, simply follow the guidelines (right).

Clubhead lie
The sole of the clubhead needs to sit flat on the ground at address.

Lie angle

Clubhead

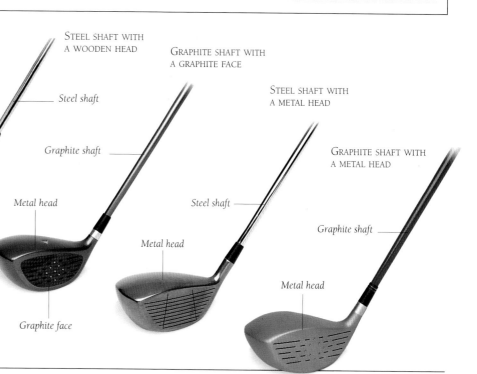

Grip size
To check the ideal size of grip, hold the club normally, but only with the left hand. The two middle fingers should just touch the heel of the palm.

Length of shaft is adjusted to suit height and posture

CHECKING THE LIE

By sticking some tape to the clubhead and hitting a dozen or so balls, it is possible to establish if the ball is being struck in the sweet spot, and if the lie of the club is correct.

The ball will mark the tape and show whether the ball is hitting the centre of the clubface.

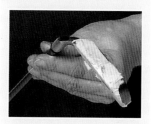

If the majority of the marks are close to the heel, the lie is too upright (and vice versa).

Driver options
Carbon-fibre technology is now a major influence in driver design. Heads and faces can be made of graphite, or used in combination with steel, while graphite-shafted clubs are now commonplace with tour professionals. Try out a selection of steel, graphite, and wooden drivers, but be guided by the professional's advice.

STEEL SHAFT WITH A WOODEN HEAD

Steel shaft

GRAPHITE SHAFT WITH A GRAPHITE FACE

Graphite shaft

Wooden head

Plastic insert protects face

Metal head

Graphite face

STEEL SHAFT WITH A METAL HEAD

Steel shaft

Metal head

GRAPHITE SHAFT WITH A METAL HEAD

Graphite shaft

Metal head

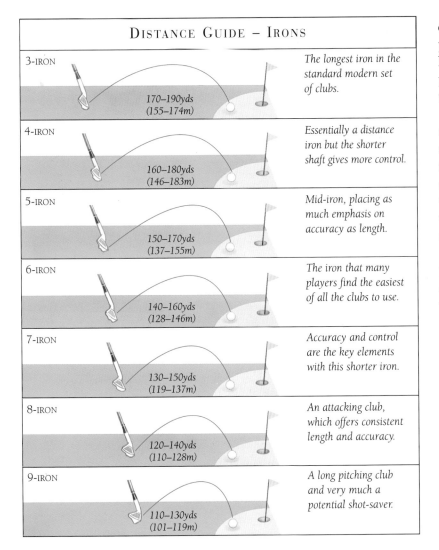

DISTANCE GUIDE – IRONS

3-IRON	170–190yds (155–174m)	*The longest iron in the standard modern set of clubs.*
4-IRON	160–180yds (146–183m)	*Essentially a distance iron but the shorter shaft gives more control.*
5-IRON	150–170yds (137–155m)	*Mid-iron, placing as much emphasis on accuracy as length.*
6-IRON	140–160yds (128–146m)	*The iron that many players find the easiest of all the clubs to use.*
7-IRON	130–150yds (119–137m)	*Accuracy and control are the key elements with this shorter iron.*
8-IRON	120–140yds (110–128m)	*An attacking club, which offers consistent length and accuracy.*
9-IRON	110–130yds (101–119m)	*A long pitching club and very much a potential shot-saver.*

The wider weight distribution in the oversize head creates a larger effective hitting area in the face; in fact, a bigger *sweet spot*. That means the club will be more forgiving. Good contacts will always result in good shots, but slightly off-centre contacts will still result in a shot flying reasonably true.

FINDING THE RIGHT SHAFT

The advances in carbon-fibre technology now allow players greater scope in selecting a shaft matched to their particular requirements. Getting the right components for clubs is as important as getting a suit made-to-measure. Off the shelf will do, but major improvements can still be made.

It can be folly to choose a new set based purely on aesthetics and a few trial hits. The club may feel fine on demonstration,

encouraging a purchase, but there are strong possibilities that some customization could help a player's game dramatically. After all, few people would buy a suit that was too long in the trousers, would they?

The ideal shaft has a direct relation to the speed and power of one's swing; get it wrong, and the game can be much more difficult than it need be. Too stiff a shaft can result in the clubhead being behind the hands at impact, which in turn will push the ball right. A shaft with too much flex will have the opposite effect, with the ball tending to fly left.

So o how do we decide which is best? As a rule of thumb, a stiff-shafted club is more suitable for a powerful, high-speed swing, while a weaker, more deliberate swing requires a little more flexibility. The local professional should be able to assess your swing specifications from watching you hit some demonstration shots, and from a check on the clubhead lie (see page 33). But make sure that he explains his choice – particularly if it means extra expense for you. While the majority of players still use steel shafts, the shift towards graphite is growing, particularly for those with less powerful swings.

CAVITY-BACK IRONS

Once the ideal shaft has been selected, the next consideration should be the best type of clubheads to accompany them. As with woods, the direction of development in iron clubs has moved towards the production of oversized clubheads.

BLADED

CAVITY-BACK

Cavity versus blade
More and more players are moving away from the traditional bladed club and instead choosing the peripherally weighted cavity-back iron.

Plenty of wedge
More renowned for his power play than for his touch around the green, John Daly has been known to use as many as four wedges in a round.

This is a direct result of the development of the cavity-back club. The oversized cavity-back iron suits golfers who need a little help from their clubs; for just as the oversized woods offer forgiveness to mis-hit shots, so too do oversized cavity-back irons. This makes them the ideal club for players of all levels.

The alternative is the bladed iron. Until the arrival of the cavity-back model, the bladed iron – made from forged steel – was the only type of clubhead available, and is still looked upon by many as the classic golf club.

However, blades are now generally used by better golfers only, and that means very low handicap players and professionals. This is because blades are said to offer better touch and feel for well-struck shots, but hit an off-centre shot and there is no forgiveness. A bad shot always stays bad.

SHORTER IRONS

It is more than likely that a bad approach shot will leave a golfer reaching for a wedge. For many years that meant a simple choice between a pitching or sand variety, but these days the choice is far greater. Specialist wedges are now produced to cover just about every possible situation. As well as a wide range of lofts, wedges can now feature brass or graphite inserts in the clubhead designed to give extra

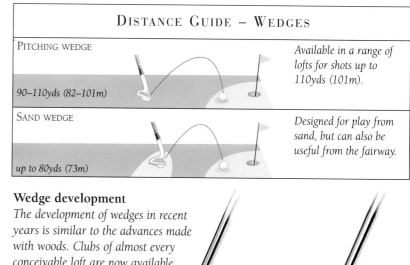

DISTANCE GUIDE – WEDGES

PITCHING WEDGE	
90–110yds (82–101m)	*Available in a range of lofts for shots up to 110yds (101m).*
SAND WEDGE	
up to 80yds (73m)	*Designed for play from sand, but can also be useful from the fairway.*

Wedge development
The development of wedges in recent years is similar to the advances made with woods. Clubs of almost every conceivable loft are now available, and now feature brass and graphite inserts to help improve the contact between club and ball.

Graphite insert

Brass insert

control. It is not uncommon for lower handicap players to carry three wedges instead of the standard two. Indeed, some leading tour players will even sacrifice a wood or a longer iron in order to accommodate a plethora of wedges. John Daly, who has a strong short game, is able to add a third wedge and leave one of his longer clubs out of the bag. Some pros even carry as many as four short irons in their bag on certain courses.

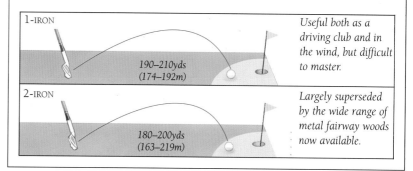

SPECIALITY CLUBS

Though popular in the early days of golf, long irons have become much more of a rarity and are not usually included in a standard set of clubs. The length of shaft, together with the relative lack of loft, leaves little room for error, with the consequence that most players opt for a more forgiving fairway wood.

1-IRON	
190–210yds (174–192m)	*Useful both as a driving club and in the wind, but difficult to master.*
2-IRON	
180–200yds (163–219m)	*Largely superseded by the wide range of metal fairway woods now available.*

Choosing the right putter

If it feels right, it probably is right. The choice of putter is the most personal decision the golfer has to make when selecting equipment, and there are no hard and fast rules.

PUTTER TYPES

There is one club that, in terms of shaft and clubhead design, frequently bears little relation to its fellow clubs in the bag: the putter. Putting, perhaps more than any other part of golf, is influenced by the individual characteristics of the player.

No other club has inspired so many strange designs as the putter (peripheral weighting was first tried out on putters many years in advance of cavity-back irons). Despite manufacturers' best attempts to prove otherwise, there are no hard and fast rules; long handles, short handles, moulded grips, centre-of-gravity adjustments – they can all be of use if they create confidence and feel comfortable. Test as many types as possible before deciding upon a favourite.

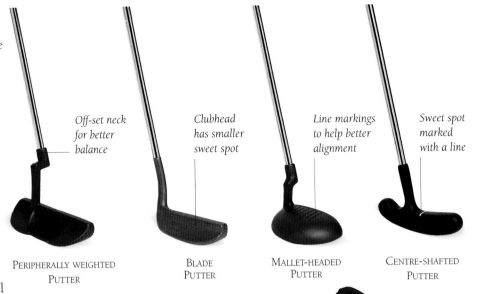

Off-set neck for better balance

Clubhead has smaller sweet spot

Line markings to help better alignment

Sweet spot marked with a line

PERIPHERALLY WEIGHTED PUTTER

BLADE PUTTER

MALLET-HEADED PUTTER

CENTRE-SHAFTED PUTTER

THE RIGHT BALL

Research has demonstrated that golfers, by and large, do not know a great deal about golf balls. And just as selecting the right clubs can help anyone's game, so too can choice of ball.

In general terms, balls are either three-piece or two-piece (see page 37), with the choice of covers between balata and surlyn. While the three-piece balata ball is the choice of most

MAINTAINING EQUIPMENT

The key point with clubheads is to keep them clean; any dirt or grass in the grooves will reduce the club's control of the ball. Try to check the club after every shot – clean away any obvious dirt with a tee-peg and wipe down with a towel. For more stubborn dirt, clean away with a brush and some soapy water after the round.

Steel is very durable, so the likelihood of breaking steel-shafted clubs is extremely small. They may warp, however, so check for any bending by holding the shaft against a straight edge. Graphite does not bend but can be prone to scuff marks. These cannot be cured so take extra care. Acquire extra-long headcovers and fit padding to bag dividers to stop shafts rubbing against each other.

The grip is probably the most neglected part of a club. Grips will get worn through excessive use, and need to be replaced; regular players should renew them annually. Grips are relatively inexpensive to buy, and most pro shops now offer a fitting service for a small extra charge; the half-cord grip is probably the best compromise.

Wipe shaft to remove dirt and grease

To get rid of mud, wash clubhead and shaft in mild soapy water

On the course, use a tee to remove mud and grass from grooves

Long putter

One of the most obvious and controversial refinements in putter design in recent years has been the long-handled putter. Several leading players, including Sam Torrance (above), now use the 'broom-handle', though many feel that it goes against the spirit of the game. It is used with the end of the handle almost resting against the chin at address.

better players, its lack of durability and high price mean that surlyn gives a better value alternative for the average club player. Though one-piece balls are still made, their use is largely confined to practice ranges.

Golf balls come in different compressions, normally expressed as 80, 90, or 100 (compression is essentially the 'hardness' of the ball). Choice of compression is related – like shafts – to the speed and power of the swing. Only very good amateur players with powerful swings will benefit from the hardest compression (100) golf ball. The 90 compression ball is well suited to the ordinary handicap player, while the 80 compression ball is the biggest help to women players.

These are, of course, only guidelines – and players need to find the ball that is most complimentary to their game. Once again, trial and error is the best advice, so don't be afraid to experiment.

THE CHOICE OF BALL

THREE-PIECE
Three-piece balls come with two types of cover. The soft balata cover offers maximum spin and control but lacks resilience, and is unlikely to last more than one round. The surlyn type, while offering a good deal more resistance, will not spin as much.

TWO-PIECE
If the ultimate thrill is to hit a golf ball as far as possible, then look no further than the two-piece ball. In terms of distance and durability, it simply can't be matched, although its lack of spin properties greatly reduces the ability to control the ball.

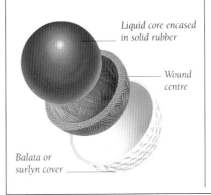

Liquid core encased in solid rubber

Wound centre

Balata or surlyn cover

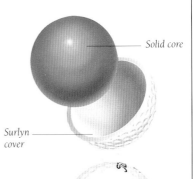

Solid core

Surlyn cover

BUYING SECOND-HAND

For those working to a restricted budget, or who are simply not satisfied with the new clubs on offer, it is well worth looking at a second-hand set. Most professional shops will have some and it is surprising what can be found.

Bear in mind that relatively minor scratches on irons can be easily treated, and that even fairly major damage on a wooden clubhead can be repaired by specialists. However, major damage to several clubs can be an indication of how they have been treated.

Once again, much of it is down to personal preference, but by using the measuring-up procedures (see page 33), and a few basic pre-purchase checks it should be feasible to avoid buying a poor quality set. The grips are more than likely to be worn, but remember that they can easily be replaced.

Wooden-headed clubs are the most susceptible to wear. Look out for cracks in the neck and wear and tear around the insert and sole-plate; there might also be loose whipping.

Iron-headed clubs are designed to stand up to some pretty rough treatment, but make sure that the grooves have not become too worn, that there are no major dents, and that the hosels are in good condition.

With **steel shafts**, look for any signs of rusting or dents, and make sure that they are straight (with graphite, check for scuffs).

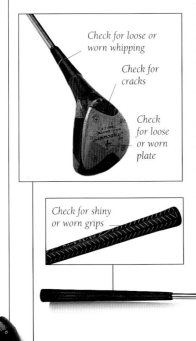

Check for loose or worn whipping

Check for cracks

Check for loose or worn plate

Check for shiny or worn grips

Check that shaft is straight and free from dents

Watch out for worn grooves

Check hosel

Check for damaged edges

Numbers game
The only numbers on balls that relate to their specific properties are those giving the compression (80, 90, or 100). The more prominent numbers are purely for identification purposes. Those in red indicate that the ball has a 90 compression while 80 and 100 compression balls will have black numbers.

Making the most of accessories

THERE IS MORE to golf equipment than clubs and balls – the accessories market is huge in itself. Much of the market is geared towards fashion, but there are elements that can have a significant effect on performance.

Dress sense
Flamboyant Payne Stewart combines fashion and practicality when choosing on-course attire.

A golfer refuses to give thought to accessories at his peril. Clubs and balls are the most vital elements in his armoury of course, but an ill-fitting glove, a badly worn-out shoe, or uncomfortable clothing can all be detrimental to a player's performance on the course – and ultimately to his scoring.

GETTING A GRIP

The majority of players now wear a glove on their 'top' hand to help keep a firmer grip on the club – a trend pioneered just prior to the Second World War. Its popularity has grown to such an extent that nearly all of today's top players use a glove – Fred Couples is probably the most famous exception. There are now gloves to suit every conceivable fashion requirement, though the major priority must be selecting one that is both

Tight against extended fingertips

Taut and raised above palm

Snug to base of finger

Hand in glove
It is not just a case of using any old glove that fits. Remember that its primary purpose is to help maintain better grip.

comfortable and affords the best grip. Gloves made of material that retains grip even in wet weather are popular and practical.

A FIRM FOUNDATION

Just as a house has to be built on strong foundations, so too does the golf swing. It is an explosive action that, if it is to work to the best effect, needs a solid platform to work on,

The right shoes for the job
While golf shoes traditionally have spikes on their soles (either permanent or removable), rubber-dimpled shoes are a more than useful alternative, particularly in warmer climates where courses are less likely to be damp and spongy.

Leather shoe with permanent spikes

Lightweight shoe with rubber grip

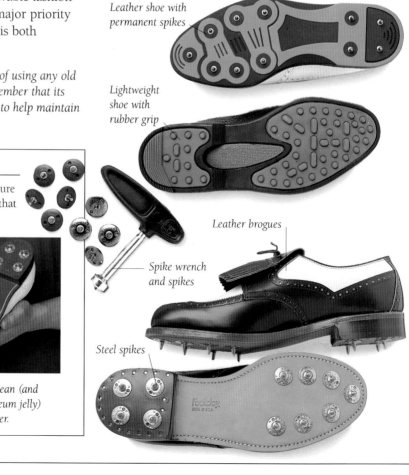

Leather brogues

Spike wrench and spikes

Steel spikes

REPAIRING YOUR SPIKES

Spikes are an extremely important part of golf equipment. Make sure that worn or missing spikes are constantly checked for, and that replacements are readily to hand.

Screw-in spikes can be easily removed using a spike wrench that, in most cases, is supplied with the shoes.

Threads should be kept clean (and can be coated with petroleum jelly) to make replacement easier.

Breathable,
lightweight
material

Elasticated
wrists

Covered zip

therefore easier to
swing a club in than,
for instance, a
standard waterproof
hiking suit. Golf
waterproofs allow
full movement with a
minimum of noise, are
lightweight, and now mostly
made of a breathable material
to give maximum comfort.
And don't forget headgear.
Whether choosing a baseball cap,
a jockey cap, a sun-visor, a knitted
hat, or a straw hat, make sure it is one
that doesn't impede the swing. Once
again, however, headgear can be
expensive, so take time and care before
purchasing. Similar criteria also apply to
general clothing. If funds are limited, put
comfort before so-called designer labels –
price does not guarantee compatibility.

Weather beater
*Protection against the cold is
just as important as keeping
dry. Stars such as Seve
Ballesteros realize that you
cannot concentrate on a
shot when you're worrying
about the weather.*

which is where a good pair of
shoes becomes essential. On a
6,500yd (5,940m) golf course,
a player will walk well in
excess of 4½ miles (7km).
Comfort, therefore, is of
paramount importance. A golfer who
is uncomfortable cannot perform at his best.

As always, of course, there is a price to
pay. A pair of golf shoes can cost a great deal
of money, and more than one pair in your
locker may be needed to cope with varying
course conditions.

JUST IN CASE

Golf is full of the
unexpected, so carry a few
'extras' to deal with any
problems that might occur
when you are well away
from the clubhouse.
• Extra set of shoelaces
• Spare spikes
• Medical tape (for blisters)
•Sun screen
• Insect repellent

Shoes must be kept
clean and supple to give
the best results. Leather
shoes, in particular,
need to be protected
against the wet in order
to avoid any cracking;
professional shops
should stock a range
of protective oils for
this purpose. And
make sure that spikes
are kept in good condition. Worn spikes not
only jeopardize the solid grip on the turf, they
are also potentially dangerous in wet and
slippery conditions.

DRESSED FOR SUCCESS

European golfers are only too aware of the
problems of playing golf in inclement weather,
and investing in a good set of golf waterproofs
is a worthwhile venture. They are specifically
designed for the rigours of golf, and are

GETTING AROUND THE COURSE

Since caddies have all but disappeared, except from a
few elite clubs, some thought needs to be given to how
clubs are going to be carried. The modern, lightweight,
polyurethane bag is ideal for carrying, in sharp contrast
to the old all-leather bags. A trolley or bag stand are
other items that can make life a lot easier.

*Furry covers help
protect heads of
woods and
graphite shafts*

*The ideal trolley should
have a light frame,
wide wheels, and be
easily folded to fit
into a car boot.*

Make sure
graphite shafts
are protected
from scuffing

Wipe
clubs after
every shot

Add a little
lubricating oil to
wheel bearings every
couple of months

*A good
umbrella is a
must for wet
conditions*

Technical assistance

THE HISTORY OF GOLF instruction is littered with teaching devices, aids, and gadgets designed to help certain aspects of the game. Many merely hinder, but some can be of real benefit because every 'invention' is usually based on simple golfing principles.

Sandy on the slide
Sandy Lyle resorted to a variety of aids and gimmicks following his dramatic slump in form in the late 1980s. Gloves, harnesses, and sighting devices were all pressed into service, with varying degrees of success.

There are teaching aids aimed at most aspects of golf. They can range in diversity from the simplest – a handkerchief held under the right arm to encourage the elbow to stay close to the body throughout the swing – to a state-of-the-art computerized swing trainer. But, for every useful aid between these two extremes, there are many more that can be best described as gimmicks.

As with golf-club technology, many of the latest gadgets actually owe their origin to well tried and tested teaching and practice aids from earlier days. Body harnesses – designed to keep the right elbow down and close

Balloon prevents elbows from separating in swing

Balloon prevents legs from separating in swing

Swing balloon
An inflatable ball or a balloon placed between the elbows is a simple but effective aid to keeping the arms close together during the swing. It helps promote a smooth takeaway, and a solid position at the top of the swing.

against the upper chest, thereby preventing it flying and throwing the club off plane – have been around for decades. The late Sir Henry Cotton was a great believer in a tight elbow, though he employed far less complicated devices than a harness in his teaching sessions.

SIMPLE BUT EFFECTIVE
Cotton's particular favourite was a handkerchief held between the right upper arm and the upper chest that had to be maintained in that position throughout the swing. Indeed, he was responsible for many classic aids to better golf, as well as techniques for improving strength – particularly in the hands and wrists. He added a mass of lead to an old driver to produce the first weighted club, which he used to build strength in the golfing muscles of the

---

PUTTING AIDS

FLEXIBLE-SHAFTED PUTTER
A putter designed with an exceptionally flexible carbon-fibre shaft can help encourage a smooth takeaway and stroke through the ball. Only a smooth stroke will allow the putt to be struck solidly. Any snatching on the downstroke will cause the putter head to leap ahead of the hands and shaft before it reaches impact.

A hurried downstroke causes putter shaft to bend

PUTTING ANALYZER
A putting analyzer is designed to create the feeling of the perfect putting stroke. It features a frame that acts as a guide rail for the putter shaft to promote a straight back-and through-stroke. In addition, it has a mirror behind the ball to show when the eyes are in the ideal position, and a scale for the length of swing.

Guide rail for putter

Mirror

For the three-quarter swing, arm is locked with hands under the shaft and elbow points to ground

The right angle
Keeping the club on plane is critical to consistent striking. This device allows the club to be swung to the ideal position at the top of the backswing, depending on the length of the swing.

shoulders, arms, and hands. Cotton believed it also helped to promote a smooth swing and was an excellent warm-up tool. The modern equivalent has a cranked shaft and a head shaped like an iron club, but the principle remains exactly the same.

In terms of teaching aids, what Cotton was instrumental in starting, the modern teaching gurus have taken a stage further. Teachers such as the Florida-based Zimbabwean, David Leadbetter, and British putting guru Harold Swash, are two of the many who have designed, developed, and marketed teaching aids. And where once Henry Cotton simply used his eyes to assess the faults of his pupils, the modern teaching professional uses a video camera and a television screen.

Harness keeps left arm bonded to upper chest to help make a full, one-piece turn

Body harness
A more sophisticated version of the balloon trick, this body harness encourages the same one-piece effect. It keeps the upper arms close to the chest and prevents the elbows from separating during the swing.

THE HINGED-SHAFT IRON

One of the most effective pieces of teaching equipment around is the club with a hinged shaft. Only by making a smooth takeaway and keeping it on the correct plane is it possible to swing the club without the hinge breaking down.

When swinging consistently, it is possible to hit full shots with this club, despite the hinge. A very effective aid, it is particularly valuable in preventing the club from being snatched away from the ball at the all-important start of the backswing.

If clubface is too open at top of backswing, its bad positioning will cause hinge to break open

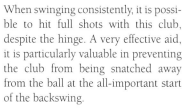

Correct swing
At the top of the swing the hinge remains firm. This is because the club is correctly on plane, the hands are set under the grip, and the clubface is square.

Too far outside
Lifting the club to the outside on the takeaway will result in the hinge breaking down.

Too far inside
Taking the club too far on the inside in the takeaway causes the hinge to break down.

CHAPTER THREE

GETTING *into* SHAPE

THE WONDERFUL THING *about golf is that anyone can play it, regardless of his or her physical attributes. Shape, or even disability in whatever form, presents no barrier to enjoying the delights of the golf course. Within the ranks of the great players over the decades there have been players of all shapes and sizes from whom we can all draw*

Simple exercises using a golf club and an old tyre can help build strength in the hands and arms

inspiration. This chapter looks at how to use your body shape to the best advantage, and how to prepare for the rigours of a round of golf.

Three-tier practice
No other nation in the world practises golf like the Japanese. Because the demand for golf courses far outstrips availability, practice facilities like this three-tier range in Tokyo are popular throughout the day and night.

A few minutes stretching and toning of the muscles each day can do wonders for body flexibility out on the course

Playing to your strengths

IT IS OBVIOUS that the short and stocky Ian Woosnam cannot swing the golf club in the same way as tall and slim Tom Weiskopf. Yet these examples of the 'long and short' of golf have both won major championships – confirmation that extremes in physical makeup are no barrier to playing golf.

Few of us have the golfing attributes of Woosnam or Weiskopf; very few of us have the suppleness of Bobby Jones, or the trained hands of Henry Cotton; and fewer still will have the delicacy of touch of Seve Ballesteros or the mental strength of Jack Nicklaus. Yet we all have strengths that can be exploited to help us play to our full potential. Learning from other players is what this book is all about. We are looking for clues from those who play golf better than we do. However, there is very little point in a successful, 55-year-old executive with an ever-expanding girth using Jose Maria Olazabal as a swing role model; or the tall, gangly, teenager modelling his style on an ageing Jack Nicklaus. We have to play with what we have been given, or, as the great Sam Snead put it a little more colourfully: "You've gotta dance with the woman ya brung"!

Marie Laure de Lorenzi
Enjoying an ideal build for a woman golfer, Marie Laure de Lorenzi has a long and elegant swing that is a product of her slim and athletic 5ft 7in (1.7m) shape.

Phil Mickelson
The 1963 British Open, won by Bob Charles, is the only major victory of a left-hander. Yet being left-handed should not make golf any more difficult – and the ideal build and sound technique of Phil Mickelson superbly illustrate this point.

Tom Watson
Five-times British Open champion Tom Watson is just about the perfect build for playing golf. Immensely strong in the shoulders, arms, and legs, his 5ft 9in (1.75m) frame gives him a low centre of gravity and a very solid base for a powerful swing – one of the reasons why Watson performs so well in windy and difficult conditions.

TALL AND THICK-SET

Players who are tall and thick-set require more room in the swing and usually have to rely on an opening and closing of the hands allied to a more rounded swing plane. Golf is certainly more difficult for people at the physical extremes, but there are always ways in which an individual can compensate. Players with this body shape need to develop good hand action and sometimes benefit from staying further back from the ball at address.

Laura Davies MBE
World number one Laura Davies is a classic example of a player making the best of her physique. At 5ft 10in (1.8m), her height gives her the advantage of a long arc. Allied to a powerful frame, her height helps her to hit the ball further than most.

TALL AND SLIM

Most of the problems for tall, slim golfers are centred on the width of the swing arc they create. The radius of the arc – the distance from the left shoulder to the clubhead – is wide; ideal for long clubs but more difficult as the length of shaft shortens.

Approach shots in particular require a narrow arc width, making life more difficult for the taller player. Many overcome this by swaying into the ball on the downswing to make the angle of attack a little steeper.

Tom Weiskopf
At 6ft 3in (1.9m) Weiskopf is one of the tallest players to win the British Open. Because of his height he has to work hard to maintain good balance in the wind.

ROTUND

A high percentage of golfers fall into this category either because of their natural body type or, more often, because the passing of the years has added considerably to their girth. As players advance in years they not only have to cope with expanding waistlines, but also tightening of the muscles and less flexibility in the joints. The swing inevitably has to be more around the body to accommodate the extra girth. Good hand action is one of the compensatory keys. It is no coincidence that players with 'flexible waistlines' invariably have an excellent short game to make up for possible deficiencies in their long game.

Bobby Locke
Four-times British Open champion Bobby Locke swung the club around his body from a very closed stance and hooked every shot. This was an ideal technique for coping with an expanding waistline.

SHORT AND STOCKY

Short and stocky players cope better than most with strong winds but their lack of height and squat figure make it difficult to create a wide enough arc, particularly for the longer clubs. They benefit from a flatter, more around-the-body swing to create width, and they often complement that with a distinct sway away from the ball in the backswing, which also widens the arc. Smaller golfers often become expert short-game players because their naturally steep arc is ideal for the pitching clubs.

Ian Woosnam
Ian Woosnam relies on technique to compensate for his 5ft 4in (1.63m) frame. He makes a huge shoulder turn and uses a flatter swing to create as wide an arc as possible, making him one of the longest hitters around.

SHORT AND SLIM

Players who are short and slim cannot hope to swing the golf club with the power of their physically bigger and more muscular counterparts. But what nature takes on one side she generally gives back on another. Short, slim players are usually very supple, allowing them to make a full shoulder turn to create a wide arc. They can be excellent pitchers of the ball because of the steeper arc, and very often have a wonderful touch around the greens to compensate for lack of length off the tee.

Jan Stephenson
Former US Women's Open champion Jan Stephenson has a kind of figure not commonly seen in top-level golf, yet she has proved herself to be one of the truly outstanding players in the history of the women's game.

SHORT AND STRONG

Strength is not always equated to size, and there are many short individuals who are extremely powerful. There are many advantages for players with this type of build. A solid platform, provided by a low centre of gravity, combined with a wide arc, helps to utilize the strength to maximum effect in the swing. A shorter stature also tends to create a good action for the fairway irons and the pitching clubs.

Gary Player
Gary Player, who is 5ft 8in (1.73m) tall but weighs only 159lb (72kg), has, by dint of intense physical exercise and self-denial, built himself into, in terms of his size, the strongest man ever to play the game of golf.

SLIGHT

Golfers who are slightly built clearly have a disadvantage in terms of strength but often compensate for their lack of length with guile and tenacity. There is always more than one way around a golf course, and players who are slight of build often develop a superb touch around the greens and are numbered among the game's best putters. Paul Runyan, one of the top players of the 1930s, weighed only 142lb (64kg) and was a notoriously short-hitter, but he defeated big-hitting 'Slammin' Sam Snead by 8 & 7 in the final of the 1938 USPGA Championship thanks largely to his play on and around the greens.

Corey Pavin
1995 US Open champion Corey Pavin is very slightly built, although he is still capable of hitting the ball a long way. His main strength, however, is being able to work the ball to suit conditions, allied with a masterly touch around the greens.

ADVANCING YEARS

Advancing years are something over which we have no control, but changes to the golf swing can be made to help keep the years at bay for as long as possible. A more rounded and flatter swing, which helps produce a drawn shot, will go some way to compensate for the shortening in length that accompanies the latter years. Jack Nicklaus was one of several top players to follow this route as he moved into senior golf. Modern equipment, too, has come to the aid of players in the later stages of life. Lofted metal woods,

graphite shafts, and high-performance golf balls have given many players a new lease of life.

Gene Sarazen
Well into his 90s, Gene Sarazen, one of golf's all-time greats, is still playing the game. An inspiration to anyone of advancing years, he is a star draw at the US Masters, where he ceremonially starts the event together with Byron Nelson and Sam Snead.

OVERCOMING PHYSICAL DISABILITIES

Many golfers are still able to play and get fulfilment from the game of golf despite congenital disability or disability through illness or injury. Indeed, there are various societies and championships for impaired golfers all over the world, including tournaments for those who are blind or partially sighted.

Several players who have sustained some permanent physical damage have not only overcome the disability but gone on to become players able to compete at the very highest level. Ben Hogan is perhaps the most famous example of a player succeeding despite, and some would suggest because of, physical disability. Perhaps more than any other sport, golf proves that natural talent and the desire to play can take on and overcome even the most debilitating of handicaps.

Ed Furgol
As a result of an accident in his youth, Ed Furgol had a left arm that was crooked, shortened, and stiff at the elbow. In spite of this disability, which forced him to swing almost totally with his right arm, he won the 1954 US Open at Baltusrol, one of the world's toughest courses.

Sir Douglas Bader
Despite having both legs amputated as a result of a flying accident, British air ace Sir Douglas Bader still managed to play golf to a low, single figure handicap; making him an inspiration to all limbless golfers.

Calvin Peete
Despite a left arm which he could not straighten, thanks to a fall from a tree, Calvin Peete, for a spell in the 1980s, was one of the most successful players on the USPGA Tour. His bent left arm did not allow him to hit the ball far but he has always been one of the straightest hitters in the game.

Jack Newton
The professional career of Jack Newton was ended by a tragic accident, in which he walked into an aeroplane propeller and lost an arm and an eye. However, that has not stopped the Australian, who was beaten by Tom Watson in a play-off for the British Open at Carnoustie in 1975, from continuing to play. Even with one arm and impaired vision, Jack is still a match for most players.

Building up your strength

ONE OF THE MOST effective, yet simple, training methods for improving strength in the hands and wrists is this set of drills invented by Sir Henry Cotton. Inspired by a chance discovery in the car park of an English golf club, these exercises can be a valuable aid to today's golfer, and require nothing more complex than a golf club and an old car tyre.

Sir Henry Cotton spent many long hours over the years playing in the deepest rough he could find on the golf course. Such behaviour is not quite as strange as it sounds. By swinging away in the long grass, which offered greater resistance to the clubhead, Cotton was able to build up the muscles in his hands and arms.

But as courses became more manicured, the amount of long grass available diminished and he was forced to find an alternative solution – both for himself and the teaching programmes that he had been steadily developing. The solution arrived one day at Temple Golf Club, near Maidenhead in England. Sir Henry drove his car into the car park and found an old tyre blocking his way.

He got out and kicked the obstruction out of the way. In a flash, Cotton realized that he had found the very equipment he needed to help develop his hand-strengthening programme.

WEIGHT TRAINING

The tyre exercises Sir Henry created are, in effect, a form of weight training for golfers. They help build strong muscles in the hands, wrists, and forearms as well as training the hands to accept the impact of a heavy blow on the clubface. Sir Henry called it 'resistance' training and these drills remain just as useful today as they were back in the 1950s. For all these exercises, it is advisable to use an old club and the oldest and most worn tyre you can find. A tyre with soft walls and as little tread left as possible is the ideal.

The maestro
One of the great players of his era, Sir Henry Cotton was also an innovator who did much to advance teaching theories and practice.

THE SINGLE-HANDED TAP

Hold a middle iron with a normal grip in the right hand only. Tap the back of the tyre on a pre-selected spot using the action of the wrist only. Do not swing the arm back but concentrate on making a square-faced connection with the tyre. Start off with 10 repetitions. Keeping the same grip, move to the other side of the tyre and repeat the exercise backhanded.

Switch hands and grip the club with the left hand only in the normal grip and repeat the exercises in the same order. Ten repetitions are sufficient to begin with, but this number can gradually be increased as you get stronger, although be careful not to do too many and strain your wrist. This is a valuable exercise to strengthen the hands, wrists, and forearms.

Wrist only
Keep arm firm and rely on wrist to move club.

Contra exercise
Repeat all exercises in opposite direction.

SWINGING AT A TYRE

This is the simplest tyre exercise on which all the others are based. It simply involves using the tyre as a replacement for a ball, and not only builds up the arm muscles but also helps you to judge the speed of your swing.

Wrists
Hinge wrists early in takeaway.

Takeaway
Take a normal stance with the tyre positioned like a large golf ball. Employing a normal grip, use a quarter swing to hit the back of the tyre, moving the clubhead as fast as possible.

Target
Always pick a spot on tyre to aim at. Mark it if necessary.

Head
Keep head still, as for a full shot.

Impact
The pitch of the swishing noise and the sound of the impact are your indicators of speed. The higher the pitch and the louder the crack, the faster the clubhead speed. The loudest crack at impact will be heard when the clubhead is released properly, similar to the way that a hammer head strikes a nail. The longer the 'hit' is delayed, the faster will be the clubhead speed.

Real shot
After several swings at tyre, step back and attack ball with the same late 'hit'.

Late 'hit'
Delay 'hit' as long as possible.

LEFT-HANDED

Sir Henry was a great believer in two-sided exercises and insisted that all exercises had to be repeated in the opposite direction so as not to develop one side of the body more than the other. Equal development on both sides particularly helps the hands and arms to work together without one overpowering the other. He also felt that exercises performed both right-handed and left-handed helped to reduce the threat of back injuries. And among his contemporaries, he was one of the very few who did not suffer from back complaints.

HEADLESS CLUB

This exercise, using an old shaft without a head, is valuable in training the hands to work more quickly. Keeping the arm stationary, use the hand and wrist only to whip the shaft against the front and back of the inside of the tyre. Concentrate on hitting the same points each time and move the shaft as quickly as possible. Then repeat using the left hand. It is important to reiterate that the arm must be kept still for the exercise to be effective.

Hold arm tight to body

Headless club

Improving your flexibility

AMONG ALL THE athletic sports golf is unique in that it does not require huge physical strength to play well. Of course, strength is a contributing factor but of much more importance is flexibility in the muscles and joints. This simple home exercise programme takes only about 10 minutes to run through and, if carried out regularly, will make a valuable contribution to game improvement.

The average golfer tends not to have the same opportunities as the tournament professional when it comes to getting really fit to play the game of golf – for most of us there just does not seem to be enough time. However, any weekend golfer who is serious about trying to improve cannot afford to ignore the benefits that warming up before a round can bring. A simple yet effective exercise programme should be part of every golfer's schedule. Warming up is just as important as work on the practice ground and can be the best insurance against injury. Those of us who rush to the first tee from the car and then lash at the first drive, not only face the probability that the ball will scuttle pathetically off the tee, we also run a serious risk of damaging muscles and tendons not warmed to the task.

This group of exercises helps improve flexibility in the back, shoulders, and neck, and improves strength in the leg and abdominal muscles – all vital elements for playing golf.

BEND AND STRETCH
Ten minutes a day with this bend and stretch programme not only makes it easier to play, but is also excellent as part of a general health and fitness programme.

NO. 1 – KNEES TO CHEST FORWARD STRETCH

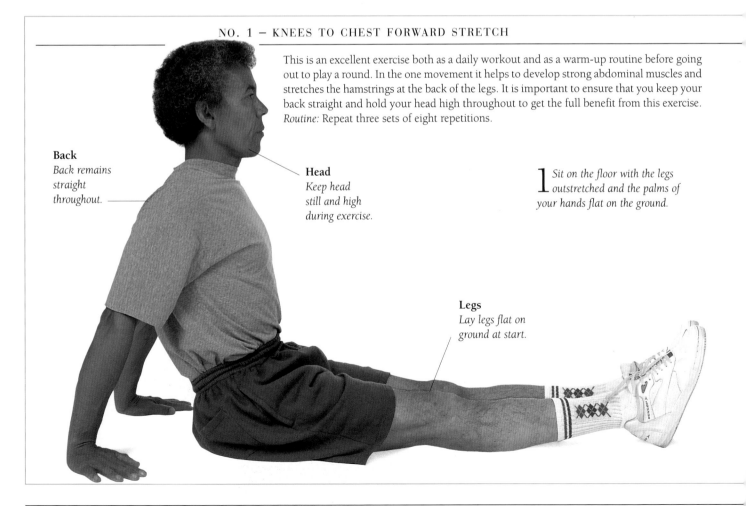

This is an excellent exercise both as a daily workout and as a warm-up routine before going out to play a round. In the one movement it helps to develop strong abdominal muscles and stretches the hamstrings at the back of the legs. It is important to ensure that you keep your back straight and hold your head high throughout to get the full benefit from this exercise. *Routine:* Repeat three sets of eight repetitions.

Back
Back remains straight throughout.

Head
Keep head still and high during exercise.

1 *Sit on the floor with the legs outstretched and the palms of your hands flat on the ground.*

Legs
Lay legs flat on ground at start.

NO. 2 — LYING HALF TWISTS

This multi-purpose exercise is designed to develop trunk rotation and flexibility, while at the same time helping to tone up and shape the midriff. The significance of performing half twists is that they largely reproduce the body movements used in both the backswing and the followthrough of the golf swing. *Routine:* Repeat three sets of six repetitions on each side.

1 *Keep feet and knees together with back pressed flat against the floor and head looking towards knees. Feet stay parallel with the floor.*

2 *Roll over to the left and then to the right, trying to keep shoulders pinned to the floor. As flexibility increases, it will become easier to keep the shoulders flat on the floor.*

Feet
Feet remain parallel to floor.

Head
Keep head up and looking at knees.

Feet
Hold feet high as knees are lifted to chest.

Body
Slight rocking action as legs are raised.

3 *Return your legs to the original position. At the same time, reach forwards with your hands to grip around the ankles, stretching the back of the legs. Repeat the exercise in one continuous movement.*

Arms
Arms reach forwards to hold ankles in forward stretch.

2 *Lift your knees towards your chest. A small rocking movement will occur as the knees and feet are held high.*

NO. 3 – THE TUMMY CRUNCH

Aimed specifically at strengthening the tummy muscles and burning off excess fat, this exercise has the additional benefit of toning the neck area. Both of these sets of muscles play a key role in the movement of the body during a golf swing, but to get the most out of the exercise, do not allow your feet to touch the floor. *Routine:* Repeat three sets with 12–20 repetitions.

1 *Lie on your back and place fingers – not hands – on back of head. Lift feet and head off the floor at the same time.*

2 *Push your back flat to the floor. With head remaining in a fixed position, work arms and legs towards each other. Return to the starting position and repeat.*

Back
Keep back flat on floor during exercise.

Feet
Feet must stay above floor throughout.

NO. 4 – THREE-WAY STRETCH

The three-way stretch is an exercise that looks more difficult than it really is. It is designed to loosen the inner part of the thighs to create more flexibility. Don't lose hope if your movement is limited. After three to four weeks there will be a marked improvement. Try to keep the legs as straight as possible throughout the exercise. *Routine:* Repeat three sets with 10 repetitions.

1 *Extend legs fully and place hands on floor to support and control stretch. Extend body forwards, aiming tummy at floor. Keep back straight throughout.*

2 *Extend the legs just short of maximum stretch. Check that the head, knee, and foot are aligned before stretching forwards, and remain as straight as possible. Then repeat on other side.*

Hands
Place hands on floor for support and control.

Legs
Extend legs as far as possible.

In line
Check head, knee, and foot are in alignment.

NO. 5 – CAT STRETCH

One of the most lithe and flexible of all animals is the cat. We can all learn from the feline world by copying the pronounced arching of the back that cats carry out regularly. This is an excellent flexibility exercise for keeping the back nice and straight – a major problem area for many golfers. *Routine:* Three sets with 10 repetitions.

Legs
Keep legs slightly apart in start position.

Back
Arch back as far as possible.

1 *Kneel on the floor with knees slightly apart. Hands should be flat on the ground.*

2 *Roll head down, looking towards your belt buckle while arching your back.*

NO. 6 – FORWARD STRETCH

This exercise is designed to stretch the hamstrings at the back of the legs. Stand with your feet slightly apart and fold your arms. Keeping your head up, gently bend forwards, ensuring that your back and legs remain straight. Sit back on your heels while bending forwards. Find your maximum stretch and hold for a count of three to five seconds. *Routine:* Repeat three sets.

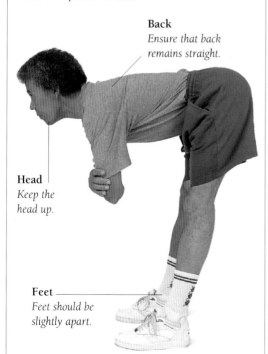

Back
Ensure that back remains straight.

Head
Keep the head up.

Feet
Feet should be slightly apart.

NO. 7 – RUNNING ON THE SPOT

This exercise is essentially to improve the cardiovascular system and to help develop stamina. Towards the end of a round a player can become physically fatigued, which in turn can affect concentration just when it is needed most. This exercise helps to delay the onset of fatigue and is excellent for general health. *Routine:* 20–30 seconds in three sessions.

Arms
Keep arm parallel to floor for each step.

Knees
Bring knees up to meet hands.

1 *Hold hands parallel to the floor as a marker. Stand as tall as possible and run on the spot.*

2 *As you change legs, ensure that your thighs make contact with your hands with each leg lift.*

Warming up your body

THERE ARE TWO main reasons why we must warm up muscles before a round of golf. The principal reason is that tense muscles, suddenly called upon to undertake violent action, are very prone to injury. Secondly, just as a car engine does not run efficiently until it reaches working temperature, the golf swing will not work at its best until the muscles involved have reached full flexibility.

USE YOUR BAG
A few simple warm-up exercises on the first tee will tune up your muscles and get rid of any stiffness.

A last-second dash down to the tee followed by a couple of quick practice swings is about as close as most of us get to a warm-up before we set out on a round. If it takes the majority of tournament professionals close on an hour to warm up, then it is hardly surprising that so many

opening tee shots in our Sunday morning fourball end up in the rough or only just make it off the teeing ground.

If we don't have time for a professional-style workout before we play, at least we should spend a few minutes on some pre-round flexibility and warm-up exercises that will

NO. 1 – SEATED TRUNK ROTATION

This is an excellent exercise for improving trunk rotation – vital to the golf swing – and for warming up the body for maximum flexibility before play. It has a double effect: it develops flexibility and tones the mid-section. The seated position (a seat or a low wall near the first tee will do) emphasizes the trunk turn with minimum hip rotation. *Routine: Repeat three sets with six to eight repetitions on each side.*

2 *Keep eyes fixed firmly ahead and turn your trunk while the hips remain in a constant position. This is the backswing position.*

1 *Sit comfortably and straddle legs as shown. This forms a platform to turn against. Place a golf club behind your neck.*

protect against injury and give us at least a chance to play at our best from the word go.

These exercises, as with the routines on pages 50–53, only take a few minutes to run through and, if we make a point of getting to the tee a couple of minutes earlier than normal, they can be done while we are waiting for our turn to play.

Getting fully warmed up is not just a matter of good preparation. From the physical and mental point of view, it could well be worth a couple of holes' start against an opponent who arrives at the first tee completely unprepared.

Rushing to the tee can easily lead to rushing through the game itself, producing a hurried tempo that is destructive to both rhythm and timing. Warming up will help relax both your muscles and your mind.

3 *Return to the starting position and make the turn in the opposite direction. This is the followthrough position.*

NO. 2 – STANDING TRUNK ROTATION

Without flexibility in the trunk it is not possible to make a full shoulder turn on the backswing. Many faults occur as a result, including the dreaded reverse pivot – hitting off the right foot. This exercise is designed to warm up the trunk muscles before play and fend off injury to the lower back, shoulders, and right upper area around the neck. *Routine:* Repeat three sets with five to eight repetitions for each leg.

1 *Place the ball of your right foot on a golf bag and the left hand just below the right knee. Rest the right hand and arm behind your back on the left hip.*

2 *Turn your body to the maximum backswing position, using your left arm to hold back the right leg, and then return. This will create maximum torque.*

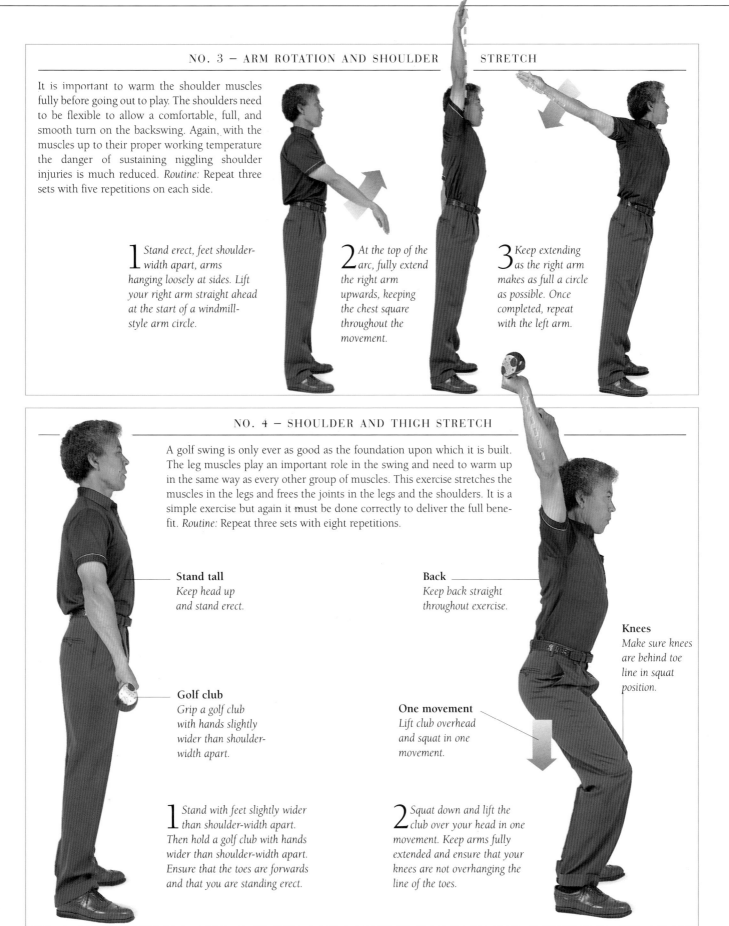

NO. 3 – ARM ROTATION AND SHOULDER STRETCH

It is important to warm the shoulder muscles fully before going out to play. The shoulders need to be flexible to allow a comfortable, full, and smooth turn on the backswing. Again, with the muscles up to their proper working temperature the danger of sustaining niggling shoulder injuries is much reduced. *Routine:* Repeat three sets with five repetitions on each side.

1 *Stand erect, feet shoulder-width apart, arms hanging loosely at sides. Lift your right arm straight ahead at the start of a windmill-style arm circle.*

2 *At the top of the arc, fully extend the right arm upwards, keeping the chest square throughout the movement.*

3 *Keep extending as the right arm makes as full a circle as possible. Once completed, repeat with the left arm.*

NO. 4 – SHOULDER AND THIGH STRETCH

A golf swing is only ever as good as the foundation upon which it is built. The leg muscles play an important role in the swing and need to warm up in the same way as every other group of muscles. This exercise stretches the muscles in the legs and frees the joints in the legs and the shoulders. It is a simple exercise but again it must be done correctly to deliver the full benefit. *Routine:* Repeat three sets with eight repetitions.

Stand tall
Keep head up and stand erect.

Back
Keep back straight throughout exercise.

Knees
Make sure knees are behind toe line in squat position.

Golf club
Grip a golf club with hands slightly wider than shoulder-width apart.

One movement
Lift club overhead and squat in one movement.

1 *Stand with feet slightly wider than shoulder-width apart. Then hold a golf club with hands wider than shoulder-width apart. Ensure that the toes are forwards and that you are standing erect.*

2 *Squat down and lift the club over your head in one movement. Keep arms fully extended and ensure that your knees are not overhanging the line of the toes.*

NO. 5 — SHOULDER SHRUG

The trapezius muscle is a triangular muscle that stretches across the back of the neck and shoulders. It is one of a large group of muscles that can become tense very easily – and tension here can be disastrous for the golf swing. This exercise helps to relax the shoulder and trapezius region before commencing play. *Routine:* Repeat three sets with 10 repetitions.

1 *Stand erect, but relaxed, with your arms hanging loosely at your sides.*

2 *Take in a deep breath as you start to lift your shoulders upwards.*

3 *As you roll your shoulders backwards and downwards begin to exhale slowly.*

NO. 6 — BACK AND SIDE STRETCH

This exercise is aimed at warming up the upper back and shoulder muscles by gently stretching them together with the joints. It is important to make sure that your arms remain fully extended throughout the exercise. *Routine:* Repeat three sets with eight to 10 repetitions.

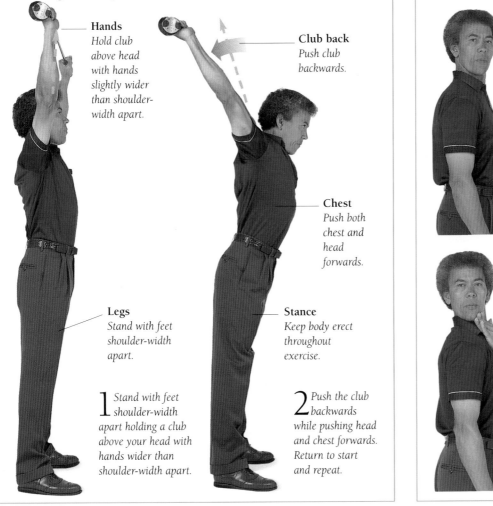

Hands
Hold club above head with hands slightly wider than shoulder-width apart.

Club back
Push club backwards.

Chest
Push both chest and head forwards.

Legs
Stand with feet shoulder-width apart.

Stance
Keep body erect throughout exercise.

1 *Stand with feet shoulder-width apart holding a club above your head with hands wider than shoulder-width apart.*

2 *Push the club backwards while pushing head and chest forwards. Return to start and repeat.*

NO. 7 — NECK TURN

Although our neck muscles are in constant use – particularly during a round of golf – lack of the right kind of stretching exercise can leave the muscles tight and inflexible. This is a simple but very effective exercise to loosen up the neck muscles before play. *Routine:* Repeat three sets with five repetitions each side.

1 *Look over the right shoulder until the neck is at full stretch. Make sure that you keep your chin up and shoulders back.*

2 *Using firm but gentle pressure from the left hand, push – don't jerk – the neck until you feel the stretch. Gently ease the pressure off and repeat.*

CHAPTER FOUR

The MASTERCLASS

Get an overview of the swing from every angle

IN THIS CHAPTER *we delve into the secrets of those who know best – the world's leading professional golfers. The lessons presented here are not the views of any one player or individual, but rather a gathering together of the common wisdom; an accumulation, distilled from many years of observation and study, not only of the swings of the masters of the game but also of their thoughts, impressions, and ideas on what makes the golf swing work best. It is important to stress that there is no single, correct way to swing a club, and what follows should not be treated as a definitive guide. However, the chapter provides an expert base from which the average player can develop his or her own individual technique.*

Learn from modern-day masters such as Ernie Els

Discover the best way of coping with difficult situations

Look and learn
Thousands descended upon the Olympic Club in California to watch and learn from watching the game's leading players in action at the 1987 US Open.

40%   60%

Key stages of the swing

EVERY SWING, WHETHER it be for a full-blooded drive or the shortest putt, shares the same key elements. Set-up, takeaway, downswing, impact, and followthrough are common stages in all swings – only the club used and the length of swing are variables. Of course, as we have already seen, no two golf swings are identical and there are always variations on a theme, but the key stages shown here should be as common to your swing as they are to that of Greg Norman or Ernie Els in the present day, or to those of Old Tom Morris and Harry Vardon in years gone by.

Line of feet

Feet
Feet are parallel with target line.

Target line

Ball
Ball is correctly positioned – opposite left heel for driver.

Shoulders
Shoulders turn in unison with hands and arms.

1 The set-up
This is the basic address position, with shoulders and feet aligned parallel to the line of flight. Some players, such as Lee Trevino, adopt a much more open position, but the other elements are common to all players.

Club
Aim to get club as close as possible to parallel with target line.

2 The takeaway
The first 24in (60cm) stage of the takeaway is crucial to the swing, helping to determine both its width and the clubhead's path during the swing. Mistakes here can lead to destructive compensations later on.

Hands
Hands and arms take club away in one-piece movement.

3 At the top
A good, one-piece takeaway and a full shoulder turn take the club to the top of the backswing (known as the slot). Here all the backswing elements combine to produce the ideal position from which to deliver a square blow to the ball.

TAKEAWAY ZONE

Left knee
Left knee works in towards ball.

6 Followthrough
The impetus of the club through impact carries the club round in a free-wheeling motion. The followthrough is a good indicator of the quality of the shot, with a high and balanced finish highlighting a controlled swing.

Heel
Right heel comes off ground after weight moves to left side.

Club
Club remains in control in a balanced finish.

Head
Head remains behind ball at impact.

Shoulders
Shoulders turn in unison with hands and arms.

Left foot
Weight moves onto left foot ready for impact.

5 Point of impact
The impact position is the one common position among all the great players, no matter what the rest of their swing may look like. This position is very similar to that at address, except that the weight has moved to the left side.

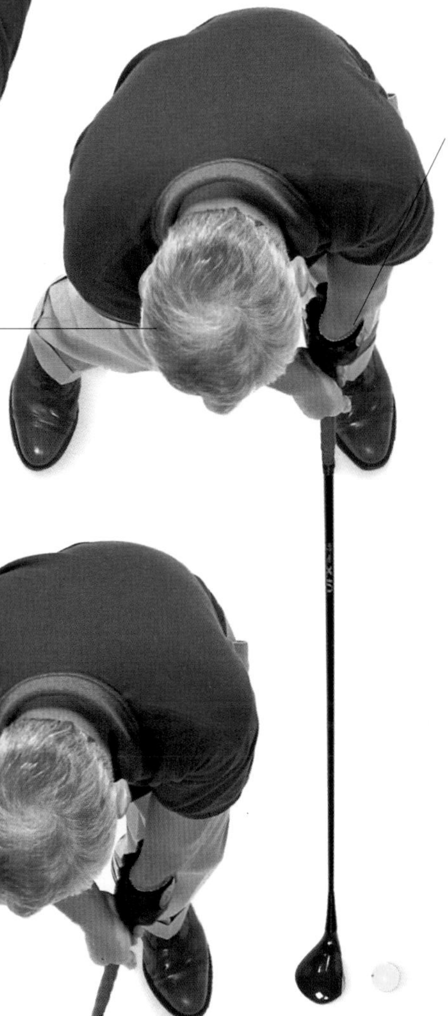

Hands
Hands and arms continue down target line before moving inside as body rotates through impact.

IMPACT ZONE

4 Downswing weight transfer
This is where the club changes direction from backwards to forwards and the weight transfers onto the left side. It is vital that this move is smooth. Any jerkiness can throw the club off its correct arc or plane.

DOWNSWING ZONE

Different strokes

TO WATCH, FOR INSTANCE, Nick Price, Ian Woosnam, and Lee Trevino swing the golf club is to see three entirely different types of golf swing. Each, however, succeeds in delivering the clubhead square to, and along, the target line, and at the right angle of attack. Whether it be in developing a consistent set-up, finding a constant rhythm, or gaining insight into better bunker play, there is always something to be learned from every great player.

Wide takeaway – Ian Woosnam
Because of his short, stocky build, Ian Woosnam needs width in his swing to generate clubhead speed. He has a wide takeaway and swings the club around his body on a slightly flatter plane.

The classic swing – Nick Price

Nick Price is a first-class example of a player with a classic swing. It is an uncomplicated action and is hugely efficient. He sets up squarely to the intended line of flight and makes a brisk, one-piece takeaway. From a neutral position at the top, he drops the club marginally inside the line on the downswing to attack the ball from the inside through impact. Simple, smooth, yet fast and highly effective.

The unconventional swing – Lee Trevino

Lee Trevino is undoubtedly one of the most controlled strikers of the golf ball there has been – despite a highly unconventional swing. He always sets up with his body aiming left of target but with the clubface square to the intended line. He then takes the clubhead back immediately outside the line. From the top, Lee drops his hands down inside the line (indicated by an aggressive lower body action). This allows him to attack the ball slightly from the inside, driving the ball out on a low trajectory.

Body
Shoulders, feet, and hips all point left of target at address.

Takeaway
Arms, hands, and shoulders turn together at start of takeaway.

Clubface
Trevino takes club immediately back outside the line.

Extraordinary swinger – Eamonn Darcy

Irish Ryder Cup player Eamonn Darcy is an extreme example of the 'flying right elbow' – the right arm coming well away from the body in the backswing. From a very unconventional position at the top, Darcy attacks the ball with a strange chopping motion. But in fact, like all the finest players, he succeeds in returning the clubhead to the ball square to the line of flight, pointing at the target and at the right angle of attack: the essential ingredients of a solid strike.

Right elbow
Right arm comes well away from body in backswing.

Impact
Clubface is square to line of flight at impact.

Downswing
Price drops club onto a flatter plane as he moves into downswing.

Followthrough
Price's excellent tempo is reflected in a perfectly balanced followthrough.

Downswing
Trevino drops hands down inside his backswing line as he moves into downswing.

Body and club
Despite a very different route, note how Trevino has moved into the same position as Price.

Followthrough
Trevino swings through in his own, distinctive style.

How to use The Masterclass

THE MASTERCLASS IS a unique guide to golf improvement. There are countless theories on how best to play the game but the most reliable place to look is where theory has been successfully put into practice – among the great exponents of the game. The Masterclass breaks down the game into nine areas, with each section containing a series of lessons based on the thoughts, theories, and techniques of golf's most successful performers. By careful study of this wisdom we can not only unlock some of their individual secrets but also explore alternative methods which could well have a dramatic effect on our game.

INTRODUCTORY SPREAD
Each of the nine sections of The Masterclass opens with a spread introducing you to the main elements covered.

LESSON SPREAD
Each section is divided into lessons, taking you through all the aspects of golf in which you can fine-tune your game.

LESSON TWO

Improving the downsw

THE TRANSITION FROM completing the backswing to starting the downswing is a critical point in the overall swing. And while the downswing is largely a reaction,

rathe
are s
can
dow

KEY 1 GET 'IN THE SLOT'
The position at the top is largely a product of the work done in the first part of the backswing. If, after the initial takeaway and turn, the club is 'set' into the ideal position (see page 81), all the difficult work is done. Rotating the body until the shoulders complete a 90° turn, while the arms continue upwards, takes the club naturally into the slot at the top.

FAULT-FINDER
DON'T SNATCH FROM THE TOP

Rushing the downswing is one of the biggest power-killers in golf. The moment the club is 'snatched' from the top, the downswing becomes too narrow and too cramped. There is nowhere to go except steeply down on top of the ball, losing power and direction – exactly the opposite of what is required with the driver.

Ri
Ke
fle
'res
sw

Right foot
Majority of weight moves onto right foot.

82

75%

FAU
DON'T SNAT

Rushing the downswing
in golf. The moment th
the downswing become
There is nowhere to go e
ball, losing power and d
what is required with th

ESSENTIALS OF CONSISTENT IRON PLAY

ESSENTIALS OF CONSISTENT IRON PLAY

LONG IRONS ARE what might be called 'anywhere-on-the-green' clubs. Even the top players hit relatively few of these shots close to the hole. When you move into the mid-iron range, though, you need to set your sights higher. The long drivers and the streak putters may grab the headlines, but solid iron play is just as important. From the classical action of Ernie Els to the unique style of Raymond Floyd, consistency remains the common factor uniting all the great iron players.

DAVID GRAHAM
Doggedly accurate iron play has helped Australian David Graham land two majors and a host of wins around the world. His 1981 US Open success at Merion was built on pinpoint accuracy with his irons and hitting every fairway bar one during his final round of 67.

ERNIE ELS
Ernie Els is one of the best players in world golf today, and the fact that he has such a good iron game is no coincidence. He does everything systematically to give himself the best chance of hitting good iron shots.

RAYMOND FLOYD
Despite a swing that can hardly be described as classical, Ray Floyd is deadly with his iron approach shots – proof of the value of a repeating technique, irrespective of how it looks.

1 THE ADDRESS
Ernie Els emphasizes the importance of good posture and a comfortable, relaxed set-up to the ball. Like all the best players, his head is kept up at address and his arms hang down naturally, free of tension, from the shoulders.

2 TURN AND SET
Having made the perfect one-piece takeaway, Ernie cocks the wrists, setting the club on an ideal plane. His upper body starts to rotate, with his left shoulder turning under the chin.

3 AT THE TOP
This is a superb position at the top of the backswing, and is a model for anyone working to improve their swing. The shoulders have made a full 90° turn, the hips and knees resisting the rotary motion of the upper body.

4 THE DOWNSWING
In all the best swings the club drops slightly inside the line on the way down. Note how Ernie maintains perfect balance and rhythm, placing him in the ideal position to attack the back of the ball.

5 THROUGH IMPACT
Once again this is the perfect position – one that handicap players should visualize and copy. Ernie's head maintains its position slightly behind the impact point while the club freewheels into the followthrough.

1 THE FOLLOW-THROUGH
A perfectly balanced finish, as demonstrated here, is a sure confirmation that all the elements of the swing have been put together correctly – a major key to solid and consistent iron play.

THE LESSONS
The lessons that follow in this section will help you develop a solid and consistent swing for playing long- and mid-iron shots.

Page 92
LESSON ONE
Checking the set-up
KEY 1: SET CORRECT POSTURE
KEY 2: WORK OUT THE BALL POSITION
KEY 3: MAINTAIN A CONSISTENT ADDRESS POSITION

Page 94
LESSON TWO
Building a repeating swing
KEY 1: STAY CONNECTED
KEY 2: SET THE CLUB ON THE CORRECT PLANE
KEY 3: SWING INTO THE SLOT
KEY 4: RETAIN THE POWER IN THE SWING

Page 98
LESSON THREE
Concentrating on impact
KEY 1: COLLECT THE BALL
KEY 2: OPEN THE SHOULDERS AT IMPACT

Page 100
LESSON FOUR
Swinging to a balanced finish
KEY 1: FIRE THE RIGHT SHOULDER
KEY 2: FOLLOWTHROUGH IN PERFECT BALANCE

Page 102
LESSON FIVE
Getting in tune
KEY 1: USE THE FULL ALLOWANCE
KEY 2: IDENTIFY A TARGET
KEY 3: ESTABLISH PERFECT PARALLEL ALIGNMENT

90

91

Fault-finder box
A valuable guide to curing the faults and errors that affect even the best golfers at some stage in their careers.

Professional sequence
Each introductory spread features examples from top professionals of the shots covered in the lessons.

Section contents list
Each introductory spread contains an at-a-glance listing of all the lessons and keys featured in the section.

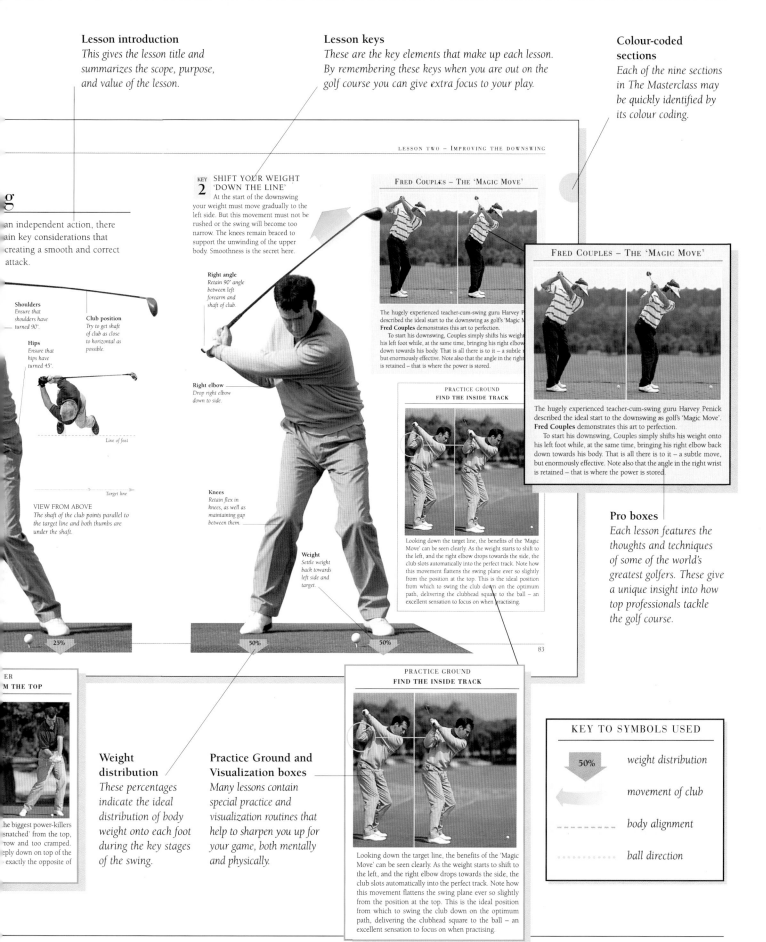

Lesson introduction
This gives the lesson title and summarizes the scope, purpose, and value of the lesson.

Lesson keys
These are the key elements that make up each lesson. By remembering these keys when you are out on the golf course you can give extra focus to your play.

Colour-coded sections
Each of the nine sections in The Masterclass may be quickly identified by its colour coding.

LESSON TWO – IMPROVING THE DOWNSWING

KEY 2 SHIFT YOUR WEIGHT 'DOWN THE LINE'
At the start of the downswing your weight must move gradually to the left side. But this movement must not be rushed or the swing will become too narrow. The knees remain braced to support the unwinding of the upper body. Smoothness is the secret here.

g

an independent action, there
ain key considerations that
creating a smooth and correct
attack.

Shoulders
Ensure that shoulders have turned 90°.

Club position
Try to get shaft of club as close to horizontal as possible.

Hips
Ensure that hips have turned 45°.

Line of feet

Target line

VIEW FROM ABOVE
The shaft of the club points parallel to the target line and both thumbs are under the shaft.

Right angle
Retain 90° angle between left forearm and shaft of club.

Right elbow
Drop right elbow down to side.

Knees
Retain flex in knees, as well as maintaining gap between them.

Weight
Settle weight back towards left side and target.

25%   50%   50%

FRED COUPLES – THE 'MAGIC MOVE'

The hugely experienced teacher-cum-swing guru Harvey P
described the ideal start to the downswing as golf's 'Magic M
Fred Couples demonstrates this art to perfection.
To start his downswing, Couples simply shifts his weight
his left foot while, at the same time, bringing his right elbow
down towards his body. That is all there is to it – a subtle
but enormously effective. Note also that the angle in the right
is retained – that is where the power is stored.

FRED COUPLES – THE 'MAGIC MOVE'

The hugely experienced teacher-cum-swing guru Harvey Penick described the ideal start to the downswing as golf's 'Magic Move'. **Fred Couples** demonstrates this art to perfection.
To start his downswing, Couples simply shifts his weight onto his left foot while, at the same time, bringing his right elbow back down towards his body. That is all there is to it – a subtle move, but enormously effective. Note also that the angle in the right wrist is retained – that is where the power is stored.

**PRACTICE GROUND
FIND THE INSIDE TRACK**

Looking down the target line, the benefits of the 'Magic Move' can be seen clearly. As the weight starts to shift to the left, and the right elbow drops towards the side, the club slots automatically into the perfect track. Note how this movement flattens the swing plane ever so slightly from the position at the top. This is the ideal position from which to swing the club down on the optimum path, delivering the clubhead square to the ball – an excellent sensation to focus on when practising.

83

Pro boxes
Each lesson features the thoughts and techniques of some of the world's greatest golfers. These give a unique insight into how top professionals tackle the golf course.

ER
M THE TOP

he biggest power-killers
snatched' from the top,
row and too cramped.
eply down on top of the
exactly the opposite of

Weight distribution
These percentages indicate the ideal distribution of body weight onto each foot during the key stages of the swing.

Practice Ground and Visualization boxes
Many lessons contain special practice and visualization routines that help to sharpen you up for your game, both mentally and physically.

**PRACTICE GROUND
FIND THE INSIDE TRACK**

Looking down the target line, the benefits of the 'Magic Move' can be seen clearly. As the weight starts to shift to the left, and the right elbow drops towards the side, the club slots automatically into the perfect track. Note how this movement flattens the swing plane ever so slightly from the position at the top. This is the ideal position from which to swing the club down on the optimum path, delivering the clubhead square to the ball – an excellent sensation to focus on when practising.

KEY TO SYMBOLS USED

50%	*weight distribution*
	movement of club
	body alignment
	ball direction

FUNDAMENTALS OF GOOD SET-UP

WITHOUT A GOOD and settled set-up no one, not even the greatest of talents, has any hope of playing the game of golf well and consistently. The set-up, or address position, is vital preparation for the production of a good swing – and is the one element of the game over which every player has total control. So before we even start thinking about swinging the club, let's take a look at the fundamentals of set-up common to all the great players of the present day. Size and stature matter little here, the main consideration is to give your swing the best chance of success.

NICK FALDO
Nick Faldo demonstrates the ideal set-up. His alignment is perfectly square with his shoulders, hips, and feet all parallel to the intended line of flight. He is relaxed and in perfect balance to make a smooth, unhurried backswing.

NICK PRICE
Zimbabwe's Nick Price demonstrates a perfect address position for a short iron shot. The ball is positioned midway in the stance, the hands are slightly ahead of the ball, the knees are flexed, and the body nicely poised.

IAN WOOSNAM
Because Ian Woosnam is short in stature he stands a little further from the ball at address than, for instance, Nick Faldo, and swings the club on a slightly flatter plane. Nevertheless he makes full use of his height, keeping his back straight and head up.

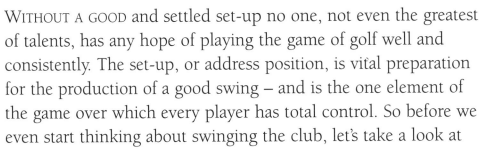

MARK McNULTY
Mark McNulty stands tall and keeps his chin up from his chest to make room for his left shoulder to turn under in the backswing – a major contributing factor in making him one of the straightest hitters on tour.

FRANK NOBILO
New Zealand's Frank Nobilo shows the perfect posture in the set-up. He has bent forwards from the hips, keeping his back straight. His head is held high while the arms hang down naturally from his shoulders.

ERNIE ELS
Ernie Els emphasizes the importance of good posture and a comfortably relaxed set-up to the ball. His heels are shoulder-width apart while the ball is ideally positioned for a long iron shot.

LESSON ONE

Building a solid grip

THE LEGENDARY CHAMPION Ben Hogan summed up perfectly the importance of the grip when he said, "a player with a bad grip doesn't want a good swing". The way the hands are placed on the grip determines the shape of the swing and, more importantly, precisely where the clubface is pointing at impact. And that dictates the direction in which the ball flies. To hit accurate golf shots, it is essential to build a good grip.

Right hand
Hold butt-end of club steady.

Left hand
Lay club diagonally across palm of left hand.

Right hand
Make sure palm of right hand faces target.

GRIP THICKNESS
A grip is ideally suited to you when the tips of the fingers on the left hand just touch the fleshy pad of the palm.

KEY 1 FORM THE GRIP

Whichever style of grip suits best, the procedure for placing the hands on the club in the correct fashion is essentially the same. The hands must be in a neutral position on the grip; palms facing one another, square to the target line. This allows the hands to work in unison throughout the swing. Bring the left hand from its natural hanging position and, holding it flat against the grip with the back of the hand facing the target, lay the club diagonally across the palm.

KEY 2 CLOSE FINGERS AROUND THE GRIP

Close the hand around the grip so that the butt of the club rests against the fleshy pad in the palm of the left hand. Looking down, it should be apparent that the left thumb is sitting fractionally to the right of centre on the grip. Once in place, waggle the clubhead back and forth to ensure a snug, secure fit.

RONAN RAFFERTY, NICK FALDO, AND JACK NICKLAUS – DIFFERENT GRIPS

THE BASEBALL GRIP

Up until the turn of the century, the baseball, or two-handed, grip was the only way to hold a club. Nowadays there are three accepted styles of gripping the club. The baseball grip is ideal for young golfers or those who have arthritic problems in their hands. At the highest level, though, only a handful of modern-day professionals favour this style; European Ryder Cup player **Ronan Rafferty** (below) is probably the best known modern-day exponent.

THE OVERLAPPING GRIP

By far the most popular style of holding the club is the overlapping grip, where the little finger of the right hand literally rides 'piggy-back' on the forefinger of the left hand. Also known as the Vardon grip (see page 16), this is the most widely adopted method, favoured by players such as **Nick Faldo** (below), Seve Ballesteros, and Ernie Els. They all subscribe to the theory that it is the most neutral of all the grip options, allowing the hands to work as one cohesive unit.

THE INTERLOCKING GRIP

A slight variation to the overlapping method is the interlocking grip, where the little finger of the right hand is entwined with the fore-finger of the left. As with the overlapping grip, this grip encourages the hands to work in harmony throughout the swing. It has proved hugely successful for players such as the great **Jack Nicklaus** (below), 1992 US Open champion Tom Kite, and 1995 British Open champion John Daly – not a bad three-some to emulate.

KEY 3 RIGHT PALM FACES THE TARGET
Now introduce the right hand onto the grip, with the palm facing the target. Nestle the grip in the base of the fingers and close the hand around the grip. In the final stages of securing the grip, sense that the right forefinger and thumb form a 'trigger' position.

Right hand
Nestle club in fingers of right hand.

Check the 'Vs'
Make sure 'Vs' are pointing towards right shoulder.

KEY 4 BRING HANDS TOGETHER
Check in a mirror that the 'Vs' formed by the thumb and forefinger on each hand point up somewhere between the right shoulder and right eye. Ideally, two knuckles should be seen on each hand. Finally, grip lightly. Apply just enough pressure to provide a secure hold and really feel the weight of the clubhead in the fingers.

LESSON TWO

Improving posture

THE BODY ANGLES created at address, known as posture, have a significant effect on the shape and quality of the swing. Work hard at getting them right and a better golf swing will surely follow. If, however, the factor of body posture is neglected, then the swing will forever be full of compensatory moves, and achieving any level of consistency in the swing will be a constant struggle.

Club
Hold club lightly out in front of you.

Arms
Keep arms free from tension.

KEY 1 STAND UP STRAIGHT WITH ARMS EXTENDED

This is a routine you can rehearse on the practice ground, in the garden, or any other place where the opportunity arises. Its purpose is to help create familiarity with the feeling of perfect posture. The more comfortable this address position feels, the greater the chance of automatically repeating it on the course, which is where it really matters. Stand upright with your arms comfortably extended out in front of you at chest height.

Stance
Stand upright and comfortably.

PRACTICE GROUND
ESTABLISH A ROCK-SOLID BASE

Keeping balance throughout the swing is a major element in hitting good shots. And good balance stems from perfect weight distribution at address, so it is essential to create a solid base from which to start. This drill helps to establish good weight distribution. Address the ball as normal and have a friend shove you firmly from either side, or from behind. If you don't stagger off balance, then the weight distribution must be evenly spread. If it is incorrect, your friend will find it all too easy to push you. Depending on which way you stagger, you will be able to identify and rectify the imbalance.

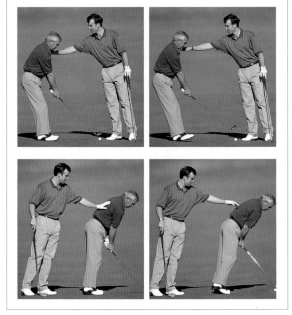

70

Upper body
*Angle body
forwards and
bend from waist.*

Grip
*Maintain
a light hold
of club.*

Clubhead
*Lower club
and rest gently
on ground.*

PRACTICE GROUND CREATE THE RIGHT ANGLES

This is a simple drill to help check that the correct body angles are being created at address, irrespective of size or weight. Assume the address position as normal, then get someone to hold the butt of a club against the middle of your right shoulder so that it hangs vertically downwards. If the shaft extends through a point level with the right knee, the posture is spot-on. If the bottom of the shaft is either side of that point, then it is time to make some adjustments.

Head
*Keep head up to
make room for
shoulder turn.*

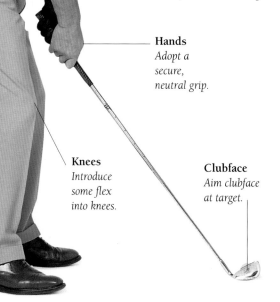

KEY 3 FLEX THE KNEES

When the clubhead makes contact with the ground, flex the knees just enough to create a little tension in the thighs. Stick out the backside a little and 'draw in' the tummy. The correct posture will create quite a 'bouncy' feeling. It will be relaxed, but not slumped.

Hands
*Adopt a
secure,
neutral grip.*

Knees
*Introduce
some flex
into knees.*

Clubface
*Aim clubface
at target.*

KEY 2 BEND FROM THE WAIST

Slowly lower the clubhead to the ground by bending from the waist, being careful not to alter the relationship between the arms and upper body. Simply wait for the clubhead to make contact with the ground.

ERNIE ELS – BIG MAN, PERFECT POSTURE

There is no better exponent of perfect posture than the young South African star **Ernie Els**. And this in spite of a 6ft 3in (1.9m), 15 stone (95kg) frame; hardly the ideal build for golf. This is because he pays attention to the basics. All the key elements of posture are clearly visible in this photograph of the 1994 US Open champion.

LESSON THREE

Establishing a better stance and ball position

THE WIDTH OF the stance – the distance the feet are apart at address – is determined by the club being used, and is a major factor in consistent set-up. Just as important is ball position, because it influences the path and angle of attack of the clubhead at impact. These keys encourage a uniform set-up and ball position, leading to more consistent ball-striking.

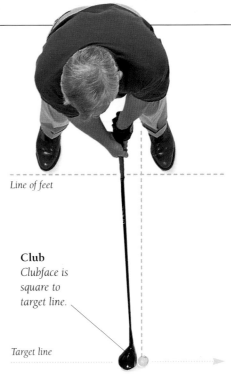

Line of feet

Club
Clubface is square to target line.

Target line

KEY 1 — A SOLID BASE FOR THE DRIVER

With the longest club in the bag, the driver, it is logical that the feet should be wider apart than for other clubs, with the ball positioned just inside the left heel.

Hands
Position hands level with, or near to, ball at address.

Knees
Introduce flex into knees.

Stance
Make sure heels are same width apart as shoulders.

BALL POSITION

The ideal ball position for the driver is just inside the left heel. This greatly increases the chances of the clubhead meeting the ball at the correct angle of attack and on the right path towards the target.

FAULT-FINDER BAD BALL POSITION

The position of the ball in your stance has a direct influence on the path of the clubhead at impact, which then determines the initial direction of shots. This overhead view shows the effect a badly positioned ball can have on the initial direction of shots.

*If the ball is **too far back**, the clubhead is likely to be on an in-to-out path at the point of impact, sending the ball to the right of target.*

*If the ball is **too far forwards**, then the clubhead will be travelling on an out-to-in path at impact, sending the ball to the left of target.*

FAULT-FINDER **WRONG WIDTH OF STANCE**

Just as a good set-up helps produce a good swing, even the slightest mistakes at address can cause major problems in the swing itself. Take the width of stance for instance. If the feet are **too far apart**, it becomes impossible to turn the hips and shoulders to the necessary extent. Inevitably, the backswing will be restricted.

If the feet are **too close together** in the stance it is just as serious. A narrow stance does not provide a sufficiently stable base for the swing. It allows plenty of room to turn your upper body, but it will be ineffective in terms of generating the leverage and power necessary in the golf swing. Balance will almost certainly be lost, too.

GREG NORMAN – IMPROVISE FOR A BETTER TURN

Greg Norman has a fairly orthodox swing, but he knows the value of improvisation. At address, he sometimes splays his left toe out, which enables him to clear his left side a little better through impact. It also prevents him over-rotating in the backswing, creating resistance as his upper body coils 'over' his legs. Follow his example and try splaying the left toe out. Alternatively, if body flexibility is a problem, splay the right toe for a better turn away in the backswing.

KEY 2 NARROW THE STANCE FOR A WEDGE

At the opposite end of the scale to the driver, the feet should be close together when using a wedge. The very nature of this shot, and the relatively short swing required, means that the demands on keeping balance are not so great. Somewhere between a driver and a wedge lies the ideal width of stance for every other club in the bag. Trial and error should decide what feels most comfortable.

Shoulders
Sense that left shoulder is higher than the right.

Hands
Make sure hands are ahead of ball.

Stance
Adopt a narrow stance with a wedge.

LESSON FOUR

Fine-tuning for accuracy

AS OFTEN AS tour professionals play, they constantly monitor their aim and alignment. If a gun is not aimed correctly, the bullet will not hit the target, and this principle applies just as much to the golf swing. The clubface must be aimed at the target and the alignment of the body must match the angle of the clubface – known as perfect parallel alignment. These are the keys to help establish that alignment.

KEY 1 **VISUALIZE TO REALIZE**
Stand behind the ball and look down the target line. Picture the type of shot that is required, how it will travel through the air, and exactly where it will land.

KEY 2 **AIM THE CLUBFACE**
With a clear picture in mind of the intended shot, pick out an intermediate target, such as a divot-mark or a leaf, a club-length or so in front of the ball along the intended target line. Aim the clubface over that point, rather than at a distant flag.

Ball
Pick out an intended landing spot for ball.

Vision
Fix line of sight over an intermediate target.

Target
Direct line to ultimate target.

Club
Aim club directly over an intermediate target.

KEY 3 BUILD A CLASSIC STANCE

Once a square clubface position has been established, the next stage is to build a stance around it. To hit a straight shot, with no curvature through the air, try to ensure that the feet, hips, and shoulders are square to that clubface position. This is known as perfect parallel alignment, and will have a positive effect on the shape and quality of the entire swing.

Arms
A good spine angle encourages arms to hang down freely.

Clubhead
Sit club squarely behind ball.

Left hand
Ensure back of hand faces target.

Feet
Make sure toe-line runs parallel with target line.

FAULT-FINDER
PERILS OF POOR ALIGNMENT

Alignment is one of the easiest pre-swing factors to get wrong and, if not remedied, it can destroy the entire path of the swing. In a closed stance (below left), with everything aiming right of target, it is inevitable that the club will be taken back too far on the inside. Similarly, from an open stance (below right) there is every chance that the clubhead will travel outside the line on the way back. Again, far from ideal. Remember, the golf swing is a chain reaction. Start badly, and it is very difficult to recover. The whole swing becomes a series of compensations, and that is something to be avoided at all costs.

PRACTICE GROUND
CHECK YOUR ALIGNMENT

Whenever practising, always lay some clubs on the ground to indicate perfect alignment. This helps to align the feet automatically and correctly in relation to the target. Practising shots to a target when alignment is not correct will only result in ingraining faults into the swing. And that defeats the whole object of practising in the first place.

JAMIE SPENCE – BUILD A POSITIVE MENTAL PICTURE

Visualizing a shot in the mind's eye before address is an essential part of any successful pre-shot routine. All the top players do this, Englishman **Jamie Spence** included, usually choosing to stand directly behind the ball as they picture the flight and trajectory of the shot. Visualization is a good habit to get into. It focuses the mind totally on the shot in hand. It helps establish a kind of tunnel vision, excluding all the distractions that can play havoc during a round – such as wondering about the depth of the pond on the right of the green! For a better mental approach and fewer wayward shots, get into the habit of thinking: "Visualize to realize".

LESSON FIVE

Triggering the swing into action

THE FINAL ADDRESS position should feel athletic and 'ready to go'. Once set, many players develop what is known as a 'swing trigger'. This encourages a smooth first move away from the ball. For players with a tendency to 'freeze' over the ball, or who start the backswing too quickly, developing a swing trigger is the best antidote.

Eyes
Focus all senses on honing in on intended target.

PLAYER, PALMER, NICKLAUS – GREAT SWING TRIGGERS

It is easier to perpetuate motion than it is to start it. That is why many great players start their swing with a slight move to trigger the swing into action. **Gary Player** (left) kicks in his right knee; **Arnold Palmer** (centre) gives the club one final, aggressive waggle before he launches the ball into the distance; **Jack Nicklaus** (right) turns his head to the right – Nick Faldo does the same. All of these movements have one thing in common: they help the player make a smooth start to the backswing, preventing any sudden, jerky movements that can destroy the all-important linkage in the swing. Take a moment to experiment with each of these moves – developing an effective trigger can make all the difference.

Hands
Exert only light pressure with grip.

KEY 1 TAKE DEAD AIM
Employ tunnel vision. Try to focus on the target, to the exclusion of everything else around you.

Feet
Spread weight on balls of both feet.

Clubhead
Rest club gently behind ball.

PRACTICE GROUND
HOW TO STAY RELAXED

Gripping the club too tightly can destroy a swing before it has even started. Tense hands lead to tense arms, leading in turn to tense shoulders – causing a restricted turn in the swing, as is clearly shown below.

Regardless of the club, it is vital to learn to grip lightly. Try this exercise to help stay relaxed. Stand as normal to hit a shot and let your arms hang down naturally. Now rehearse a normal backswing movement. The arms can be swung to the top easily, and the shoulders and upper body turn more readily – delivering a perfect free-flowing movement away from the ball.

KEY 2 GET READY TO GO

Waggle the club to prevent any tension creeping into the hands and arms, and feel the weight of the clubhead in the hands. Shuffle the feet slightly to keep the legs lively and poised, ready to drive the weight back and forth in the swing.

Head
Rotate head right to allow room for full shoulder turn.

RELIEVE TENSION
Waggle the club back and forth to ensure that no tension creeps up through your hands into your arms and shoulders.

Hands
Grip lightly and initiate waggle with hands.

Clubhead
Make sure waggle mirrors path of intended swing.

Feet
Shuffle feet into perfect position.

TECHNIQUES OF LONGER DRIVING

FOR SHEER SATISFACTION there is no other shot that comes close to matching the full-blooded drive that soars into the distance and finishes in the middle of the fairway. It is savoured by accomplished players and envied by those desperate to emulate it. But length from the tee is often confused with strength and muscle power. While we might have to accept that we will never be able to hit the ball as long or as impressively as, say, Greg Norman or John Daly, we can still improve our driving considerably by developing a sounder technique from the tee.

TOM WATSON
A free-flowing swing, which generates immense clubhead speed rather than great strength, is the secret behind Tom Watson's ball-striking success down the years.

GREG NORMAN
Australian Greg Norman is one of the finest drivers of the golf ball the game has ever seen. He is strong, certainly, but his length off the tee, and more importantly his accuracy, come from sound technique rather than brute strength.

1 THE ADDRESS
Norman's set-up is geared to a powerful swing. He hovers the clubhead above the ground for a smooth takeaway and turns the left toe towards the hole to encourage his left side to clear out of the way more easily through impact.

2 THE TAKEAWAY
This is a perfect example of the one-piece takeaway. It promotes a wide arc and builds rhythm into the swing, necessary ingredients for generating the power to drive the ball further.

3 AT THE TOP
Greg's position at the top of the backswing is perfect, and a model for everyone. The shoulders have turned a full 90°, his back is facing the target, and the club is perfectly on line.

JOHN DALY
John Daly is the man everyone wants to see 'let fly' with a driver. He sends the ball remarkable distances thanks to a massive turn of the shoulders and a very long swing. But the key is the harnessing of this power to a good technique.

6 THE FOLLOW-THROUGH
The clubhead freewheels into a high followthrough, confirming that all the elements of the swing have come together correctly. Note the perfectly balanced finish.

5 THROUGH IMPACT
Here lies another clue to Greg Norman's length and accuracy. With the left side out of the way, the hands and arms fully extend down the line. Note that Greg's head maintains its position slightly behind the impact point.

4 THE DOWNSWING
Into the downswing Greg has dropped the club onto a slightly flatter plane, enabling him to attack the ball from the inside. His right arm stays close to his body, his left side has cleared out of the way, and his head remains behind the ball.

THE LESSONS

The lessons that follow in this section will help you to work on all aspects of driving; from finding extra length off the tee to planning the right strategy.

LESSON ONE

Building a better backswing

ANNIKA SORENSTAM – SHIFT WEIGHT FOR MAXIMUM POWER

Power is best generated by allowing weight to move back and forwards in harmony with the direction of the swing. If the upper body coil and the weight shifted are both correct in the backswing, the natural movement is a lateral one onto the right foot. The 1995 US Women's Open champion **Annika Sorenstam** is a good example. Note the position of her head at address and compare it with the top of the backswing position. It has moved a good 5–6in (12–15cm), enabling her to 'get behind the ball'.

THE GOLF SWING is very much a chain reaction, in that one good move tends to lead naturally on to another. The first few links in the chain are obviously the most important. They determine not only the shape, but also the quality of the entire swing. A good set-up and start to the swing immediately increases the chances of making a good, complete swing – and therefore more consistent shotmaking.

KEY 1 MAKE A PRE-FLIGHT CHECK

It is important to get into the habit of ticking-off the fundamentals in a pre-swing checklist. Start by checking for correct posture (see page 70); check for even distribution of weight – slightly favour the right side when using the longer clubs; make sure that the ball is opposite the inside of the left heel; and finally, check the tee-height.

Club
Sense that shaft of club is an extension of left arm.

Grip
Make a neutral grip with two knuckles showing on each hand.

CHECK THE TEE-HEIGHT
Don't waste the benefits of the tee-peg; make sure it is at the correct height. As a general rule, the top edge of the driver should be level with the equator of the ball. This applies irrespective of the size and design of the driver head. It is also applicable to lofted clubs such as a 'spoon' or 3-wood used from the tee.

Knees
Make sure knees are comfortably flexed at address.

Heels
Position heels approximately shoulder-width apart.

55%   45%

KEY 2 THINK 'ALL ARMS'

Building the feeling of 'all arms' in the first 30in (75cm) of the club's initial movement away from the ball reaps major dividends. The 'all arms' takeaway pulls the left shoulder, left knee, and left hip in towards the ball. The upper body also responds to the swinging of the arms while the hands and wrists remain passive.

Chin
Keep chin up and away from chest.

Club
Sweep club away slowly on wide arc.

Legs
Keep legs firm at start of takeaway.

PRACTICE GROUND LIFT IF YOU WISH

There are really no hard and fast rules as to whether the left heel should stay grounded in the backswing. In the early 1900s it was the done thing, probably due to the restrictive nature of clothing. Nowadays, it depends on how flexible the player is. If the left heel needs to lift to complete a full body turn, it should be lifted. However, delay the 'lift off' for as long as possible to help create the resistance in the swing.

Right angle
Form a 90° angle between shaft and left forearm.

Upper body
Turn back naturally towards target.

Hips
Turn right hip away from ball.

Left knee
Point left knee and hip in towards ball in response to turning motion of upper body.

Right knee
Turn around a flexed knee.

Weight
Weight moves slightly onto right foot.

60%   40%

ERNIE ELS – THE ONE-PIECE TAKEAWAY

Good players sweep the club back low and slow in the early stages of the takeaway. It is known as the classic one-piece action. This introduces width and co-ordination in the swing immediately – essential for all full shots, but particularly with the longer clubs.

Look at the takeaway of the 1994 US Open champion **Ernie Els**. His upper body, hands, arms, and the club all move away from the ball in harmony. The wrists are almost completely passive – they only start to hinge as the hands reach a point just beyond the right hip; the ideal takeaway to emulate.

KEY 3 TURN AND SET

The wrists hinge as the body continues to turn and the arms swing the club up on plane. A good checkpoint in the swing occurs at the '9 o'clock position' (see page 168), where the clubhead points to the sky.

LESSON TWO

Improving the downswing

THE TRANSITION FROM completing the backswing to starting the downswing is a critical point in the overall swing. And while the downswing is largely a reaction, rather than an independent action, there are still certain key considerations that can help in creating a smooth and correct downswing attack.

KEY 1 **GET 'IN THE SLOT'**
The position at the top is largely a product of the work done in the first part of the backswing. If, after the initial takeaway and turn, the club is 'set' into the ideal position (see page 81), all the difficult work is done. Rotating the body until the shoulders complete a 90° turn, while the arms continue upwards, takes the club naturally into the slot at the top.

FAULT-FINDER
DON'T SNATCH FROM THE TOP

Rushing the downswing is one of the biggest power-killers in golf. The moment the club is 'snatched' from the top, the downswing becomes too narrow and too cramped. There is nowhere to go except steeply down on top of the ball, losing power and direction – exactly the opposite of what is required with the driver.

Shoulders
Ensure that shoulders have turned 90°.

Club position
Try to get shaft of club as close to horizontal as possible.

Hips
Ensure that hips have turned 45°.

Line of feet

Target line

VIEW FROM ABOVE
The shaft of the club points parallel to the target line and both thumbs are under the shaft.

Right knee
Keep right knee flexed to create 'resistance' in swing.

Right foot
Majority of weight moves onto right foot.

75%   25%

KEY 2 SHIFT YOUR WEIGHT 'DOWN THE LINE'

At the start of the downswing your weight must move gradually to the left side. But this movement must not be rushed or the swing will become too narrow. The knees remain braced to support the unwinding of the upper body. Smoothness is the secret here.

Right angle
Retain 90° angle between left forearm and shaft of club.

Right elbow
Drop right elbow down to side.

Knees
Retain flex in knees, as well as maintaining gap between them.

Weight
Settle weight back towards left side and target.

50%　　50%

FRED COUPLES – THE 'MAGIC MOVE'

The hugely experienced teacher-cum-swing guru Harvey Penick described the ideal start to the downswing as golf's 'Magic Move'. **Fred Couples** demonstrates this art to perfection.

To start his downswing, Couples simply shifts his weight onto his left foot while, at the same time, bringing his right elbow back down towards his body. That is all there is to it – a subtle move, but enormously effective. Note also that the angle in the right wrist is retained – that is where the power is stored.

PRACTICE GROUND
FIND THE INSIDE TRACK

Looking down the target line, the benefits of the 'Magic Move' can be seen clearly. As the weight starts to shift to the left, and the right elbow drops towards the side, the club slots automatically into the perfect track. Note how this movement flattens the swing plane ever so slightly from the position at the top. This is the ideal position from which to swing the club down on the optimum path, delivering the clubhead square to the ball – an excellent sensation to focus on when practising.

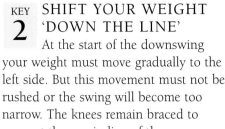

LESSON THREE

Making better impact

THE COMMON FACTOR among all history's great drivers has been the position at impact. From the fast, jerky action of Harold Hilton at the turn of the century to the smooth, big-hitting of Fred Couples and Ernie Els, the position when club meets ball has changed very little.

A straight left arm is not vital in the backswing but it is crucial to good impact on the down-swing. It enables the clubhead to be returned to the ball squarely and at the right angle of attack. This is known as re-establishing the radius of the swing. A look at former US Open champion **Curtis Strange** shows a perfect example of this move. The fact that here he is using an iron rather than a driver is irrelevant. At the top of the backswing the left elbow is clearly bent, but look at the position through impact – the left arm has straightened, re-establishing the radius of his swing, and so producing solid contact.

KEY 1 MAKE CONTACT

Perfect impact is not a position that is swung to – it is a position to swing through (and this is true of all clubs). Nevertheless, this is still a good image to have in mind as the driver moves through impact – emphasising the key elements at this critical stage of the swing. But do remember, swing through it, and not to it.

Head
Keep head behind point of impact through hitting zone.

Right shoulder
Move right shoulder under chin through impact.

Arms
Fully extend arms to re-establish radius of swing.

Right heel
Allow right heel to come off ground as upper body rotates back through ball.

Angle of shaft at impact

25%

75%

PRACTICE GROUND
WALK THROUGH TO A BETTER FINISH

Just as a boxer must move his weight from the back foot to the front foot to land a powerful punch, so must the golfer train to use his weight to the best effect, particularly with distance shots. This exercise focuses on the correct use of weight in the critical area through the hitting zone and on to the finish.

1 Address the ball normally, but perhaps choke down on the grip – this is only an exercise.

2 Swing back, make a good turn, and a real effort to transfer the weight on to the right side.

3 Shift the weight onto the front foot through the hitting zone. Sense being over the ball through impact.

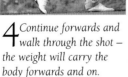

4 Continue forwards and walk through the shot – the weight will carry the body forwards and on.

KEY 2 FREE-WHEEL THROUGH IMPACT

This point, well past impact, is no more than a free-wheeling stage as the momentum of the club pulls the arms through impact. The driver is the most dynamic club in the bag and requires the most powerful swing, but perfect balance is still maintained. There must never be a feeling of instability. If there is, change down a gear and reduce the swing to 75% power.

KEY 3 FINISH IN BALANCE

The driver needs smoothness and rhythm to give length and accuracy. A followthrough in perfect balance is confirmation that this has been achieved. The feeling of posing in the perfect finish position concentrates the thoughts and increases the chances of a controlled swing.

Shoulders
Drive right shoulder past chin.

Spine
Keep spine angle relatively straight to ease strain on lower back.

10%   90%

Balance
Support majority of body weight on left leg.

20%   80%

LESSON FOUR

Finding that extra distance

THE SECRET OF achieving extra distance with the driver lies, quite simply, in better technique. The latest high-tech driver won't make any difference unless it is swung properly. Hitting the ball further means focusing on the key moves and sensations that promote power where it matters – at impact with the ball.

KEY 1 — THINK 'WIDTH'

For extra length, widen the stance a little to give greater stability to support a more powerful action. A little more weight on the right side at address, roughly in a 60–40 ratio, promotes a good turn away from the ball and also a powerful coil. Just as important, it guards against the dreaded reverse pivot, leaving the weight on the left leg on the backswing – the biggest destroyer of distance in golf.

JOHN DALY – THE ULTIMATE TURN

The 1995 British Open champion **John Daly** is arguably the longest hitter in golf. An unfeasibly long backswing, combined with a mighty downswing assault, launches the ball almost impossible distances. His swing is certainly not to be recommended for the average player, but there are aspects of his technique that can be beneficial. For instance, don't be afraid of the overswing: it is better than swinging too short. Remember, however, that the longer the backswing the smoother the rhythm must be, particularly in the transition from backswing to downswing.

PRACTICE GROUND KEEP YOUR CHIN UP

The term 'keep your head down' is one of the most damaging pieces of advice. Concentrating on keeping the head fixed in one spot creates a restriction in virtually every other area of the swing – particularly in the shoulder turn and weight transfer, two critical areas. Thinking of keeping the chin up instead will create more room to turn the left shoulder under the chin, encouraging a better coil.

CREATE GOOD ANGLES
Posture is crucial. Flex the knees and bend comfortably from the waist to encourage the arms to hang down in a relaxed fashion. Good body angles promote a good shape to the swing.

Clubhead
Hover clubhead behind ball to promote a smooth takeaway.

Stance
Widen stance a fraction more than for other shots.

60%   40%

KEY 2 STRETCH OUT IN THE TAKEAWAY

It is vital to make as wide a takeaway as possible. The club should be swept away from the ball wide and slow. The extension of the arms pulls the left shoulder under the chin, while the muscles in the lower left side stretch out as the body coils.

Left arm
Rotate left forearm to help ensure that clubface stays square to path of swing.

VIEW FROM ABOVE
Settle the weight gradually onto the right side, with the knees braced to support the coiling of the upper body in the backswing.

Create width
Sweep club away from ball on a wide arc – low and slow.

70% 30%

GREG NORMAN – HOVER THE CLUBHEAD FOR A SMOOTH, WIDE TAKEAWAY

Many players, **Greg Norman** and Jack Nicklaus among them, hover the clubhead above the ground at address. While it might not be the easiest technique to master, it does have the significant benefit of encouraging a smooth, wide takeaway. This is particularly important when looking for extra distance with the driver. The benefits to be gained from this technique are well worth the time spent perfecting it. One additional tip: make sure that the ball is positioned opposite the left heel. This helps to ensure that the clubhead sweeps the ball off the tee-peg, the ideal impact to make full use of the available loft on the driver.

KEY 3 HIT HARD WITH THE RIGHT HAND

Start down smoothly (see the 'Magic Move', page 83), but then really hit hard with the right hand through impact. Henry Cotton said that it was not possible to hit too hard with the right hand provided the left hand worked in unison. There should be a sense of the right forearm crossing over the left through impact and on up to a high finish.

Weight
Move weight onto left side into impact.

LESSON FIVE

Planning strategy on the tee

THE TEEING GROUND is the one area on the course where the player can decide where to place the ball. Think first and make the most

of it. Some tactical planning at this stage will pay dividends; here are the key elements to take into account before driving off.

KEY 1 TEE IT UP FOR HIGHER FLIGHT
Teeing the ball at different heights can encourage a better swing shape and help move the ball more easily through the air. When playing a hole downwind, and assuming that the requirement is maximum distance, tee the ball higher than normal. This helps to generate a higher ball-flight with more carry through the air so that you can take advantage of the tailwind.

Back
Keep back straight despite standing further from ball.

WITH THE WIND
Use a following wind to add extra distance. Teeing higher allows the wind to 'take' the ball, thereby carrying it that much further.

Encourage a draw
Grip as long as possible and tee ball up.

Stance
Stand about 2in (5cm) further from ball to provide a more rounded swing plane.

Normal feet position

ERNIE ELS – POWER IN RESERVE

Most professionals, like **Ernie Els**, leave some power in reserve when they tee off. Far better to be in the middle of the fairway than 40yds (35m) further up in the rough. Unless the situation is desperate and something dramatic is required, always swing at 70 or 80% power. This will help to promote a solid strike that, on most occasions, provides all the necessary distance.

A ROUNDED SWING-SHAPE
Teeing the ball higher encourages a more rounded swing-shape, which promotes a tendency to draw the shot.

KEY 2 TEE DOWN FOR A PENETRATING FLIGHT

Playing into a stiff breeze is a major distance-killer. The lower the ball can be kept, the less of an effect the wind will have on a drive. Tee the ball down to promote a lower, more penetrating trajectory. But avoid chopping down too steeply on a ball teed low. Doing so creates excessive backspin, which has the effect of making the ball climb higher.

Head
Keep head as still as possible.

Back
Back must still be kept straight in a slightly more upright stance.

Legs
Feel tension in thighs at address.

Normal feet position

Fading
To encourage a fade, stand a fraction closer to ball in order to further promote a more upright swing plane.

Fight the hook
Grip down on club, and tee ball lower than normal, to encourage a more upright swing plane. This helps reduce likelihood of a hook shot.

COLIN MONTGOMERIE – HITTING THE FAIRWAY

Colin Montgomerie is well known for being one of the straightest hitters around. This can be attributed to cultivating a certain shape of shot, and trusting it. Montgomerie fav-ours a slight left-to-right fade off the tee. With this in mind, he tees the ball up on the right-hand side, and aims down the left side of the fairway. If the shot goes to plan, the ball works its way back to the middle of the fairway. Even if the ball flies dead straight, it finishes in the left half of the fairway – the edge of the light rough at worst. And if by some chance he over-exaggerates his fade, the ball finishes in the right half of the fairway, or the light rough on a bad day. Discovering what shape of shot suits you is the key to consistency.

INTO THE WIND
Hitting the ball into a strong wind can severely affect distance. By teeing low, the ball, in effect, flies under the wind.

A MORE UPRIGHT SWING
Just as a high tee encourages a draw, so a ball teed lower than normal promotes a more upright swing and therefore a tendency to fade the shot. On a hole with dangers on the left, tee the ball low and grip down on the club.

ESSENTIALS OF CONSISTENT IRON PLAY

LONG IRONS ARE what might be called 'anywhere-on-the-green' clubs. Even the top players hit relatively few of these shots close to the hole. When you move into the mid-iron range, though, you need to set your sights higher. The long drivers and the streak putters may grab the headlines, but solid iron play is just as important. From the classical action of Ernie Els to the unique style of Raymond Floyd, consistency remains the common factor uniting all the great iron players.

DAVID GRAHAM
Doggedly accurate iron play has helped Australian David Graham land two majors and a host of wins around the world. His 1981 US Open success at Merion was built on pinpoint accuracy with his irons and hitting every fairway bar one during his final round of 67.

ERNIE ELS
Ernie Els is one of the best players in world golf today, and the fact that he has such a good iron game is no coincidence. He does everything systematically to give himself the best chance of hitting good iron shots.

1 THE ADDRESS
Ernie Els emphasizes the importance of good posture and a comfortable, relaxed set-up to the ball. Like all the best players, his head is kept up at address and his arms hang down naturally, free of tension, from the shoulders.

2 TURN AND SET
Having made the perfect one-piece takeaway, Ernie cocks the wrists, setting the club on an ideal plane. His upper body starts to rotate, with his left shoulder turning under the chin.

3 AT THE TOP
This is a superb position at the top of the backswing, and is a model for anyone working to improve their swing. The shoulders have made a full 90° turn, the hips and knees resisting the rotary motion of the upper body.

RAYMOND FLOYD
Despite a swing that can hardly be described as classical, Ray Floyd is deadly with his iron approach shots – proof of the value of a repeating technique, irrespective of how it looks.

6 THE FOLLOW-THROUGH
A perfectly balanced finish, as demonstrated here, is a sure confirmation that all the elements of the swing have been put together correctly – a major key to solid and consistent iron play.

5 THROUGH IMPACT
Once again this is the perfect position – one that handicap players should visualize and copy. Ernie's head maintains its position slightly behind the impact point while the club freewheels into the followthrough.

4 THE DOWNSWING
In all the best swings the club drops slightly inside the line on the way down. Note how Ernie maintains perfect balance and rhythm, placing him in the ideal position to attack the back of the ball.

LESSON ONE

Checking the set-up

THE SET-UP POSITION is a vital, but often overlooked, element in good iron play. It is something over which we have total control and so there is little excuse for getting it wrong. All the great players have a set-up routine that they go through for every shot. Each has his own way of achieving the same end; the idiosyncrasies of the individual do not matter so long as they are consistent. What is important is to develop good set-up habits.

KEY 1 SET CORRECT POSTURE

The ideal posture is determined by the length of the shaft. With the long shaft of a 3-iron the stance is further from the ball and the angle of the spine more upright, rather as it is with the driver (see page 72). By comparison, the 6-iron is some 2in (5cm) shorter in the shaft and requires a closer stance and more bending from the waist. The 9-iron is shorter still, meaning an even closer stance to the ball and a further bending of the waist to encourage a more upright swing plane.

3-iron

6-iron

9-iron

PRACTICE GROUND FIND A CONSISTENT ADDRESS POSITION

1 Start by standing behind the ball facing towards the target. Then pick out a point to aim for.

2 Hold the club at the top in the right hand. Rest the club behind the ball, with the elbow against the hip.

3 Without moving in relation to the ball, take a normal grip. Bend at the waist and settle club behind ball.

4 Flex the knees to make the legs active in a comfortable stance. This routine ensures a consistent position.

FAIRWAY WOODS
Effective though they are, long irons are not always the best option on the fairway. From a bare lie, for instance, a small-headed fairway wood is far more forgiving than a long iron. Also, in wet conditions, lofted woods make it easier to sweep the ball away, and to achieve more carry through the air. In conditions where the ground is particularly soggy underfoot, getting maximum carry is essential.

7-WOOD

KEY 2 WORK OUT THE BALL POSITION

Ball position, to a large extent, dictates the angle of attack. With the 3-iron, where a sweeping action produces the best results, the ball position is much the same as for the driver – opposite the left heel at address. The 9-iron requires a much steeper angle of attack, so the ball benefits from being further back to encourage a crisp strike. The 6-iron falls between the two and that is reflected in the ball position. These are useful benchmarks but do not be afraid to experiment a little.

3-iron
Just inside, or opposite, left heel is ideal.

6-iron
Mid-range ball position.

9-iron
4in (10cm) inside heel is a good guide.

KEY 3 MAINTAIN A CONSISTENT ADDRESS POSITION

A consistent address is the vital factor in setting-up with irons. Creating, and keeping to, a set-up routine that suits the individual is the key. The feet and shoulders in parallel alignment, weight evenly distributed, and the hands over, or just ahead of, the ball, are the basics common to all the great players. The choice between the conventional ball position, as shown below with the 5-iron, or the Jack Nicklaus version, is up to the individual.

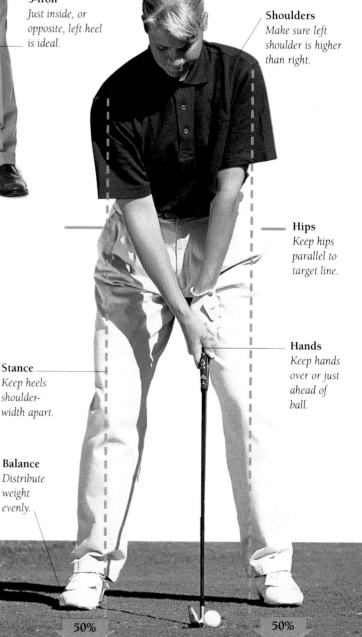

Shoulders
Make sure left shoulder is higher than right.

Hips
Keep hips parallel to target line.

Hands
Keep hands over or just ahead of ball.

Stance
Keep heels shoulder-width apart.

Balance
Distribute weight evenly.

50%   50%

JACK NICKLAUS – CONSTANT BALL POSITION

Jack Nicklaus is unusual among the great players in that he advocates a constant ball position, regardless of the club he is using. The Nicklaus view is that the ball opposite the left heel is the only spot where the clubhead will ever be travelling parallel to the target line. Any other position towards the right foot means that the ball will be struck too early in the downswing – when the club is still travelling from inside to out.

Instead, he favours an open stance for his shorter irons, and progressively pulls his right foot back, to make his stance wider and squarer, as the shaft-length of the club increases.

LESSON TWO

Building a repeating swing

THE LEGENDARY Ben Hogan hit the ball consistently straighter than just about anyone else. He once commented: "I want to be remembered as the man who hit them the straightest – not the longest." It was a clear, if rare, insight into the great man's way of thinking, and one we can all learn from. The more we can repeat the swing, the more often we will achieve a predictable result – the key to our assault on the golf course.

BEN HOGAN – ACCURACY BEFORE LENGTH

Ben Hogan rifled his iron shots through the air in a piece of the sky that seemed to belong to him alone. By swinging the club in exactly the same way he was able to repeat this time after time. Never was there a hint of forcing the shot, it was all about accuracy and consistency – a lesson to us all. By taking one club more than logic would initially suggest, and swinging smoothly and easily, accuracy can be gained because the quality of the strike is so much better and more consistent.

KEY 1 **STAY CONNECTED**
One of the common factors among all the great iron players is the one-piece start to the backswing – known as 'staying connected'. This means making sure that the shoulders, arms, hands, and the club all move away from the ball smoothly in unison as the backswing commences. Any kind of loose connections at this stage can be disastrous.

Body
Allow left side to work in towards ball.

The initial takeaway
Keep clubhead parallel to line of feet for first 12in (30cm) of takeaway.

Takeaway
Move hands, arms, and club away together.

Weight transfer
Feel weight flowing from left foot over to the right.

Clubhead
Employing the one-piece takeaway ensures clubhead travels on a wide arc away from ball.

Right knee
Retain flex in right knee.

60% 40%

KEY 2 SET THE CLUB ON THE CORRECT PLANE

The next stage in the backswing is to hinge, or cock, the wrists to set the club in the correct plane. As the arms continue to swing, and the body continues to turn, the wrists cock and start to point the clubhead up towards the sky. The angle of the shaft at this stage should ideally be the same as it was at address.

Clubhead
Clubface remains square to path of swing.

Head
Keep head at same level as it was at address.

Wrists
Hinge wrists as arms continue to swing.

Shoulders
Turn left shoulder to where right shoulder was at address.

Upper body
Turn upper body in harmony with swinging motion of arms.

Right knee
Retain flex in right knee.

Left heel
Lift left heel off ground if necessary.

FAULT-FINDER
CLUBFACE OUT OF POSITION

Closed face *A hooded, or closed, clubface is usually caused by a lack of hand and forearm rotation away from the ball. As a result, the chances of returning the clubface back to a square position become more remote.*

Open face *Equally damaging, although probably less common, is fanning the clubface into an excessively open position. This forces a host of compensatory moves in order to return the clubface squarely to the ball.*

PRACTICE GROUND
SELF-ANALYSIS

One of the main problems when it comes to self-analysis of faults is the inability to actually see the swing and check the various elements. Swinging in front of a mirror or a window can be helpful to check club position and swing plane. But by far the best check is photographic evidence. A video of the complete swing is the perfect answer, but getting a friend to take still photographs at various points in the backswing is almost as good.

Swing shot
Ask a friend to photograph your swing from several different angles.

Building a repeating swing

KEY 3 **SWING INTO THE TOP SLOT**

This position at the top needs to be checked in a mirror or be monitored by a friend. It is important that the shaft of the club, if it is horizontal to the ground, is parallel to the target-line. The angle of the clubface should match that of the forearm. This angle is known as square, or neutral, and is the ideal position to aim for. Also maintain the original spine angle and head position.

Square at the top
Set shaft parallel to target line at top of swing and ensure that clubface and forearm are at same angle.

SHUT FACE
Clubface is closed, or shut, and could well result in a pulled or hooked shot.

OPEN FACE
Here, clubface is open and may cause player to push or slice shot.

Head
Keep head at same level throughout swing.

**PRACTICE GROUND
90° CHECKPOINT**

It is important that the clubface stays square to the path of the swing from start to finish. This simple drill makes it easy to check the clubface position, at least in the earliest stage of the backswing.

1 *Start by addressing the ball as normal. Any club will do, although a mid-iron is preferable.*

2 *Then move into the takeaway, but stop when the shaft is horizontal to the ground.*

3 *Now turn 90° to the right, lower the arms, bend from the waist, and ground the club.*

4 *Without re-gripping the club, the clubface should still be square to the stance as before.*

A POWERFUL TURN
Note the power ratio. The shoulders have turned 90° and the hips 45°. Most of the body weight is now clearly over the right foot.

Right knee
Feel resistance in both right knee and right thigh.

Target line

JOSE MARIA OLAZABAL – PURPOSE IN PRACTICE

The late, great American teacher Harvey Penick was a strong believer in practice swinging with a purpose. Many players just waft the club backwards and forwards without any real intention.

Take a leaf out of **Jose Maria Olazabal's** book. Make a practice swing with a purpose. Aim at a specific point, such as a divot or a particular blade of grass, and pretend that it is the ball. Close your eyes and feel a smooth rhythm. Grip lightly and listen to the sound of the clubhead 'swishing' through the hitting area. Use these precious seconds to build composure before swinging for real.

Using the baseball grip (see page 69), swing two irons together. Swing them back and through, slowly and smoothly, concentrating on maintaining good rhythm and perfect balance. Feel that the muscles used in the swing are being stretched out, and becoming accustomed to the swinging motion.

Shaft drops
Flatten plane of swing very slightly.

Elbows
Drop right elbow down to side of body.

Left wrist
Retain 90° angle between left wrist and shaft of club for as long as possible.

Right heel
Allow right heel to come off ground as weight shifts to left side.

KEY 4 RETAIN THE POWER IN THE SWING

The 'Magic Move' applies to iron play, just as it does to the driver. Settle the weight, smoothly but purposefully, back towards the left side, and start to unwind the upper body. The right elbow should be dropped down to the side, but don't worry about the hands yet – they will come into play in the hitting area (see page 98).

SHIFT AND UNWIND
Moving into the downswing, feel the sensation of the left shoulder pulling away from the chin. Then start to unwind the upper body.

LESSON THREE

Concentrating on impact

FAULT-FINDER
POOR BALL POSITION

With the ball **too far forwards** in the stance the chances are that the clubhead will reach the bottom of the arc before the ball. The outcome is likely to be a 'heavy' shot where the club hits the ground before the ball, or a topped shot.

With the ball **too far back** in the stance the results can be similarly catastrophic. The clubhead makes contact with the ball before it has had time to reach the bottom of its arc. The result is likely to be iron shots that are 'thinned' when the ball is struck around its equator.

IMPACT IS THE moment of truth when it comes to clean, crisp iron shots. Everything in the swing is channelled into this one split-second and critical moment. The quality of the shot can only be determined by the quality of the impact. However, it is important to realize that these images are positions within motion; the swing is through them and not to them.

Head
Keep head behind point of impact.

KEY 1 COLLECT THE BALL

All iron shots must be struck with a descending blow if they are to fly consistently and accurately. With the long irons, the descending blow is less acute than with the shorter ones. A good image to have in mind is of the clubhead 'collecting' the ball on the way through the hitting zone. Don't think 'hit': think 'collect'. With good ball position, and the right angle of attack, the ball-then-turf strike will produce crisp and clean shots.

Left wrist
Keep left wrist firm through ball.

Arms
Extend arms fully through impact.

Impact position
Ensure hands lead clubhead into ball at impact.

Right heel
Lifting right heel off ground is a good indication that body weight is flowing towards target.

35%   65%

BALLESTEROS, TREVINO, WOOSNAM – THE PERFECT IMPACT

There are as many golf swings as there are people playing the game. But the best players have an almost identical position at impact. Here we see **Seve Ballesteros** (left), **Lee Trevino** (centre), and **Ian Woosnam** (right), three great golfers who are built differently and who have their own unique swings, yet at the point of impact the common elements are clearly seen. In each case, the left hip has cleared out of the way, the weight is on the front foot, and the left wrist is firm.

KEY 2 OPEN THE SHOULDERS AT IMPACT

It is a common fallacy that the body has to return to a square position at impact in order to make a square contact with the ball. In fact, the hips, body, and shoulders are slightly open to the target line at impact. This creates the necessary room for the arms to release the club down the correct path through the ball. The body has to 'get out of the way' for consistent striking.

Knee
Kick in right knee at impact.

Right heel
Lift heel as body weight transfers onto left side.

Hands
Hands and arms deliver clubface squarely to back of ball on desired path.

Clubhead
Clubhead makes perfect ball-then-turf contact.

PRACTICE GROUND
STRIKE IT CLEAN AND CRISP

A clean and crisp strike is all-important in iron play, so it is vital to avoid 'hitting heavy' – this is when a turf-then-ball contact is made rather than the other way round. Work on this drill to keep the strike clean. Start by pre-setting the ideal impact position at address. Shift the weight on to the left foot and lift the right heel off the ground a fraction. Remember, the hips and shoulders should be slightly open with the head and body more over the ball. This creates the feeling of a good impact position, albeit in freeze-frame.

1 *Address the ball in a 'freeze-frame' of the impact position.*

2 *Move through the backswing, shifting your weight onto the right side.*

3 *Return weight to the left, swinging through original address position.*

4 *Move through to a balanced position, with the weight on the front foot.*

LESSON FOUR

Swinging to a balanced finish

PRACTICE GROUND
TRAIN FOR A BETTER TURN

In order to transfer the weight correctly in the swing, the head will start to move to the right in the backswing. However, too much lateral movement in the lower half of the body will cause problems if the timing is not quite right. This is a useful drill to encourage a more effective, rotary body action. Start by sticking a golf umbrella or an old clubshaft into the ground, roughly 6in (15cm) to the side of the left hip.

1 Set-up as normal and swing back with the weight on the right knee.

2 The left hip starts to move away in the hitting zone.

3 Follow through without sliding or disturbing the umbrella.

4 Finish in perfect balance, leaving the umbrella undisturbed.

ALTHOUGH THERE IS nothing that can be done to influence the flight of the ball after it has been struck, the followthrough is still an important part of the overall swing. Concentrating on certain 'post-impact factors' during the swing very often encourages improvements in the nature of the swing itself – influencing both impact and accuracy.

Shoulder
Fire right shoulder through, past chin.

KEY **1** FIRE THE RIGHT SHOULDER
Try to stay with the ball for as long as is comfortable through impact. Drive the right shoulder past the chin and through towards the target. Known as 'good extension', this is a positive image to have in mind as the club swings down through the hitting zone.

Hands
Natural movement of crossing right hand over left indicates a good release through impact.

Hips
Continue to unwind hips and upper body through hitting zone.

Legs
Maintain balance as club swings down and through impact.

20%   80%

PRACTICE GROUND THE SWISH DRILL

This is a particularly useful exercise, used by many top players, to help maintain, or even regain, rhythm and tempo during a round. From a normal stance, hover the clubhead roughly 2ft (60cm) above the ground. Swish the clubhead back and through impact. Concentrate on the sound of the clubhead as it moves through the hitting zone. Without the ball to get in the way of the free-flow of the swing, it should make an impressive 'whoosh'. By repeating this continually, the body will start to 'free up'. This encourages a smooth acceleration of the clubhead in the downswing and through impact. Then go ahead and re-create this feeling in an actual swing.

KEY 2 FOLLOWTHROUGH IN PERFECT BALANCE

Maintaining balance is critical for good iron play. The swing should finish with the spine straight, and the right shoulder over the left foot. Any stumbling or toppling off balance is a sure sign that there was something wrong in the swing. Often poor balance comes as a result of swinging too fast or too hard. Curb the power and stay in balance.

Back
Finish with spine as straight as possible.

Right foot
Show spikes in follow-through.

5%   95%

Right shoulder over left foot

View from above
The body is in perfect balance at the finish.

LANNY WADKINS AND FRED COUPLES – SWING SPEEDS

Different players have different swing speeds. **Lanny Wadkins** (left) is as quick as anyone in the professional game – no sooner does he have the club in his hands than the ball is rifling off towards the target. **Fred Couples** (right), on the other hand, has a much slower swing and an altogether more languid approach to the game.

Despite the difference in speed, they each swing at a tempo that allows them to control the club. One way of determining swing speed is the percentage drill. Go to the practice ground and hit 10 balls at 50% power, then 10 balls at 60% power, and so on up to full power. This test will help determine which swing leads to the greatest level of consistency, both in terms of quality of strike and distance achieved.

LESSON FIVE

Getting in tune

UNFORTUNATELY, IT IS not possible to read what goes on in a professional's mind during a tournament. This is a pity because experience and wisdom are just as important as a good-looking swing. But there is still much to be learned by studying professionals, and the ways in which they plot their course through 18 holes. Much can be learned through careful study of course management – which is another key element in good iron play.

LARRY MIZE – THE DREAM START

The opening tee shot often sets the tone for the rest of the round, as **Larry Mize** demonstrated to dazzling effect in the final round of the 1994 British Open at Turnberry. With two bunkers flanking the first fairway at driving distance, the landing area was perilously narrow. Despite the obvious advantage of trying to get as close as possible to the green on this short par 4, Mize left the driver in the bag and took an iron from the tee. From the safety of the fairway, he then holed his second shot for an eagle two. It is important to get off to a good start consistently. Take a club that will find the first fairway from the tee. This early in the round, it is accuracy that is important, not distance.

PRACTICE GROUND
LEARN DISTANCES

It is important to know how far you hit every iron in the bag. Most golfers have a rough idea, but for significant improvement in iron play, distances must be worked out more precisely. This drill establishes a bench-mark for each club, vital information to take out onto the course. Hit 20 balls with each club, discard the longest five and the shortest five. The cluster of 10 remaining balls indicates an average distance for each club you test in this way.

KEY 1 ## USE THE FULL ALLOWANCE
It is important to make full use of the teeing area for iron shots on short holes. The Rules of Golf allow for a full two club lengths' distance back from the tee markers, and this extra space should be put to good use. Invariably, the ground to the rear of where most players have teed up will be less worn and more even. Also experiment using the full width of the teeing ground. Playing in from a different angle can offer a more direct route to the flag.

Full distance
Ball can be positioned up to two club lengths back from tee markers.

Feet position
Provided ball is teed within area defined by the two markers, feet can be positioned outside that area.

VIJAY SINGH – HARD WORK AT PRACTICE

It is no coincidence that Fiji's **Vijay Singh** is one of the best players around in the world today, and also practises harder than just about any other player on tour. Vijay has reaped the rewards of hours of hard work on the practice ground.

There is much to learn from his work ethic. However, practice purely for its own sake will bring little, if any, reward. There must be a clearly defined purpose to every practice session. If the iron shots are not clean and crisp, check the elements detailed in the previous pages, seek out the cause, and then practise the cure. Even in the unlikely event of being happy with all aspects of your game, always go into a practice round with a purpose – and come away with a positive result.

Dead aim
Aim clubface over an old divot mark between ball and target.

KEY 3 ESTABLISH PERFECT PARALLEL ALIGNMENT
Get into the habit of building the stance around the position of the clubface, square to the target line. Learn to match a square stance to a square clubface by aligning with floorboards at home, or with a particular carpet pattern. Do this as often as possible until perfect parallel alignment becomes almost second nature.

KEY 2 IDENTIFY A TARGET
Any teeing ground on a par 3 has its share of divot marks. Rather than regarding these as an eyesore, use them as a visual aid to alignment. Find one that corresponds with the target line and line up the ball behind it. Line up the clubface over that point to ensure perfect aim, every time. Alternatively, use the same divot mark and, this time, tee up the ball ahead of it. Now swing the clubhead down along the line of the divot mark and through into impact. This helps promote an on-line attack, and therefore, more on-line shots.

Feet
Make sure feet are in perfect parallel alignment.

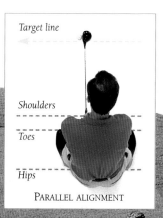

Target line

Shoulders

Toes

Hips

PARALLEL ALIGNMENT

BASICS OF BETTER PITCHING

ALTHOUGH WE MAY never emulate the powerful hitting of the likes of John Daly or Greg Norman, there is no reason why we cannot come close to matching them when it comes to pitching and the short game. This is a key area when it comes to lower scoring. There are no physical restrictions to hold us back, and pitching the ball close to the hole is within the capability of every golfer. In this section we study the techniques that make the top players deadly accurate with the pitching clubs and identify the lessons we can learn for our own game improvement plan.

TOM KITE
It is Tom Kite's accuracy in his approach shots that has helped him to become one of the leading money winners in the history of golf, proof that distance off the tee is not a prerequisite for success.

NICK FALDO
Britain's Nick Faldo is a master of the short game and has a wonderfully deft touch with the pitching clubs. His smooth rhythm helps to explain why so many of his pitch shots end up within such close range of the hole.

1 THE ADDRESS
Although he is a tall man, Nick does not allow himself to crouch over the ball at address. He bends naturally from the hips, keeping his knees flexed, his chin up, and his head perfectly still as he takes the club away.

2 THE TAKEAWAY
Like all the great players, Nick has an excellent one-piece takeaway with the club, hands, arms, and shoulders moving away from the ball in unison. His wrists do not start to 'break' until his hands are almost waist high.

3 AT THE TOP
A three-quarter backswing is the secret behind controlling a pitch shot. Nick makes a full shoulder turn but the hands only reach shoulder height. The length of the shot is controlled by the length of the swing.

SANDY LYLE
Although renowned for the prodigious distances he can hit the ball, particularly with his long irons, Sandy Lyle is also a superb pitcher of the ball. Much of his control comes from a relatively short backswing and a smooth rhythm.

6 THE FOLLOW-THROUGH

The momentum of the swing carries the club up to a perfectly balanced finish. As the club freewheels to the top of the followthrough, it automatically brings Nick's head up to watch the flight of the ball.

5 THROUGH IMPACT

This is the perfect position through impact. Nick's head remains still as he releases the club freely through the ball – his body weight flowing onto the left side.

4 THE DOWNSWING

Nick's slightly open stance, an essential ingredient of good pitching, helps him to clear his left side in the downswing, delivering the clubface square to the back of the ball on the ideal path and angle of attack.

LESSON ONE

Pitching for accuracy

ONE OF THE principal keys to lower scores is accurate pitching. Turning three strokes into two by pitching close is a major weapon in the battle for improvement. The main element is control. Bad pitchers struggle because they hit the ball 'flat out', assuming that a pitch is played like any other shot. It is not. Control of length and accuracy are what matter.

JOSE MARIA OLAZABAL – FINDING A PITCHING ZONE

Even better than knowing how far to hit a club is developing a favourite distance – a 'pitching zone' that you can play to. In a well-documented incident, **Jose Maria Olazabal** had driven into trouble off the tee and was then heard to ask his caddie, "What club gives me 92yds to the flag for my next shot?" Thinking one step ahead enabled Olazabal to leave himself in a position where he was confident of making a pitch-and-putt save. Hours spent on the practice range hitting balls does pay dividends. Establishing a personal pitching distance gives a strength to play to. It provides another weapon in the armoury to get the ball close and help save some strokes.

KEY 1 MAKE SUBTLE CHANGES AT ADDRESS

Preparation is important here. The ball position needs to be around the middle of the stance (see page 93) – this ensures that the ball is struck crisply on a slightly descending angle of attack. It is also important to check that the shaft and the left arm are in a straight line at address – this also encourages a crisp, ball-then-turf contact.

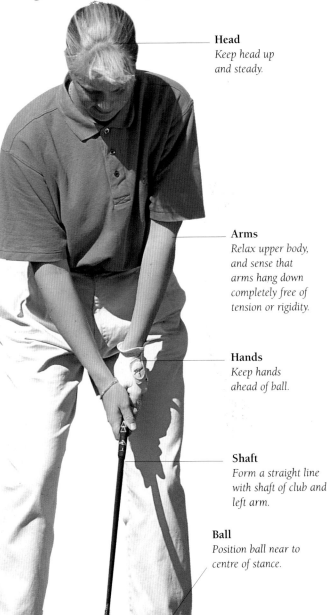

Head
Keep head up and steady.

Arms
Relax upper body, and sense that arms hang down completely free of tension or rigidity.

Hands
Keep hands ahead of ball.

Shaft
Form a straight line with shaft of club and left arm.

Ball
Position ball near to centre of stance.

50%   50%

KEY 2 OPEN THE STANCE

One major difference between the pitch shot and any ordinary full shot is in the address position. Alignment should be a little open at address to help the left side clear through impact. It is not a major shift but enough to make a difference. The other important aspect in this set-up is that, despite the open alignment, the clubface must still be aimed directly at the target.

Back
Angle spine comfortably forwards.

Shoulders
Make sure right shoulder is over outside of right knee.

Grip
Adopt a secure, but light, grip.

Stance
Open feet slightly more than usual at address.

Clubface
Aim clubface at intended target.

PRACTICE GROUND WORK ON A ONE-PIECE MOVE

One of the biggest mistakes that golfers make when hitting short pitch shots is getting too wristy in the early part of the takeaway. This results in a loss of co-ordination and inconsistency in judging both line and length. To avoid getting too wristy this drill to promote greater synchronization of the club, hands, arms, and torso away from the ball. This will help achieve a more consistent ball-strike and with it the ability to judge distance.

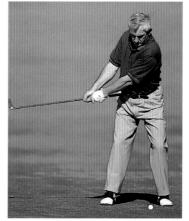

1 *Address the ball as normal and feed the shaft of the club up through the hands so that the butt of the grip fits snugly against the midriff. Keep the posture the same.*

2 *Now start to move the club away without altering the relationship between the arms, the club, and the torso. Simply turn the upper body, stopping as you see the hands move past the right knee.*

GARY PLAYER – CHOOSE THE RIGHT EQUIPMENT

Gary Player, one of only four golfers to have won all four Major championships is fond of the saying that "Seventy per cent of all shots are played within one hundred yards (90 metres) of the green"; a startling but accurate statistic. All the more baffling, then, that so many club golfers head out onto the course ill-equipped to meet the demands of a game that places so much emphasis on the short shots. Don't fall into this trap. Carry three wedges in the golf bag, a pitching wedge from the regular set plus two utility wedges. There is a range of lofts available between 52–60° that should provide for any eventuality.

LESSON TWO

Building a better action

THERE ARE TWO stages to developing a good pitching action. The first is to build a technique that produces a consistently accurate ball-flight.

The second phase is learning to judge distance. This lesson will help develop technique, but judgement of distance comes only with experience and practice.

Right thigh
Feel some tension in right thigh.

FROM THE FRONT
Good weight transfer and upper-body rotation are as vital to the 100yd (90m) pitch as they are to the 300yd (275m) drive.

Right knee
Retain flex in right knee.

Left foot
Keep left heel planted on ground.

KEY 1 · MAKE A TIDY BACKSWING

Opening the stance slightly helps to curb the movement of the lower body, and this helps to create resistance as the upper body is coiled. Gripping further down the shaft also reduces the backswing to a tidy, compact, three-quarter position, giving more control over the shot. But despite the shorter swing, the weight still needs to be transferred correctly. There should be a sense of loading the weight into the right knee and thigh.

NICK FALDO – A SHORTER BACKSWING

For playing a less-than-full pitch shot, where accuracy is at a premium, choking down the grip can have several benefits, as **Nick Faldo** demonstrates here. Firstly, it brings the hands closer to the clubhead and the ball, thereby enhancing control. It also automatically shortens the backswing to a three-quarter position, which reduces the distance the ball flies without any conscious effort required; so just choke down, and let the club do the work.

KEY 2 CLEAR THE LEFT SIDE

Because the swing is relatively short, the body has less time to turn out of the way in the downswing. By opening the stance slightly it is easier to clear the left side out of the way. In a sense it gives the left side a head start – which is exactly what is needed in order to swing the clubhead down on the correct path.

Clubhead
Keep clubface square to swing path.

Upper body
Unwind upper body in downswing.

Hands
Feel hands leading clubhead down to ball.

Hips
Re-rotate hips, clearing left side in readiness for perfect impact.

Knees
Retain gap between knees long into downswing.

PRACTICE GROUND TRAIN A ROTARY ACTION

Body action is the engine room of the swing, regardless of the shot being played. Visualizing the torso as a rotating drum, with the arms simply moving in harmony with it, is a good image to maintain.

Problems will only arise if the body and the arms start to work independently of each other. This drill encourages an all-round better action, with the body and arms working closely together throughout. Address the ball with the feet closer together – no more than 6in (15cm) apart – and hit a series of three-quarter pitch shots. Because of this stance, any swing abnormalities will result in a loss of balance.

In order to maintain balance, the body is forced to coil in the backswing before unwinding in the downswing. This produces a more effective rotary action, with the arms working in perfect harmony.

FRED COUPLES – KEEPING THE SAME RHYTHM

Fred Couples is a wonderful pitcher of the ball. The consistent rhythm of his swing is immediately obvious. It stays the same for every pitch he plays. To vary the distance of a shot, Couples does not change the pace of the swing – he simply changes its length.

This is the key to consistent judgement of distance. When practising pitch shots, link the length of the swing to the intended distance, but at the same time keep the rhythm exactly the same for every shot.

Building a better action

KEY 3 STRIKE IT SQUARELY

As the left side clears, the arms have sufficient room to deliver the clubface squarely to the ball and on the correct path. If a square stance is adopted for pitching, there is not sufficient time to move the left side into this position.

KEY 4 RELEASE THE CLUBHEAD

From a good position just before impact the clubhead is released freely towards the target. There is no fear of the ball flying left, and no steering of the clubhead through the hitting zone. All the good work earlier on now pays dividends.

Shoulders
Keep shoulders slightly open through impact.

Hands
Make sure hands are slightly ahead of ball at impact.

Clubhead
Clubhead meets ball squarely and on ideal swing path.

PRACTICE GROUND ELIMINATE THE SHANK

The shank is not only the most destructive shot in golf, it is also the most dreaded. It is usually caused by an excessively out-to-in swing path, with the ball flying wildly right off the hosel of the clubhead. By the very nature of the downswing attack required for pitch shots, the chances of hitting a shank are greatly increased.

This drill helps to eliminate the shank by encouraging a swing inside the line while, at the same time, maintaining the necessary descending attack on the ball.

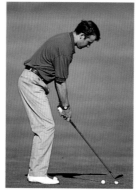

1 *Assume a normal stance but place another ball outside the target ball. Address the outer ball without changing the stance.*

2 *Swing down and hit the inner ball. This automatically encourages a swing down from inside the ball-to-target line.*

KEY 5 MOVE INTO THE FOLLOWTHROUGH

Moving into the followthrough, check that the weight has moved over to the left foot and that the right shoulder has moved through towards the hole.

PRACTICE GROUND LEARN TO STRIKE THE BALL FIRST

For those having difficulty in making a clean contact with the ball before the turf, this drill will help to promote a far crisper strike. Start by placing a headcover approximately 18in (45cm) behind the ball. Then hit several pitch shots, making sure that the clubhead does not make contact with the cover on the downswing. The cover forces the hands to stay ahead of the clubhead just a little longer and encourages a slightly steeper angle of attack on the ball. By repeating the drill, this soon becomes a more comfortable movement. That is good practice, gradually training a better swing.

Right shoulder
Right shoulder moves through towards hole.

Hips
Rotate hips to face target.

Right knee
Move right knee into shot.

Right heel
Right heel comes off ground as weight transfers.

Spine
Keep spine straight, ensuring there is no strain on lower back.

Left foot
Continue to move weight over onto left foot.

FOLLOW RIGHT THROUGH
The majority of the weight should now be on the left side, with the right shoulder over the left foot, and the spikes on the right foot in full view.

LESSON THREE

Pitching from bad lies

WE ALL HAVE to accept our share of bad lies, whether in the rough or on the fairway. It is part and parcel of the game of golf. But, as players such as Seve Ballesteros often demonstrate, these situations can appear more daunting than they really are. A few simple adjustments should be enough to remove the fear from the majority of difficult lies.

SHOT SELECTION LIE FACTORS

The first thing to understand about bad lies is that no single club is ideal for all shots. Selecting the right club is almost as important as developing an effective technique. The first instinct with a bad lie is often to reach for the sand wedge, but that is not always wise. In most cases, what is needed is a sharp leading edge to cut through to the back of the ball. From a bare lie, a divot mark, or when the ball is buried in deep rough, it is often best to take out a pitching wedge or even a 9-iron. The sharper leading edge allows the club to cut through the interference, providing the best chance of catching the ball squarely – and successfully.

Bare lie   *Divot mark*   *Thick rough*

KEY 1 **A STEEPER ATTACK**
The key in thick rough is a steeper angle of attack. Position the ball 1in (2.5cm) or so back in the stance – this sets the hands well ahead of the clubhead. Sense that the weight is set a little more onto the left foot than it would be for a standard pitch – a ratio of 60-40 is a good guide.

Hands
Set hands well ahead of ball.

Shaft
Make sure that shaft of club and left arm form a straight line down to ball.

Stance
Assume normal width stance with ball positioned towards middle.

CURTIS STRANGE – THUMP OUT OF ROUGH

As double US Open champion **Curtis Strange** demonstrates, a ball lying in heavy clumps of rough is one of the few occasions in golf where brute force comes into play. As long as the lie is not too deep, aim to dislodge as much grass from around the ball as possible. Don't change the rhythm of the swing, just put a little extra muscle power into it at the bottom. Try to take all of the grass with the shot, and swing through to a balanced finish.

40%   60%

Weight
Keep weight centred over ball.

Right knee
Coil upper body over flexed right knee.

50% 50%

KEY 2 TURN AND SWING TO THE TOP

Make a normal backswing. The only discernible variations from a normal pitch should be the setting of the wrists a fraction earlier in the takeaway and the centring of the weight over the ball at the top of the backswing. These factors combine to encourage a sharper, descending blow, exactly what is needed to force the ball out.

SEVE BALLESTEROS – CREATIVITY AND INVENTION

There is no one more adept at escaping from bad lies than **Seve Ballesteros**. Follow his example, and don't be afraid to experiment with clubs, even during a round. Not every pitch shot has to descend onto the flag from a height of 150ft (46m). Try landing the ball onto the green from different heights; use the contours of the ground to sweep the ball in towards the flag; and apply various levels of spin. Above all, use some imagination.

KEY 3 PUNCH THE CLUBHEAD DOWN

Now punch the clubhead down into the back of the ball with force, driving it forwards. Most of the weight should be on the left foot at impact and the head should be over the ball as the clubhead cuts through the grass.

Left hand
Keep left hand and wrist firm.

HANDS DICTATE
Look at this impact photograph taken as the ball is driven forwards out of an old divot mark. Notice the angle of the shaft relative to the ground – it is slanted forwards quite dramatically. This confirms that the hands are leading the clubhead through impact.

30% 70%

PRINCIPLES OF ACCURATE CHIPPING

THE MOST STRIKING aspect of professional play around the greens is just how simple the great players make it look. When Jose Maria Olazabal steps up to a chip-and-run shot just off the green he is looking to hole it, not just get it close. In actual fact the chip shot is one of the simplest shots to learn in golf. Good technique and touch, allied to confidence and a little imagination, are the main ingredients required.

LARRY NELSON
Larry Nelson is a player who seldom lands in trouble. But when he misses a green he has a great short game to get him back on track. He was 21 before he first hit a golf ball, and subsequently learned how to play from a book.

JOSE MARIA OLAZABAL
Jose Maria Olazabal, like his fellow countryman Seve Ballesteros, is a master craftsman around the greens. His combination of a wonderful touch, imagination, and a perfect understanding of how the ball will behave makes him one of the best in the business.

1 THE ADDRESS
Jose Maria addresses the ball off the left heel for this 'floating' chip shot. He is completely relaxed and has already decided the exact spot on which he wants the ball to land.

2 THE TAKEAWAY
The one-piece takeaway, vital for all shots, is very evident here. Jose Maria keeps his head still, with his weight slightly favouring the left side. There is little or no weight transfer needed for this shot.

3 THE BACKSWING
The length of the backswing determines the length of the shot. Jose Maria takes the club back slowly and smoothly, allowing the wrists to hinge naturally. His weight remains predominantly on the left side.

WAYNE GRADY
Wayne Grady for many years had an unenviable reputation for always finishing second. But one thing he did win was a well-deserved reputation for his sharp short game. His chipping touch around the greens is one of the reasons why he won the 1990 USPGA Championship.

6 FOLLOWTHROUGH
Perfectly poised, with his weight mainly on his left side, Jose Maria takes the club into a controlled followthrough. His hands have travelled a little higher than they did on the backswing, indicating that the club has been accelerated through the ball.

5 THROUGH IMPACT
Through impact Jose Maria has 'held the clubhead off' by not allowing his right hand to cross over his left. This technique keeps the clubface open through impact and creates a higher and softer landing shot with little roll.

4 THE DOWNSWING
Jose Maria makes sure that his hands stay ahead of the clubhead in the downswing to ensure a crisp ball-before-turf contact. His aim is literally to slide the clubface under the ball, taking just a wafer-thin sliver of turf in the process.

LESSON ONE

Understanding ball behaviour

BEING ABLE TO predict just how the golf ball will behave when playing a chip shot is just as important as the ability to play the shot itself. Spin, trajectory, and roll all have to be taken into account – for each has an effect on how close the ball will finish to the hole. The following keys, together with experience and practice, will help make predicting ball behaviour much easier.

SHOT SELECTION **LIE FACTORS**

Many golfers are unaware of how much influence the lie of the ball has on its flight through the air. A bare lie, for instance, where there is little or no grass beneath the ball or where the grass is tightly mown, produces a lower than normal flight. Therefore, the high cut-up shot should never be attempted from this type of lie. In longer grass, however, the opposite applies. The ball will come out of this kind of lie with a relatively high flight, although with a lot less backspin because grass gets between the face of the club and the ball. When the ball is sitting relatively well in this lie, a more varied selection of shots can be attempted.

Bare lie

Fluffy lie in long grass

USE LESS LOFT ON AN UPSLOPE
On an upslope, the slope itself effectively adds loft to the club. Always select a longer iron than normal – the exact choice depending on the incline. Position the ball forwards in the stance.

Torso
Rotate upper body in harmony with arm swing.

Takeaway
Make a shorter length of backswing.

Balance
Keep weight distribution central throughout shot.

Knees
Retain original flex in left knee.

KEY 1 COPE WITH AN UPSLOPE
Using a less lofted club on an upslope will result in a shorter, softer swing, making it easier to control distance. The ball will also shoot forwards on a fairly low trajectory, with little backspin – making it easier to judge the running speed of the ball.

Wrists
Keep left wrist firm through ball.

Trajectory
Less lofted club creates lower ball flight.

50%

50%

KEY 2 COPE WITH A DOWNSLOPE

On a downslope lie, the ball has a tendency to fly out on a low trajectory, making it difficult to control. Selecting a club with as much loft as possible will help to compensate. The sand wedge is often the ideal club for the job. It replaces some of the control that is naturally lost on a downslope, at the same time creating enough elevation on the ball to ensure a soft landing.

USE MORE LOFT ON A DOWNSLOPE
Select a more lofted iron on a downslope to counteract the effect of the decline. Position the ball back in the stance.

COLIN MONTGOMERIE – HIT THE SPOT

All professionals play shots differently around the green, using a variety of clubs or a range of shots. But one thing they all do is select an exact spot to land the ball on – before they even think about taking a club out of the bag. Scotsman **Colin Montgomerie** is no exception. When he plays a chip shot he knows where the ball will land and where it will finish, and he keeps the technique nice and simple.

This is the best approach to follow for chip shots. Start by visualizing the shot, taking into account what the ball will do; focus on a precise landing spot, preferably on the green to ensure an even bounce; and then select the club that best performs that function. Hitting the spot consistently equates to lower scores.

Body
Stay down on shot for as long as possible.

Trajectory
Good technique creates plenty of height and control.

Takeaway
Hinge wrists in backswing to help create necessary steep angle of attack.

Clubhead
Slide clubhead through grass and under ball.

Weight
Keep weight on lower leg throughout swing.

40%

60%

LESSON TWO

Perfecting the chip shot

THE BASIC CHIP shot is just that – basic. It is not a complicated technique, and the simpler things are kept the better. The shot's sole function is to loft the ball over any uneven ground ahead, and on to the relatively even surface of the putting green, rolling smoothly towards the hole. This is how to fine-tune chipping technique with the least fuss and the most accuracy.

KEY 1 SET THE RIGHT ADDRESS

The ideal address for chipping is summed up in one sentence: 'Ball back, hands forwards, and weight forwards.' This promotes the slightly descending angle of attack and crisp strike necessary to produce good chip shots. Choke down on the club 2in (5cm) or so, nudge the body – weight over on to the left foot, and maintain a light grip pressure.

PRACTICE GROUND
THE RANDOM CHIPPING EXERCISE

An effective practice session should aim to re-create as closely as possible an on-course situation. The feeling should be of playing a proper round, experiencing the 'one-shot' pressures associated with competitive play. Here is a useful exercise to sharpen up performance around the greens.

Throw several balls randomly around a green, and then play each ball as it lies. Have three or four clubs to hand, and picture each shot before addressing the ball. This will help to determine which clubs work best in certain situations. The benefits of this drill will be reaped during competitive play when the requirement really is to get up and down in two.

Hands
Choke down on grip and nudge hands ahead of ball.

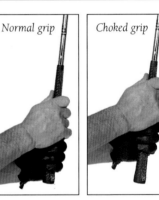

Normal grip   *Choked grip*

GRIPPING DOWN THE CLUB
While longer irons are gripped towards the end of the shaft (left), the hands need to be further down the grip for chips and short shots (right). This brings the hands closer to the ball and enhances control over the shot.

Stance
Adopt a stance slightly more open than for a normal iron shot.

Weight
Shift weight towards left foot to promote a downward strike.

Ball
Ball is positioned further back in stance.

40%   60%

Shoulders
Control stroke with a gentle rocking of the shoulders.

Right wrist
Hinge right wrist to set hands in dominant position.

Balance
Continue to keep body weight forwards on left side.

40%   60%

COREY PAVIN – A SOFT TOUCH FROM CLOSE RANGE

The 1995 US Open champion **Corey Pavin** is known for being a gritty competitor. He is also renowned for his razor-sharp short game. Under the toughest conditions he can still threaten the hole from the most unlikely positions. Pavin's chipping action is an education in itself. Just look how relaxed he is. His grip is 'soft' and his posture is relaxed and comfortable – without being sloppy.

Follow Pavin's example, and try to stay relaxed over the ball. Grip softly and stay loose, and the ability to judge the weight of chip shots will become that much sharper.

KEY 2 HINGE THE RIGHT WRIST ON THE TAKEAWAY
This shot requires an arms-type movement, essentially controlled by a gentle rocking of the shoulders. Also create a slight hinge in the back of the right wrist as the club moves away from the ball. This angle helps set the hands in a dominant position to lead the clubhead down into the ball.

KEY 3 HANDS LEAD IN THE HITTING ZONE
For a crisp strike, try to return the hands, arms, and the clubhead exactly to where they were at address. The weight should have stayed on the left side throughout. This helps produce a ball-then-turf contact, squeezing the ball out towards the target.

KEEP LEFT WRIST FIRM THROUGH IMPACT
Try to hold the angle of both wrists through the ball. This helps prevent the clubhead overtaking the hands, which could lead to a disastrous scoop at the ball.

Impact
A crisp downward strike produces low trajectory with a hint of spin.

40%   60%

119

LESSON THREE

Chipping for extra height

A CHIP FROM a troublesome lie normally leaves a player with two alternatives. The low shot is basically the standard chip shot, played with a less-lofted club. However, the high shot, the only option for 'carrying' over hazards, has its own unique requirements. Here we see how going high can keep scores low.

Backswing
Make a relatively long swing for a shot of this length.

KEY 1 SET UP TO GO HIGH

Start by gripping softly and opening the clubface. Position the hands more over the ball – this retains the loft and prevents an excessive downward strike. Also open the stance to encourage a slightly out-to-in swing path, which helps give the shot a soft, floating flight.

Wrists
Set wrists in backswing.

Upper body
Allow upper body to rotate in response to swinging motion of arms.

Stance
Adopt a wider stance than for a normal chip.

Ball
Position ball inside left heel.

Weight
Keep weight evenly distributed.

SEVE BALLESTEROS – LOFT IT AND LET IT RUN

Somewhere between the chip-and-run and the high, cut-up shot lies the stroke of genius that **Seve Ballesteros** pulled off on the 72nd hole of the 1993 European Masters at Crans-sur-Sierre. The chip shot itself is one we can all hope to play – reproducing the timing is another matter. Having carved his drive into the trees on the right of the fairway, he played an improbable recovery through a tiny gap in the branches, over a wall, and up to within 20ft (6m) of the putting surface. From there, he played the most exquisite lofted, running chip straight into the hole for surely one of the most unlikely birdies in history. It is amazing what a little imagination, a lot of practice, and a large dose of genius can achieve.

KEY 2 KEEP THE SWING LONG

Confidence to make a long swing for what is a fairly short shot is the key here. Sense that the clubhead traces a path along the line of the feet for the first 18in (45cm) of the takeaway. Then allow the wrists to hinge up, and the clubhead to move inside the line, as the backswing is completed.

Shoulders
Rotate left shoulder out of the way through hitting zone.

Swing
Swing to, and through, original address position.

Clubhead
Slide clubhead through grass and under ball.

TOM WATSON – FLY HIGH, LAND SOFTLY

In the final round of the 1982 US Open at Pebble Beach, **Tom Watson** played one of the great cut-up shots of all time. Holding a one-stroke lead over Jack Nicklaus, Watson missed the green in a terrible spot at the treacherous 17th. Given the lie and the lack of green between him and the pin, a costly bogey seemed inevitable. Somehow, though, Watson conjured up a miraculous shot, landing the ball in the fringe, from where it trickled into the hole for a tournament-clinching birdie. The lesson is, no matter how difficult the shot may be, pick a spot and be committed to landing the ball on it.

KEY 3
SLIDE THE CLUBHEAD UNDER
Imagine trying to slice a wafer-thin sliver of turf from under the ball through impact; as if 'cutting the legs away' from under the ball. Be positive, and accelerate the clubhead smoothly through the ball. Remember, there needs to be a fair bit of grass around the ball to play this shot – don't contemplate it from a bare lie.

Hands and body
Body continues to unwind as hands swing through.

Trajectory
Despite long swing, ball pops up high and travels only a short distance.

KEY 4
KEEP RHYTHM SMOOTH
Accelerating through impact, the clubhead almost overtakes the ball. Try to picture this as the clubhead slides under the ball and through. The ball pops up high – so softly, in fact, that it is almost possible to run forwards and catch it before it lands. Continual practice will help develop the nerve to swing the club long and slow – and the confidence to play some audacious chip shots.

Weight
Sense that weight hangs back more than normal in through-swing.

LESSON FOUR

Chipping from the edge of the green

GREG NORMAN – 'BRUSH' AND RUN

Surprisingly enough, chipping with a lofted wood has several benefits. As **Greg Norman** proved in the 1994 Dubai Desert Classic, it is actually a viable, and profitable, shot – subtly lofting the ball onto the putting surface, from where it can roll smoothly towards the hole, just like a putt. And for those who struggle to play the chip-and-run, this shot represents a great alternative. The sole of a lofted wood is flat, making it literally impossible to stub the clubhead into the ground behind the ball. Instead, the club glides across the turf.

KEY 1 SET UP WITH A PUTTING GRIP

As this shot is a mixture of a chip and a putt, start by trying a putting grip, or at least experiment with it to see how it feels. This enhances control in chip shots and prevents excessive wrist action, which, from close range, can cause inconsistencies and erratic ball-striking.

HOVER THE CLUBHEAD
Take a short iron and address the ball just as if it were a putt, except that the blade of the club is hovered just above the ball's equator.

WHEN THE BALL rests up against the collar of rough surrounding the fringe of a green, it can be a nasty predicament. Strangely, the more manicured the course, the harder the shot is. In the mind, it is seemingly neither a putt nor a chip, and indeed that is exactly how it should be treated – as a mixture of the two.

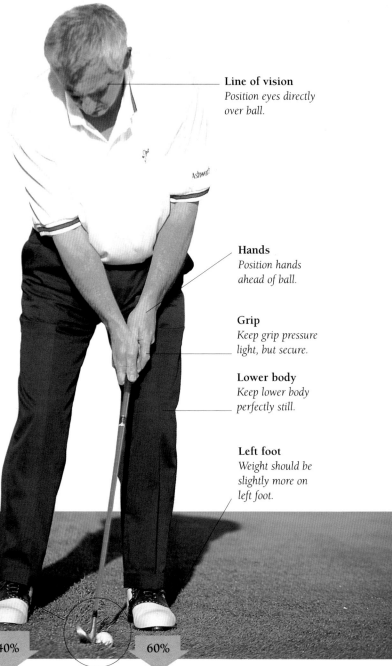

Line of vision
Position eyes directly over ball.

Hands
Position hands ahead of ball.

Grip
Keep grip pressure light, but secure.

Lower body
Keep lower body perfectly still.

Left foot
Weight should be slightly more on left foot.

40%   60%

Focal point
Focus on an intended point of impact.

Wrists
Keep wrist movement to a minimum.

Left wrist
Maintain original angle in left wrist.

Takeaway
Keep clubhead low to ground in takeaway.

Ball's equator

PRACTICE GROUND THE CHEEKY 'CHIP-PUTT'

There is a cheeky alternative to 'blading' the ball from the collar of rough around the green. Swivel the grip of the putter in the hands so that the toe sits directly behind the ball. This cannot be done with all types of putter, but it is well worth giving the shot a try if at all possible.

1 *Address the ball as if for a straightforward putt. Then swivel your grip so that the toe of the putter is hovering behind the ball as squarely as possible.*

2 *Repeat the normal putting stroke, aiming to strike the ball around its equator. Though the ball may well hop briefly into the air, it should then settle and roll relatively smoothly towards the hole.*

Head
Keep head and shoulders as still as possible throughout swing.

Hands
Smoothly accelerate hands and clubhead through ball.

Followthrough
Imagine clubhead travelling low to ground through impact.

KEY 2 STRIKE THE BALL'S EQUATOR

Make a compact backswing with very little 'wrist-break'. Aim to strike just above the ball's equator with the leading edge of the clubhead. Do not 'flip' at the ball – just keep the wrists firm, as you would for a putting stroke. The nature of this type of action ensures that there is no interference, or snagging, of the clubhead in the rough. This helps to encourage as clean a contact as possible.

KEY 3 ROLL IT LIKE A PUTT

The greatest benefit of all with this shot is that it creates a smooth roll on the ball, which is obviously just what is required when the green is in such close proximity. Played correctly, the ball will roll across the green just like a putt.

ANSWERS TO BUNKER PLAY

A BALL LYING in sand holds a special fear for the average golfer, yet many professionals would actually prefer to be in a bunker than in rough beside the green. They are confident they can get the ball close from the sand to save par. In this section we learn some of the tricks of the trade that have made players like Bernhard Langer and, of course, the master bunker specialist Gary Player, so outstanding in this department of the game.

HUBERT GREEN
Former US Open and USPGA champion Hubert Green gives a perfect lesson of how to play a standard 'splash' shot from a bunker. Good technique enables him to slide the clubhead through the sand, literally 'splashing' the ball out of the bunker.

BERNHARD LANGER
One of the finest golfers Europe has ever produced, Bernhard Langer has no real weaknesses in his game, only strengths. One of them is certainly his ability to recover from sand. He possesses a wonderful touch from bunkers backed up by an excellent technique.

1 THE ADDRESS
For this longer-range bunker shot, Bernhard stands tall to the ball in order to ensure as clean a contact as possible. He is careful to keep the clubhead above the sand at address.

2 THE TAKEAWAY
A wide, one-piece takeaway is very evident here. Clubhead, hands, arms, and shoulders have moved away from the ball in one piece, as for a conventional shot from the fairway.

3 AT THE TOP
This is a perfect position at the top of the backswing. Bernhard has made a full shoulder turn, the club is exactly on line, his hips are resisting nicely, and he is perfectly poised to swing the club down into the back of the ball.

6 THE FOLLOWTHROUGH
This is a classic followthrough position. The club has freewheeled on through impact to this poised and perfectly balanced position, a clear indication that everything in the swing is under control.

5 INTO THE FOLLOWTHROUGH
Here we see a full extension through the ball. Bernhard has moved his weight onto his left side through impact and driven his right shoulder past his chin. His head has just started to rise to see the outcome of the shot.

4 THROUGH IMPACT
Because this is a longer bunker shot, Bernhard contacts the ball before the sand just as he would with a normal fairway shot. For a short bunker shot the clubhead would contact the sand first and 'splash' the ball out on a cushion of sand.

THE LESSONS

The lessons that follow in this section will help you develop your technique for most of the kinds of bunker shot you are likely to be faced with.

LESSON ONE

Setting up with the sand wedge

NO OTHER GOLF club is designed to work as specifically in the player's favour as much as the sand wedge. Few golfers, however, make the best use of the club's potential. Understanding just how this special wedge works is vital to becoming a more accomplished bunker player.

KEY 1	OPEN THE FACE AND FORM THE GRIP

How and where the club is gripped are crucial here. Start by opening the clubface, and then forming a grip – this ensures that the clubface stays open in the swing. Do not open the face simply by swivelling the hands to the right – this will cause the clubface to return to square at impact. Also choke well down on the grip.

Right hand
Hold club and ensure clubface is open before forming any grip.

Clubhead
Open clubface and hover it above sand.

GENE SARAZEN – FATHER OF THE SAND WEDGE

The sand wedge was born way back in the 1930s when **Gene Sarazen** – who despite having won several major titles, considered himself a relatively poor bunker player – decided to refine his equipment. He filed away the sharp leading edge of his wedge, which tended to encourage the head to dig too deeply into the sand. In its place came a more rounded design, with a wide flange on the sole of the club that sat below the level of the leading edge. Experimenting with this, he discovered that as soon as the clubhead entered the sand, the flange on the sole forced it upwards and out. It created a splash effect, throwing the ball out on a cushion of sand.

CHOKE DOWN
Choking down on the grip both improves control and compensates for the fact that the feet are lower than the level of the ball.

KEY 2 OPEN THE STANCE

To play greenside bunker shots, both the stance and the clubface must be open to the target line. Opening the stance involves aligning the feet, hips, and shoulders left of target. Conversely, opening the clubface means aiming it right of the line of the stance. However, these opposing factors will actually combine to produce a straight shot.

KEY 3 DIG A SOLID FOUNDATION

Shuffle the feet down into the sand to provide a secure base and guard against any slipping in mid-swing. Burying the feet also gives a feeling for the depth and texture of the sand, which gives a valuable clue as to how the clubhead will react at impact and how the ball will come out.

Hands
Maintain a light grip pressure.

Feet
Establish a firm footing in sand.

Upper body
Align shoulders, torso, and hips to left of target line at address.

Hands
Weaken grip a fraction and place hands over ball.

Knees
Flex knees to provide steady base for swing.

Feet
Open stance to encourage desired out-to-in swing path.

Open stance

Clubhead
Ensure that clubhead does not make contact with sand at address.

Target line

Open stance

Target line

FROM ABOVE
With the feet and body aligned left of target, the clubhead follows an out-to-in swing path. Combined with an open clubface, this produces a straight shot with a soft, floating trajectory.

LESSON TWO

Building better bunker technique

THE TECHNIQUE FOR better bunker play is quite straightforward once there is an understanding of how the sand wedge works and of the fundamentals of set-up and posture. The application of a sound technique will remove the basic fear so many golfers have of bunker play.

KEY 1 — MOVE AWAY IN UNISON

Resist the temptation to get too steep in the early stages of the takeaway. Keep the wrists fairly passive as the club is swept away from the ball, trying to harmonize the arm-swing and the body-turn. Feel that the first part of the takeaway is a one-piece movement, the clubhead tracing a path along the line of the feet for at least 18in (45cm) or so.

BERNHARD LANGER – THE SAME SPOT

Assuming the texture of the sand is consistent, the club should hit the same spot behind the ball for all bunker shots up to a maximum of about 30yds (27m). That is the system **Bernhard Langer** adopts and it does have the huge benefit of simplifying matters. Maintain the same rhythm and tempo for all short-range bunker shots. Pick the spot behind the ball and always accelerate into impact. The only aspect of the backswing that changes is its length.

The initial takeaway
Clubhead remains parallel to line of feet for first 12in (30cm) of takeaway.

Line of feet

TAKE THE RIGHT PATH
For at least the first 18in (45cm) of the takeaway, make sure that the clubhead traces a path away from the ball parallel to the line of the toes.

KEY 2 ROTATE AND OPEN

As the swing continues, sense that the left wrist and left forearm rotate, rather like turning the arm to look at a watch-face. This 'cranks' open the clubface and will help make maximum use of the bounce effect on the sand wedge at impact.

Head
Keep head as still as possible throughout backswing.

Upper body
Turn back towards target.

Shoulder
Turn left shoulder in under chin.

Clubhead
Maintain open clubface.

Knees
Maintain original flex in knees.

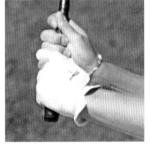

SEVE BALLESTEROS – KEEP A LEVEL HEAD

While long-range golf shots need a little lateral movement, shorter shots require the head to be kept as still as possible. Here is a great example. Look how steady **Seve Ballesteros's** head position remains from address to the top of his backswing position. It hasn't moved at all – there is a wonderful grace and poise about it. Try to emulate this stillness, and keep a level head when playing out of sand.

SET THE WRISTS
Start to hinge the wrists as the hands reach a point just beyond the right thigh. This helps to set the club into the slot at the top of the backswing.

SWING IN HARMONY
As with all shots, success from sand depends on the arms swinging up in harmony with the turning of the upper body.

Building better bunker technique

KEY 3 **TURN TO THE TOP**
As the body continues to turn, sense that the clubhead is 'cocked' up towards the sky. Keep the knees flexed, with your body weight central over the ball.

Takeaway
Move club back in a wide, smooth takeaway.

Downswing
Swing club down on a flatter plane and into sand behind ball.

PRACTICE GROUND HIT DOWN AND THROUGH

Gene Sarazen put a lot of thought and hard work into designing the sand wedge, so make sure that it is working for you, not against you. This exercise is useful for establishing the feeling of how the sand wedge should really work. Stand in a bunker and make continuous swings – back and forth – slapping the clubhead firmly down into the sand. Do not hit a ball. Just get used to the sensation of the clubhead splashing through the sand, not digging in. Become comfortable with this and then throw a few balls into the sand and try to re-create that exact same feeling. Just let the ball get in the way of the swing.

SET THE WRISTS
Cock the wrists fully at the top of the backswing to create a 90° angle between the left wrist and the shaft of the club.

NICK PRICE – JUDGING DISTANCE

One of the keys to judging distance from bunkers lies in the followthrough. As Zimbabwe's **Nick Price** demonstrates, swing through to a full finish for long greenside bunker shots. And when the pin is cut close to the bunker, make a short followthrough. This will help gauge the tempo of the downswing and, with that, the distance the ball flies.

VISUALIZATION MAKING THE RIGHT CONTACT

Visualizing the exact impact point is particularly important from sand. Imagine that the ball is lying on top of a tee-peg hidden beneath the sand. In a sense, forget the ball, and instead focus on trying to clip the tee-peg. Executed properly, this will propel the ball forwards with the right amount of sand.

PRACTICE GROUND SPLASH BETWEEN THE LINES

Focusing on the spot where the clubhead hits the sand can lead to inattention as to where it emerges, resulting in a nasty digging action and a fluffed shot. Try this drill to avoid that. Draw two lines in the sand, approximately 7in (18cm) apart.

The lines indicate the point of entry and the spot where the clubhead is meant to resurface. Now line up a series of balls between the lines and simply swing the clubhead down into the first line and out through the second line.

KEY **4** **CREATE A CONTROLLED EXPLOSION**
Smoothly accelerate the club down into a point roughly 2in (5cm) behind the ball. As the body unwinds in the downswing, feel the hands drag left, pulling the clubhead across the line through impact. Make certain that the right hand does not cross over the left.

Spine
Maintain original spine angle.

Hip
Clear left hip through impact.

Knees
Maintain flex in knees.

Weight
Keep weight on left side through impact.

Clubhead
Imagine clubhead sliding through sand and under ball.

SLIDE THE CLUBHEAD
The geometry of good bunker play is now apparent. If the stance and clubface are both open, and the swing is along the line of the feet, the ball will fly straight. The trajectory should be quite high – soft, too, almost floating.

LESSON THREE

Dealing with a plugged lie

ONE OF THE MOST daunting lies in golf is the plugged
ball in the bunker. Often referred to as a 'fried egg'
because of its appearance in the sand, it usually
results from a high shot that pitches straight into
soft sand, causing the ball to become half-buried.
It looks, and is, a difficult lie but escape is always
possible. This sequence shows how.

KEY 1 SQUARE THE STANCE AND THE CLUBFACE

Playing a shot from a plugged
lie goes totally against the techniques
required for almost every other bunker
shot. For a start, the clubface needs to
be square to the target rather than open.
The ball is positioned further back in the
stance, rather than opposite the left heel,
and the weight is even more on the left
side. Also, stand square to the target.

Wrists
*Hinge wrists earlier
than normal in
backswing.*

Clubface
*Keep clubface
square, rather
than open, on
the way back.*

Square stance

Target line

KEY 2 KEEP THE BACKSWING STEEP

The downswing here has
to be a lot steeper than for most
bunker shots – it is altogether a
much more punchy, stabbing
action. To pre-set a steeper angle
of attack, pick the club up more
steeply in the takeaway. Hinge the
wrists and point the clubhead at
the sky earlier than normal.

Balance
Feel that body is over ball at top of backswing.

SANDY LYLE – LONG-DISTANCE SAND PLAY

The long bunker shot is a tough one, but professionals often make it look easy. Never more so than when **Sandy Lyle** blasted a 7-iron from the fairway bunker on the final hole of the 1988 US Masters, a shot that ultimately won him the championship. Lyle made several key adjustments to his standard bunker shot, adjustments valid for anyone playing a long-range shot from sand.

Select a club that has sufficient loft to clear the front lip, but try to take one more club than would be usual from the same distance on the fairway. Position the ball a fraction further back in the stance and choke further down on the grip.

Keep to a three-quarter swing and concentrate on clipping the ball off the surface cleanly. Pitch the ball well up to allow for backspin.

KEY 3 · KEEP THE WEIGHT CENTRED

At the top of the backswing, the body weight must be centred over the ball – perhaps even favouring the left side just a fraction. This helps to promote a steeper than normal angle of downswing attack.

KEY 4 · THUMP DOWN THE CLUBHEAD

Plenty of clubhead speed needs to be generated to force the ball up and out to safety. Be aggressive and bang the clubhead down into the sand – don't worry too much about the followthrough. The ball will come out pretty low and, crucially, with little backspin, so allow for some run on landing.

KEEP THE WRISTS ROCK SOLID
With this shot, where there is plenty of interference from the sand, it is vital to grip the club firmly and to keep the wrists rock solid through the hitting zone, as shown above. Any weakness will result in the ball staying in the bunker.

LESSON FOUR

Playing from lies above the feet

WHEN THE BALL comes to rest on any kind of slope in sand, the address position, the swing, and the flight of the ball are all affected. With the ball above the level of the feet, there are several factors that can make the difference between success and failure. The biggest danger is taking far too much sand and leaving the ball in the bunker.

KEY 1 GRIP DOWN AND AIM RIGHT

The address position here is obviously quite different to that of any other greenside bunker shot, and the following adjustments are absolutely essential for a successful outcome. The ball is closer to head height than normal, so grip well down to bring the clubhead up to the same level as the ball (the right hand may almost touch the shaft on a severe slope). The spine angle will automatically be straighter, while the weight needs to be moved forwards on to the toes to help maintain balance throughout the swing. Aim a little right of target, too.

Clubhead
Hover clubhead above point behind ball where it is intended to strike sand.

Grip
Choke down on grip, right down to metal if necessary on steep slopes.

KEY 2 SWING BACK WITH THE SLOPE

An upright spine angle, with the ball above the feet, can mean one thing – and one thing only: the club will be swung more around the body, creating a tendency for the ball to fly left of aim. That is why it is vital to aim to the right of the flag. The accepted bunker play practice of an out-to-in swing path is not appropriate from this lie. Instead, just swing in line with the slope, following an in-to-out path.

Weight forwards
Move weight forwards on to toes to counteract effect of slope.

KEY 3 KEEP SPINE ANGLE CONSTANT

Here we see one of the most crucial factors in playing effective shots from sloping lies – the spine angle remains exactly as it was at address, all the way to the top. Keeping the head at the same level throughout the swing ensures a constant spine angle, and increases the chances of achieving the desired strike.

BOBBY JONES – POSITIVE IN SAND

There are many who believe that the only credible challenger to Jack Nicklaus as the greatest golfer of all time is **Bobby Jones**. Jones once commented: "The difference between a bunker and a water hazard is the same as the difference between a car crash and a plane crash. You at least have a chance to recover from a car crash." In other words, don't despair if you land in a bunker, things could be worse. Follow this advice: always think positively, work on technique, and don't be frightened of the sand. There is nothing to fear in sand except fear itself.

KEY 4 SWING DOWN ON AN INSIDE TRACK

Now simply retrace the same path into impact, concentrating solely on striking the sand roughly 2in (5cm) behind the ball. Do not try to guide or steer the ball – rely on alignment and the natural shape of the swing.

Impact
Splash clubhead down behind ball.

Inside line
Sense that club approaches impact from inside ball-to-target line.

Height
Maintain height throughout swing.

KEY 5 FOLLOW ON THROUGH

Accelerate the clubhead all the way through impact and allow for the ball to fly left, which, if the stance has been closed, will be straight at the target. It is a good idea to allow for the ball kicking a fraction left on landing on the longer greenside bunker shots.

LESSON FIVE

Playing from lies below the feet

THE PROBLEMS FACED here are exactly the opposite difficulties to those on pages 134–135. The ball is positioned well below the level of the feet, although not quite enough to make standing in the bunker impossible. Even so, this is probably the tougher of the two shots for there is a very real danger of thinning the ball.

KEY 1 GRIP AS LONG AS POSSIBLE
The key to success here, as with lies above the feet, is all in the set-up. Start by holding the club as 'long' as possible to help lower the clubhead down to the level of the ball. Bend from the waist more, too, and aim left to allow for the inevitable push-flight that the slope and set-up will produce. Also select the spot where the club will enter the sand.

Steep plane
Set club on a steeper plane in order to swing it on an out-to-in path.

Spine
Maintain a constant spine angle.

Wrists
Hinge wrists earlier than for a normal sand shot.

Left shoulder
Turn shoulder under chin.

Spine
Keep a constant spine angle throughout swing.

Weight
Position weight back towards heels a fraction more than normal to prevent any loss of balance down slope during swing.

Grip
Grip as 'long' as possible to bring clubhead down close to ball.

Feet
Dig feet in to form a stable base for swing.

KEY 2 STAY DOWN IN THE BACKSWING
The key in the backswing is to keep the head at the same level throughout. Take the club back outside the line, then hinge the wrists, setting the shaft on an upright plane. Again, focus on a steady head position – standing up, even just a tiny fraction, will be disastrous.

GARY PLAYER – PRACTISE TO IMPROVISE

There are times when a highly unorthodox bunker shot is the only solution, as **Gary Player** found at the 1994 British Seniors Open at Royal Lytham and St Annes. Just getting the ball out was quite an achievement, yet this is a just reward for the years of hard work and dedication he has invested into his bunker play. So whenever there is an opportunity to practise, don't be restricted to hitting regular splash shots. Exercise the imagination and test it to the limit, ready for seemingly impossible situations in real play.

KEY 3 SPLASH DOWN BEHIND THE BALL

Now simply focus on that crucial spot in the sand behind the ball, and splash the clubhead down. Once again, stay down as long as possible – at least until the ball is on its way. Remember, it will come out a little right of aim, with a trace of slice-spin, so make allowances.

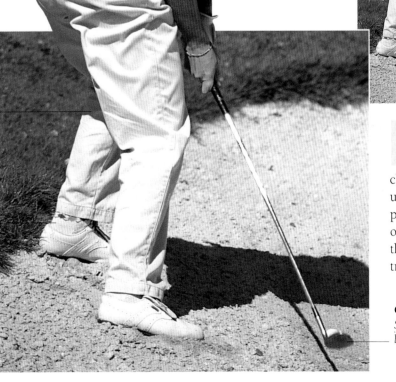

Height
Retain original height throughout swing.

Knees
Utilize flex in knees to help get down to ball.

Balance
Stay down on shot for as long as possible and rely on club to generate height.

KEY 4 HIT DOWN AND THROUGH

Try to swing the clubhead through the sand under the ball along a line parallel with the feet. This out-to-in path should set the ball on a low but direct trajectory towards the flag.

Clubhead
Slide clubhead across line from out-to-in.

LESSON SIX

Playing from an upslope lie

WHEN THE BALL stops on an upslope lie, a simple readjustment of stance and set-up is usually all that is required to cope with a situation that often looks worse than it really is. Remember that the upslope will cause the ball to fly higher when it comes out, making it sit down quickly on the green, which at least allows an aggressive shot to be played.

Weight
Keep your weight on right side all the way to top of backswing.

KEY 1 MATCH THE STANCE TO THE UPSLOPE

The key in this situation is to get the spine angle as close as possible to perpendicular to the slope. Try to climb up the slope far enough to position the ball opposite the left heel, or even further forwards. And really flex the front leg to help establish a stable stance over the ball. If the forward leg is too straight, perfect balance in the swing will be lost and, with that, all hope of escaping from the bunker.

Grip
Keep a firm, relaxed grip.

Left knee
Keep front knee flexed.

Posture
Match angle of shoulders to angle of slope.

Weight
Make sure weight favours right side.

KEY 2 KEEP THE WEIGHT BACK

The key thought in the backswing is to maintain the exact weight distribution established at address. Feel that the swing goes over the right knee. Do not sway too far away from the target – and certainly do not lean on to the left side. Just aim to stand as stable as possible.

GARY PLAYER – EXPLODING OUT

When the ball is on a bunker upslope, many golfers make the mistake of hitting into the slope at too steep an angle. This error is caused by failing to alter the stance, and results in inconsistent strikes, both heavy and thin. Take another tip from the master of sand, **Gary Player**, and build a stance around the slope, allowing for as normal a swing as possible to achieve the desired result. Climb high up the slope, flex the front knee, and feel that the majority of the weight is supported over the back leg – this brings the shoulders level with the sand. If this shot is played into a stiff breeze, be prepared to be showered in sand – a small price to pay for a successful escape.

Club
Swing club right through to a full finish.

KEY 3 SWING INTO IMPACT

Now keep the weight back on the right foot in the downswing and sense that the clubhead swings up into impact, almost as though the clubhead is following the contours of the sand.

Wrists
Work extra hard to clear left side in downswing.

Weight
Keep weight behind ball.

Knees
Make sure that both knees are still well flexed.

KEY 4 SWING UP THE SLOPE

Most golfers leave the ball well short when they are playing off an upslope, so be positive and try to land the ball on top of the flag. The likelihood of over-shooting the target is small, and the ball will certainly sit down quickly with almost no run at all.

LESSON SEVEN

Playing from a downslope lie

A LIE ON the downslope of a bunker is tough to handle. It is difficult to generate much height from this type of lie – a serious problem as most bunkers have a sizeable front lip to be cleared. Do not be tempted into trying to help the ball into the air – that can only result in disaster. Follow these keys and turn the nightmare of the downslope into a far more pleasant experience.

Knee
Keep plenty of flex in right knee.

30%

70%

Every golfer should know that the club cannot be grounded in a hazard at address. But what tends to be forgotten is that it is also a breach of the Rules of Golf, resulting in a one-stroke penalty, to touch the sand during the backswing. In a steep downhill lie in a bunker there is a real danger of this happening – so take extra care to make sure it does not occur.

KEY 1 PUT THE BALL BACK IN THE STANCE

Position the ball back in the stance, at the very least central to it, in order to create as steep an angle of attack as possible. There are several other elements that need to be introduced to the set-up, too, elements not applicable to any other shot. Shift the weight way over onto the left side, feeling some tension in the left thigh. Also, grip well down on the club for maximum control.

Clubhead
Open clubface as far as it will go.

Balance
Position weight predominantly on left foot.

STEEPER ATTACK
This shot relies on a far steeper angle of attack than in any other sand shot, enabling the clubhead to be splashed down in the sand behind the ball.

Wrists
Hinge wrists, trying to point shaft as vertically as possible.

30%

70%

BERNHARD LANGER – KEEPING BALANCE ON A SLOPE

Bernhard Langer, a keen skier in addition to his more obvious talents on the golf course, likens the art of keeping balance in the sand to riding the humps, bumps, and turns of a ski slope. It is just a question of converting his theories and sensations from the snow to the sand. The point is, travelling at speed, keeping one's balance is more of an instinctive reaction – the weight naturally transfers onto the lower leg. On slopes (regardless of whether they are up or down) in the bunker, the same applies – the weight needs to be predominantly on the lower leg, supplying the ideal platform on which to maintain perfect balance. This also helps to bring the shoulders into line with the angle of the slope, making it natural to swing with the slope.

KEY 2 CREATE A STEEP ARC
In the backswing, pick the club up steeper than for any other shot. Hinge the wrists at the start of the takeaway to ensure that the clubhead avoids the back lip of the bunker. This builds a necessarily steep arc into the swing.

KEY 3 HIT DOWN HARD TO CREATE HEIGHT
Stab the clubhead down into the sand behind the ball. Make sure the hands are playing the lead, with the clubhead retracing the exact same path that it took away from the ball in the backswing. The best image to have in mind is that of the clubhead creating an explosion just behind the ball. Be positive, and sense the clubhead chasing the ball down the slope as it travels through impact. And really stay down on the shot.

STAY IN BALANCE
Stay forwards on the left side – this is probably the only shot in golf, except for a putt, where there should be absolutely no weight transfer away from the target in the swing.

Upper body
Stay down on shot for as long as possible.

Clubhead
Sense that clubhead chases after ball, down slope.

SOLUTIONS FOR PROBLEM SHOTS

NO MATTER HOW good they are, even the greatest players in the game find trouble on occasions. This is where the average golfer identifies with them most, and it is from the way that the great players handle these situations that we can learn. The main requirement when the ball is buried deep in the rough or stymied behind a tree is to get it back into play as quickly as possible. The best advice is to take the medicine for a wayward shot and limit the damage as much as possible. Sometimes, though, identifying the best course of action is difficult and in this section we look at some short cuts that can help when the going gets tough.

PAUL AZINGER
American Paul Azinger is literally up to his knees in deep rough here. But he has escaped by forcing the ball out with a steep swing, keeping a strong grip on the club and a firm left wrist through impact.

COLIN MONTGOMERIE
Perched precariously in the steep banking above a bunker, Colin Montgomerie forces the ball towards the target by keeping his weight back on his right foot and swinging up the slope.

ROBERT ALLENBY
Faced with a group of trees Robert Allenby finds an escape route by keeping his weight back and smashing the ball as hard and as high as possible. Finesse takes a back seat in this very difficult situation.

IAN BAKER-FINCH
Almost covered by a tree, former British Open champion Ian Baker-Finch grips down on the metal of the shaft and bends low to play this escape shot from the undergrowth.

SEVERIANO BALLESTEROS
Master of the escape shot, Seve Ballesteros blasts the ball out of thick rough towards the target. This is one situation where there is simply no substitute for sheer strength.

LAURA DAVIES
Laura Davies needed to call on all her powers of recovery to escape from under these overhanging trees. The right hand has come off the grip as the club becomes entangled in the followthrough.

JOSE MARIA OLAZABAL
A remarkable balancing act from Spain's Jose Maria Olazabal as he extricates the ball from a seemingly impossible position, proving that no matter how serious the difficulty a way can often be found to escape.

THE LESSONS

The lessons that follow will help you prepare for the unusual lies and situations that can often occur during a round.

LESSON ONE

Playing from the 'perched' lie

ROUGH IS THE single most common form of trouble that golfers have to cope with. The ground rules for normal rough play were covered on pages 112–113, but for a perched lie – where the ball sits up on a tuft of grass – you must throw away the rule book and improvise. This shot is unlike any other from long grass, and can lead to big problems without the right technique to deal with it.

KEY 1 **GET THE RIGHT SET-UP**

The most obvious problem when the ball is perched higher than usual is to avoid chopping clean underneath it. The other main danger is striking the ball off the top edge of the clubface. To avoid this, choke down on the grip by at least 1in (2.5cm). Also, position the ball further forwards in the stance, to encourage more of a sweeping action through the 'hitting zone', and hover the clubhead at address.

HOVER THE CLUBHEAD
Hovering the clubhead helps to catch the ball 'flush' and also guards against the ball moving at address.

TOM KITE – USING A LOFTED WOOD

A lofted wood is one of the most versatile clubs to have in the bag. As the 1992 US Open champion **Tom Kite** demonstrates here, it is useful for all sorts of troublesome lies – even in quite long rough. This is because the clubhead tends to slide

through the grass more effectively, keeping the clubface looking at the target for longer at impact. A long iron, on the other hand, tends to become tangled in the grass, even before it reaches the ball, thus twisting the clubface at impact and causing a wayward shot. Make the best of rough situations and use a lofted wood.

ADJUST THE GRIP
Choking down on the grip helps to lessen the possibility of making the wrong kind of contact with the ball.

Grip
Shorten hold on grip by at least 1in (2.5cm).

Hands position
Place hands over ball, which should be further forwards than normal.

Ball
Position ball opposite left heel.

Club
Make sure club stops short of horizontal.

Shoulders
Turn left shoulder under chin.

CUT SHORT THE BACKSWING

Avoid hinging the wrists too early in the takeaway; just keep the club moving away from the ball nice and low, to provide width. The only thought should be to shorten the backswing. Choking down on the grip certainly helps, but there needs to be a conscious effort to stop the club short of horizontal.

SWEEP THE BALL AWAY

Avoid 'jumping' into the downswing. Concentrate on making a smooth transition and a gradual weight-shift towards the left. Imagine sweeping the ball cleanly off the top of a tee-peg. If the ball is struck correctly, the club will barely shave the tops off each blade of grass. Remember that this shot causes the ball to fly higher than a regular iron shot.

BALANCED FINISH
A balanced finish is just as important for this shot, with the majority of the weight moving onto the left side.

Hands
Sense that hands stay ahead of clubhead – do not scoop at ball.

Clubhead
Imagine clubhead sweeping ball away as if off a tee-peg.

40%   60%

LESSON TWO

Improvising recovery shots

MORE OFTEN THAN not, the best strategy for coping with trouble is damage limitation. In other words, 'take the medicine' and find the simplest route to safety. Sometimes, though, more adventure may be required. Prior experience of playing unorthodox recovery shots can make life a little easier.

KEY 1 PLAY THE BACK-HANDED CHIP SHOT

This is one of those situations that might occur only half-a-dozen times a year. But it might just come at the most important moment of a round, so it pays to know how to cope. Up against a tree, or maybe some other obstruction, it is impossible to address the ball as a right-hander. One option is to play this back-handed chip. Turn your back on the target and hold the club with the right hand only. Grip the club in such a way that the toe-end of the clubhead sits behind the ball, the heel clearly raised off the ground.

CLUBFACE POSITION
The ideal club to play this shot is a 7- or 8-iron. Address the ball with the toe of the club behind the ball. Make sure that the heel is off the ground.

1 PENDULUM SWING
Swing the arm back and forth, to nudge the ball towards the target. Keep it smooth and avoid trying to generate too much force in the stroke.

2 CLEAN CONTACT
The main objective is to move the ball. From this sort of spot, that in itself is a good result. Concentrate simply on making a smooth swing and clean contact.

KEY
2
TRY A LEFT-HANDED CHIP

There is another technique for moving a ball jammed up close to a tree-trunk. Once again, the ball is struck with the toe of the club – but the shot is played left-handed. It is not the easiest shot for a right-hander to perfect, but with a little practice it could well prove to be a shot-saver from a tight spot. Simply turn the club around and try to adopt as good a left-handed address position as possible. And don't forget to grip with the left hand below the right.

SEVE BALLESTEROS – IMPROVISED ESCAPE SHOTS

Even when the stakes are high, **Seve Ballesteros** has played back-handed recovery shots such as this one at the World Matchplay Championship in 1994. But while these shots seem risky, they are in fact carefully calculated exercises in damage limitation. Seve had only to make contact with the ball to consider the shot a success. Why? Because it avoided the need to take a penalty drop and also gave him an opportunity to progress the ball a little nearer to the target.

1 SHORT SWING
Again, keep the stroke as simple as possible. Make a short, arms-and-shoulders swing, keeping 'wrist-break' to a minimum.

CLUBFACE POSITION
With a sufficiently lofted club – an 8-iron is ideal – turn the clubface over and address the ball with the toe end. Do not be put off by this slightly strange appearance.

2 GET THE BALL SAFE
As with the back-handed shot, don't try to be too ambitious. Be satisfied with making a good, clean contact that nudges the ball out into a safe position.

LESSON THREE

Dealing with uphill lies

THERE ARE TWO key factors when dealing with uphill lies. One is that the trajectory of the shot will change greatly if the slope is severe. The other is that the address position needs to be adapted, which will then affect the shape of the swing. Uphill lies tend to cause shots to fly to the left, so this also needs to be taken into account.

KEY 1 TAILOR THE STANCE TO THE SLOPE

On an upslope there are certain elements that are essential to a good address position. As in the sand, the spine needs to be as close to perpendicular to the slope as possible. This tilts the shoulders back and places a little more of the weight than usual over the right knee. Weight distribution at address ultimately determines how successful shots from sloping lies will be.

SELECT THE LOFT

The effective loft of a club is changed on an upslope. In severe cases, a 7-iron becomes more like a 9-iron, changing the trajectory of the shot. Trial and error will give some clues about just how much effect slopes have on club selection.

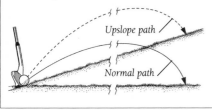

Upslope path

Normal path

PHIL MICKELSON – HOLD OFF THE CLUBFACE

With a shot from an up-slope there is a tendency to pull the ball left. To avoid this, try to hold off the clubface through impact for as long as possible, as left-hander **Phil Mickelson** does here. For a right-hander, this means delaying crossing the right hand over the left. This retains a square clubface and helps hold the ball on line.

'SIT IN' BEHIND BALL
Playing the ball from an upslope, a sense of 'sitting in' behind the ball helps to attain the correct address.

Spine angle
Make sure spine is as near to right-angles with slope as possible.

Weight
Counteract slope by shifting weight to the right.

40%

60%

Back
Turn back away from target.

THINK WIDTH
It is a costly mistake to get too narrow in the backswing when the ball is on an upslope. So concentrate on making a wide takeaway. Try to keep the wrists fairly 'quiet' in the early stages as the backswing moves up to the top.

KEY 2

KEEP THE WEIGHT THE SAME

A useful rule of thumb in the backswing is to keep the weight pretty much where it was at address. The less lateral movement there is, the greater the likelihood of making a crisp, clean contact with the ball.

Hips
Rotate hips 45°.

Head
Keep head behind point of impact.

Left knee
Allow left knee to 'work in' towards ball.

Right knee
Maintain flex in right knee.

Balance
Resist tendency to sway too far down slope.

KEEP BALANCE
The right leg supports some of the weight in the followthrough.

KEY 3

SWING DOWN WITH THE SLOPE

Because the weight is further back than normal, and the lower body less active than usual, there is a tendency to pull the ball left – caused directly by the hands getting over-active through impact. This must be avoided. Try to keep the clubface looking at the target for as long as possible, avoid drastic weight-shifts, stay stable over the ball, and keep the rhythm smooth.

50% 50%

LESSON FOUR

Dealing with downhill lies

JUST AS SHOTS from an uphill lie are more than likely to move off to the left, so shots hit from a downslope – even perfectly played – tend to fade to the right. Once again, the set-up and an understanding of the slope are the key factors in handling the situation successfully.

AT THE TOP
Maintain the same weight distribution established at address throughout the backswing. But be careful not to move the weight further down the slope.

SELECT THE LOFT

As mentioned on page 148, the effective loft of a club is changed on a slope. On severe downslopes, a 7-iron may become more like a 5-iron, changing the trajectory of the shot. Once again, hitting shots on a variety of inclines can help selection.

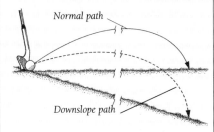

Normal path

Downslope path

KEY 1 **TAILOR THE STANCE FOR A DOWNSLOPE**
For a downslope, reposition the spine to get it as perpendicular as possible to the slope. This moves the weight forwards on to the left foot. As is the case on an upslope, the shoulders again tilt, only this time downwards – matching more closely the lie of the land.

Ball
Position ball further back in stance.

Weight
Position weight more on front foot to help promote a clean strike.

40%

60%

MAINTAIN THE ANGLE
Unwind the upper body in the downswing and maintain the angle formed between the left wrist and the shaft of the club.

Shoulders
Drive right shoulder through past chin.

Hips
Clear left hip as arms swing down and through.

Knees
Right knee 'works' in towards ball.

Through-swing
Stay down and chase ball down slope.

CURTIS STRANGE – BEATING THE SLOPES

Such are the undulations on the Old Course at St Andrews that golfers seldom have a totally flat lie – there is always some kind of slope to deal with. Despite the obvious difficulties, **Curtis Strange** dealt with these slopes extraordinarily well in the 1989 Dunhill Cup, when he broke the course record with a stunning 10 under par 62 – the lowest round ever recorded in the long history of the Old Course.

KEY 2 CHASE THE BALL DOWN

The main difficulty in a downhill lie is creating height. Resist any tendency to scoop at the ball, though. Commit yourself to hitting down – and then really feel as though you are chasing the ball down the slope, releasing the clubhead aggressively through impact. Stay with the ball for as long as possible; imagine the clubhead travelling down the slope with the right shoulder chasing the ball towards the target.

KEY 3 SWING WITH THE SLOPE

Weight transfer is obviously no problem on a downslope. The nature of the slope forces the weight over onto the front foot through impact, but avoid letting the weight transfer get out of control. It should be a smooth, gradual process through to a perfectly balanced finish.

10%

90%

LESSON FIVE

Playing the ball above the feet

JUST AS WITH uphill lies, a ball lying above the feet requires that both stance and swing will have to change. That means a different ball-flight and perhaps quite a marked one.

To make matters worse, the slope can easily make a player lose balance during the swing. Regardless of height or build, the following considerations will help to produce a balanced swing and a solid shot.

KEY 1 CHOKE DOWN AND STAND BACK

With the ball above the feet, a more upright stance than normal is required. Grip down the club 1in (2.5cm) or so and position the weight a little more on the toes than normal to counteract the destabilizing effect of the slope. Also, stand a fraction further from the ball.

KEY 2 SWING AROUND – NOT UP

An upright stance leads to a slightly flatter, more rounded swing plane. That is partly what creates the right-to-left flight that needs to be taken into account aiming at the target. Keep the rhythm, retain the original spine angle, and swing all the way to the top.

Hands
Hands choke down on grip.

Target line
Aim right of target to allow for draw that will result.

Posture
Stand a little more upright than normal.

Feet
Place more weight on toes.

Spine
Maintain spine angle as it was at address.

Weight
Work extra hard to maintain perfect balance.

KEY 3 · RETAIN THE BODY HEIGHT

As in the backswing, the body height needs to be maintained in the downswing. This is important with any shot in golf, but particularly on slopes where the danger of mis-hits is so great. If the head moves up or down into impact, altering the spine angle, all kinds of mis-hits and wayward shots will result.

Head
Keep head at same level.

Shoulders
Clear left hip in downswing.

Knees
Keep flex in both knees.

SEVE BALLESTEROS – PERFECT BALANCE IN ADVERSITY

Look at this fantastic image of **Seve Ballesteros** in action at the 1988 British Open Championship. Despite the obvious difficulties presented by a severe upslope, he is clearly in perfect balance as he hoists this iron shot towards the target. This one image alone is an object lesson in the art of playing from slopes. No matter how bad the slope, always swing the club at a pace that allows the balance to be retained throughout the swing. It is the only way to hit great shots from situations where other players might expect to struggle.

Head
Keep head behind point of impact.

Clubhead
Release clubhead through the ball.

PRACTICE GROUND
ELIMINATE THE SLICE

Believe it or not, the natural contours of a golf course can cure a particular swing fault and help a player focus on the correct feelings and sensations. For instance, time spent hitting shots with the ball above the level of your feet is helpful for anyone with a tendency to fade or slice. This exercise helps flatten the swing plane, leading to a more inside-the-line attack, which in turn encourages a draw.

KEY 4 · STRIKE 4 O'CLOCK ON THE BALL

Sense that the clubhead travels in-to-out through the 'hitting zone' – imagine that the clubface is looking right of target as it approaches impact. Refer to the clockface keys (page 168) and try to hit the ball from 4 o'clock through to 10 o'clock. The slope, along with the rounded swing, encourages this kind of impact – and remember, the ball should draw.

LESSON SIX

Playing the ball below the feet

THE TECHNIQUES INVOLVED in playing a ball from below the feet are, of course, almost a mirror image of those used on sidehill slopes. The tendency to topple down the slope remains a very real one if the weight is not properly distributed.

KEY 1 BEND FROM THE WAIST TO REACH THE BALL
To address the ball below the feet, it is necessary to bend from the waist far more than normal. Also, hold the club as far up the grip as possible. Stand a little closer to the ball and position the weight more on the heels than normal to prevent any falling down the slope in the swing.

KEY 2 MAINTAIN THE ORIGINAL SPINE ANGLE
In the backswing it is vital to maintain the spine angle established at address. Keeping the head at the same level is the most important factor in getting to grips with sloping lies. This address position encourages a more upright swing plane – creating a tendency to fade the ball to the right.

BALANCE AT THE TOP
Concentrate on maintaining perfect balance at the top of the backswing – vital for success on a slope.

Posture
Bend over from waist.

Hands
Grip club as 'long' as possible.

Feet
Align feet left of target.

Target line
Aim to left to allow for a possible fade.

Chin
Keep chin up to make room for left shoulder.

Wrists
Set wrists a little earlier in takeaway than normal.

Knees
Maintain flex in both knees.

KEY 3 — KEEP IT SMOOTH IN THE DOWNSWING

Maintain a smooth rhythm in the downswing and focus on keeping the left heel firmly planted to counteract the slope. The influence of the slope and the upright swing causes the clubhead to travel slightly out-to-in through the hitting zone. This imparts the sidespin that creates the left-to-right flight.

Knees
Maintain distance between knees.

Heels
Try to keep more weight than normal on heels.

Head
Maintain height in downswing.

Hands
Pull butt of club down towards ball.

Balance
Compensate for tendency to fall down slope.

JOHN DALY – PERFECT BALANCE

Here, 1995 British Open champion **John Daly** demonstrates just how to play from lies below the feet. As well as aiming left to allow for the natural drift to the right, he is also in perfect balance – despite being at full tilt on a slope. These two key elements are vital for striking the ball solidly.

Head
Keep head down through impact.

Spine
Maintain spine angle as it was at address.

Hips
Clear left hip to allow free arm swing.

PRACTICE GROUND
ELIMINATE THE HOOK

Players who suffer from a hook would do well to spend time hitting shots with the ball below their feet. This sets the swing on a more upright plane, and eliminates the excessively in-to-out swing path that causes big hooks. Gradually, the downswing attack is forced to become more on-line and the tendency to hook will disappear.

KEY 4 — SWINGING THROUGH IMPACT

Stay down through the hitting zone and release the clubhead down the target line. The spine angle should be the same as it was at address, with the weight on the left heel. Also remember to allow for a left-to-right flight of the ball.

FACTORS OF PRECISE PUTTING

PUTTING HAS ALWAYS been considered to be a game within a game; a skill that the great golf writer Henry Longhurst once described as the 'Black Art'. Certainly it has caused more heart-searching and more inventiveness in the search for perfection than any other department of the game. Putting represents close to half of the strokes made by most players in a full round of golf, so anything that provides improvement is eagerly sought. There is no substitute for a sound putting stroke – irrespective of how it looks.

NICK PRICE
Nick Price is one of golf's top putters. His technique is based on a locked left wrist and a shoulder-dominated stroke. Note how the putterhead still faces the initial line of the ball well after impact.

ISAO AOKI
Japan's Isao Aoki is a classic example of a player possessing a superb putting stroke locked into an outwardly strange and individual style. Confirmation, of course, that consistent results are far more important than the method used.

1 THE ADDRESS
Aoki addresses the ball with the toe of the putter high in the air. His hands are particularly low and he crouches over the ball. Like all good putters his eyes are directly over the ball.

2 THE TAKEAWAY
Aoki is very much a touch putter and uses his hands more than his shoulders. Here he takes the club back quite steeply with the right hand controlling the takeaway.

3 AT THE TOP
At the top of the backswing the putter is quite high off the ground. This is an unusual position among most of the leading putters, although it seems to work well for Aoki.

6 PERFECT FINISH
As with all other golf shots, the position at the end of the stroke is a useful indicator as to the shot's success. Note how Aoki has remained motionless except for a turn of the head to follow the ball.

CURTIS STRANGE
In marked contrast to Aoki's crouched style, Curtis Strange stands very erect, keeps his wrists firm, and uses a pendulum action controlled predominantly by the shoulders.

5 THE FOLLOW-THROUGH
The slightest body movement during the stroke can cause a putt to be missed. Here, Aoki remains motionless even after the ball has been struck.

4 THROUGH IMPACT
Aoki's wonderful touch brings the head of the putter back into a square position at impact, while his head has remained perfectly still throughout.

THE LESSONS

The lessons that follow in this section will help you to develop your own personal putting technique based on solid and consistent foundations.

LESSON ONE

Setting up to putt

THE PUTTING STROKE is in many ways a miniature version of the full golf swing. So, once again, the address position is the first stage in developing a consistent technique. A good set-up position creates the foundation for a good repeating stroke and gives the best chance of consistently striking the ball to make it run straight and true.

KEY 1	EYES OVER THE BALL

The most important ingredient in the putting set-up – irrespective of height, build, or individual style – is having the eyes over the ball. Turning the head allows a direct view down the line of the putt to the hole without any need to move the shoulders out of alignment.

BERNHARD LANGER – DEVELOP TUNNEL VISION

Distractions can make or break a putt. Total concentration is vital. The focus has to be on rolling the ball into the hole to the exclusion of everything else. **Bernhard Langer** regularly 'blinkers' his eyes as he reads a putt. This gives him a kind of 'tunnel vision' that blocks out any movements in the gallery. It helps him to focus on reading the line and visualizing the ball travelling into the hole. Though few of us will encounter the kind of crowds that follow Langer, the principle of 'tunnel vision' can be applied in every player's game.

Eyes
Keep eyes over ball.

Hands
Point thumbs down shaft.

KEEP STILL
Note how, except for the movement of the head, the alignment and body posture remain the same as the hole is viewed.

Stance
Adopt a relaxed, comfortable stance.

KEY 2 COMPLETE THE PERFECT SET-UP

There are several elements required for the ideal set-up. The ball should be placed forwards in the stance; the ideal position is opposite the left heel. You can go back a fraction, but no more than a clubhead's width. This position helps to ensure that the putter meets the ball slightly on the upward stroke. The hands need to be over the ball, at least, maybe even slightly ahead of it, and the putter face must be square to the line.

SEVE BALLESTEROS – PERFECTLY POISED

Seve Ballesteros has probably the most comfortable putting address position in the world of golf. All the elements are there; a neutral grip and a light grip pressure, bending comfortably from the waist so that his arms hang down naturally. His eyes are directly over the ball, too – it is just perfect.

It is not necessary to slavishly copy this style, but any position must be comfortable, creating the feeling that it could be maintained for a long period of time without any feeling of strain. This feeling creates a positive influence on the putting stroke itself.

Shoulders
Keep shoulders square to intended line.

Hands
Keep hands over, or just ahead of, ball.

FORM A NEUTRAL UNION
The grip is at its most effective when the palms are facing each other. This is what is described as a neutral grip, where the hands are encouraged to work together throughout the stroke. Also make sure that both thumbs point down the shaft.

Clubface
Make sure that putter face looks straight down intended line.

SQUARE UP
Viewed from above, the feet and shoulders are parallel, and the clubface is square to the line. The hands are ahead, with the eyes over the ball.

LESSON TWO

Swinging the putter smoothly

THE MOST EFFICIENT and consistent method of putting is one in which the putter swings like a pendulum, smoothly and rhythmically back and forth. The weight of the putter head creates the momentum in the swing. The body must be trained to behave so that a perfect pendulum motion can be produced time after time.

Head
Keep head steady throughout.

Upper body
Maintain imaginary triangle formed by arms and shoulders.

Hands
Keep grip pressure light.

Clubhead
Make sure putter-head travels low to ground.

KEY 1 KEEP LEFT SHOULDER DOWN
As in the full swing, the putting takeaway is a one-piece action. The arms, shoulders, and putter move away from the ball as a single unit with the hands remaining passive. Think 'left shoulder down' to produce the correct initial move.

DAVID FEHERTY – PRACTICE STROKES FOR REAL

Making a smooth practice-putting stroke is not a problem for most golfers. It is when the ball is introduced that the trouble starts. **David Feherty**, has a particularly useful practice drill which is worth copying.

Start by making a normal practice stroke. Then address the ball, close the eyes, and repeat the stroke – letting the ball get in the way. It helps make the real stroke more like the practice one, and can make a real difference to accuracy.

PRACTICE GROUND
STAY SQUARE THROUGH THE BALL

The following exercise helps to maintain a square putter-face in the hitting zone and was used by Nick Faldo in the run-up to his 1992 British Open victory.

Start by addressing a putt, from no more than 5ft (1.5m), and with as little break as possible. Brush the ball towards the hole – don't take a backswing – just sweep the putter-head forwards from a 'standing start'. If the ball goes in, then the alignment is correct. If the ball misses, then the putter-face is either off-square at address or travelling off-line at impact. Trial and error will soon reveal which is the major culprit.

Upper body
Imaginary triangle is maintained throughout stroke.

Hands
Return hands to original address position.

JACK NICKLAUS – MIND OVER MATTER

The great **Jack Nicklaus** has never missed a putt in his mind. When he lines up a putt, as far as he is concerned the ball is going in and nowhere else. There is much to be learned from this attitude. The best putting stroke in the world will not be successful without a sound pre-shot routine and 100% concentration on every putt. No one in the history of the game has concentrated more than Nicklaus and that is what made him the best.

Left wrist
Keep left wrist firm through ball.

Head
Keep head as steady as possible through stroke.

| KEY 2 | **STRIKE ON THE UPSTROKE** |

Smoothly accelerate the putter into the back of the ball. Restrict the hands to a supporting role, each applying an equal amount of grip pressure. If the ball position is correct, the pendulum action will cause the ball to be struck slightly on the up.

Followthrough
Make sure followthrough is at least as long as backswing.

| KEY 3 | **KEEP THE WRISTS FIRM** |

Few golfers give the followthrough the care and attention it deserves. One of the most important moves is to keep the left wrist 'locked' in position through the hitting zone (imagine that the lower arm is in a plaster cast). Accelerate the putterhead through towards the hole and make sure the followthrough is as long as the backswing.

LESSON THREE

Finding a cure for putting problems

PUTTING CAN CAUSE more heartbreak in golf than anything else. The 'yips' – a condition where something in the brain causes the left wrist to collapse and the right hand to take over, twitching the ball left at erratic speeds – has afflicted even the greatest players in golfing history. Many alternative methods of gripping the putter, and just as many different putting implements, have been tried in the search for a cure. But whatever alternative is used, it has to be about encouraging the pendulum action – the key element of a sound, repeating, and successful putting stroke.

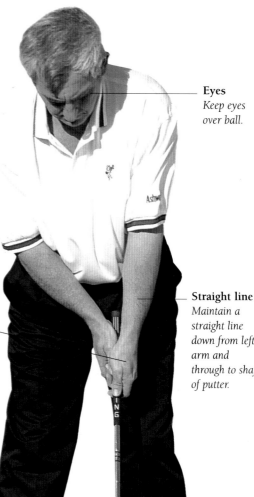

Eyes
Keep eyes over ball.

Straight line
Maintain a straight line down from left arm and through to shaft of putter.

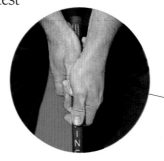

LEFT BELOW RIGHT
The cross-handed grip is the most popular cure for anyone afflicted with the dreaded yips.

BERNHARD LANGER – A TRIUMPH OVER ADVERSITY

Bernhard Langer has endured more than his fair share of agony on the greens. Twice he has been afflicted by the dreaded yips – twice he has overcome them. His latest anti-dote, the 'clamp' grip' – where the left hand reaches down the shaft and his right hand clasps his left forearm – is the ultimate measure to prevent the left wrist breaking down through impact. That is what the yips are all about: the right hand starts to dominate and the putter seems to take on a mind of its own. Stop this happening and the yips stop, too. The method may seem outlandish – but, as Langer has proved, it has had the desired effect.

KEY 1 **CHANGE THE GRIP**
The most popular 'alternative' style of putting to help eliminate the yips is the cross-handed method. Instead of gripping with the right hand below the left, the hand positions are reversed. This encourages a more pendulum-like action back and through. More importantly, it locks the left wrist throughout the stroke, preventing the yips.

Shoulders
Rock shoulders to help control stroke.

Right wrist
Allow right wrist to 'give' a little in the takeaway.

Left wrist
Continue to keep left wrist firm.

NICK FALDO – LISTEN, DON'T LOOK

Looking too soon is a major reason for missing short putts. It stems from anxiety – an urge to see if the ball is going in. The paradox is that the earlier we look, the less likely it is that we will be greeted by the sight of the ball dropping into the hole. On short putts of 5ft (1.5m) and under, **Nick Faldo** waits for the sound of the ball dropping, or until it becomes obvious that the ball is going to miss. This encourages the body to stay still over the ball for longer, which will in turn improve consistency and the quality of strike.

LOCKED UP
The positioning of the left hand below the right keeps the wrist locked in place.

Legs
Make sure legs stay completely passive throughout stroke.

KEY 2 SWING BACK AND THROUGH – LOW AND SMOOTH
The stroke itself is essentially the same as that using the orthodox putting grip. The arm-swing is controlled by a gentle rocking of the shoulders, and the hands remain passive as the putter travels back and through.

KEY 3 KEEP THE LEFT WRIST LOCKED
The left wrist stays firm through the ball, thus keeping the face square to the target line through that crucial hitting zone. This is the essence of the cross-handed method, and explains why it has proved so popular with golfers of all levels.

LESSON FOUR

Coping with slopes

SLOPING GREENS CAN be intimidating, especially if they are firm and fast. There is a tendency to be over cautious, which can lead to a jerky, timid stroke. But the line to the hole always starts as a straight one, no matter how severe the slope. It is the contour of the green that makes the ball curve, so reading the slopes correctly is vital in achieving success on the greens.

PRACTICE GROUND
LEARN TO JUDGE DEAD WEIGHT

Long-range putting is doubly hazardous when severe slopes lie between the ball and the hole. The only way to achieve a good success rate in getting the ball close to the hole is to work on 'feel' in practice, enabling better judgement on the course – and this exercise is ideal. Stand at one side of a sloping green and putt to the other side. Try to make the ball finish as close to the fringe as possible every time, without going beyond it. Competition against an opponent adds a little edge to the exercise.

GREG NORMAN – STRAIGHT PUTTING

A good method of dealing with slopes is to treat every putt as if it were a straight putt. Though this may seem bizarre, **Greg Norman** is one of several top tour professionals who favour this system, and he uses it to excellent effect.

When faced with a really sloping putt, identify a 'breaking point' – an exact spot wide of the hole that indicates the amount of break the ball will take. Then simply start the ball towards that point.

KEY 1 READ 'SUMMER' AND 'WINTER' BREAKS

The amount of break on a putt – how much the ball is affected by any slope on the green – is determined by the speed of the green and, as a consequence, the speed at which the ball is struck. Try to get used to the differences between slow and fast greens.

Summer
Ball takes more break on slick, closely mown summer greens…

Winter
…and less break on slow winter greens when grass is longer.

TOM WATSON – DEADEN THE IMPACT

Downhill putts can be worrying, particularly when there is a good chance that, if the putt is missed, the ball will end up further away from the hole than where it started. This often leads to a tentative stroke, the very circumstance that must be avoided. **Tom Watson**, who in his prime in the late 1970s through to the mid-1980s was the finest putter in the world, is a great advocate of stroking the ball off the toe of the putter on fast downhill putts. This deadens the blow, thereby allowing a more positive stroke.

PRACTICE GROUND
SQUARE-TO-SQUARE IS IDEAL

For any putt inside 5ft (1.5m), straight-back-and-through is the ideal path for the putter head to travel. Try this drill to promote a straight-back and-through stroke. Identify a straight 4ft (1.2m) putt and lay two clubs on the green so that they form parallel rails towards the hole. Simply stroke a series of putts, running the putter head back and through without touching the shafts of the clubs. If the putter face is completely square, the putt will be holed every time.

KEY 2 READ THE GREEN

Reading the slopes or borrows on greens is something that can only be learned through experience. But there are a few tricks of the trade that can speed up the learning process. Study each green as you approach it in order to get a good perspective on the general 'lie of the land.' Most greens tend to slope more one way than another, and this can give valuable clues when it comes to reading the more subtle borrows.

LOOK AND LEARN
Watch how a playing partner's ball behaves near the hole, giving you a major clue to how your putt will break as it approaches the hole.

Overall view
Take in wider view on approach to green.

Grass
Check if grass is cut with putt (light green) or against putt (darker green).

Slope
Get a feel for general slope of green.

SECRETS OF WORKING THE BALL

WHEN THE AVERAGE golfer bends the ball through the air it is more often by accident than design – his aim is usually to prevent the ball moving off a straight line, rather than deliberately to cause the curve. However, players who do not work on being able to shape the ball miss out on a significant opportunity to lower their scores. Much of being able to work the ball comes down to understanding impact mechanics – in other words, how and why the ball spins. All the top players know how, and this section unlocks some of their secrets.

JACK NICKLAUS
Possibly the finest iron player of all time, Jack's strategy was to aim at the centre of the green and 'feed' the ball into the flag by playing a draw or a fade, depending on whether the pin was positioned to the left or right.

1 THE ADDRESS
In this sequence, Seve has set up to hit a fading shot from left to right. He has pulled back his left foot slightly and stands rather more 'open' than for a normal shot, although the clubface remains square to the target.

SEVE BALLESTEROS
Severiano Ballesteros is a master at shaping shots. His ability to work the ball from left or right, or fly it high or low at will, is one of the reasons why he became one of the greats of the modern era. Much of this skill can be traced back to his early development when he learned to play every shot with just one club, a 3-iron.

2 THE TAKEAWAY
The open stance encourages the club to be taken away from the ball slightly outside the line. The takeaway is very much one-piece, with the wrists only starting to hinge as the hands reach waist height.

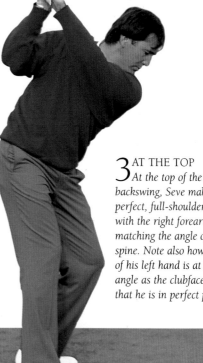

3 AT THE TOP
At the top of the backswing, Seve makes a perfect, full-shoulder turn with the right forearm matching the angle of his spine. Note also how the back of his left hand is at the same angle as the clubface – a sign that he is in perfect position.

6 FOLLOWTHROUGH
Seve swings on through to a perfectly balanced finish while the ball, having started slightly left of target, fades back onto the target line.

FRED COUPLES
Smooth-swinging Freddie Couples is another gifted exponent of ball flight. His tremendous power often overshadows his superb control with the iron clubs. The high, soft-landing fade is one of his favourite shots, and is played, more often than not, to perfection.

5 THROUGH IMPACT
Because of the open stance, the swing line is slightly across the target line, with the clubface open in relation to this path at impact – these factors combine to create the left-to-right spin.

4 THE DOWNSWING
Seve drops the club into a perfect plane in the downswing as he starts to move his weight smoothly over to the left side. Note how his right elbow stays close to his body.

LESSON ONE

Hitting left-to-right

HITTING THE BALL so that it follows a left-to-right path through the air is known as a fade or slice. This is produced by an out-to-in swing path, combined with a slightly open clubface that imparts the necessary sidespin. Here we look at how to put these factors together.

NICK FALDO – GETTING AROUND CORNERS

The ideal lie for playing a fade is a closely mown area, or even a bare lie. This makes it possible to get 'more of the ball' and create as much curve on the ball as is required. Using a straight-faced club makes it easier to generate sidespin.

Nick Faldo used all of these factors to his advantage during the final round of the Volvo PGA at Wentworth in 1989. Completely blocked out on the right side of the 15th hole, he hit a magnificent low, cut-fade around the corner onto the green, from where he holed for a birdie.

KEY 1 PRE-SET THE CORRECT IMPACT
The set-up, to a large degree, determines the nature of the impact position. And to move the ball left-to-right means an out-to-in swing path combined with a clubface position that is open to that path. Aim the clubface directly at the target and align the feet, hips, and shoulders left of target – how open the stance is depends on how much fade is required. This stance creates the correct position to swing the club across the line through impact.

Upper body
Open body and hips in relation to target.

VISUALIZATION CLOCKFACE KEYS

To strike the ball in the right place, try imagining it as a clockface and aim to strike different 'hours' to create the desired swing path. For instance, if a straight shot is required, strike 3 o'clock. To move a shot right-to-left through the air, strike 4 o'clock. This encourages an in-to-out swing path, which helps put the necessary sidespin on the ball to promote a draw or hook. Striking the ball at 2 o'clock moves the ball the other way, left-to-right.

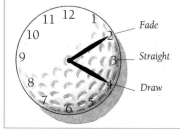

Fade — 2
Straight — 3
Draw — 4

IDEAL ADDRESS
In the takeaway, swing the clubhead along a path parallel to the line of your feet for the first 20in (51cm) or so, before it inevitably arcs inside the line in harmony with the turning motion of your body.

Target line

Line of feet

Feet
Align feet to left of target.

Target line

Clubhead
Aim clubface straight at target.

KEY 2 GO ACROSS THE LINE AT THE TOP

The outside-the-line takeaway produces a position at the top of the backswing where the club-shaft points left of target – just as it should. The body will still be fully coiled, with the weight supported over a flexed right knee.

Knees
Right knee is flexed, supporting weight.

SWING THROUGH LEFT OF TARGET
Swing through to a position where the belt buckle points left of target and, as always, the weight is supported almost entirely over the front foot.

Body
Open body to promote good contact.

Shoulder
Pull left shoulder away from chin.

Swing path
Clubhead approaches impact from outside target line.

Ball
Ball starts left before swinging back towards target.

Club
Swing club from out-to-in across target line.

KEY 3 CLEAR THE LEFT HIP

Unwind the body in the downswing as with any other full shot. Sense that the left hip is starting to clear as the club is dropped down on the correct plane.

KEY 4 STRIKE 2 O'CLOCK

Aim to strike 2 o'clock on the ball (see page 168). As the clubhead travels across the line, try to hold-off the clubface through impact. The swing path should be out-to-in with the ball starting fractionally left of target, before the spin brings it back on line.

LESSON TWO

Hitting right-to-left

THE DRAW OR hook shot (which moves the ball from right-to-left through the air) is the exact opposite of the fade. Here, an in-to-out swing path is combined with a closed clubface position in relation to the swing path. The execution may not be simple, but the ability to play this shot is extremely valuable.

KEY 1 CLOSE THE STANCE
As with the fade, the clubface aims directly along the target line, but the stance is closed. With everything aligned to the right of the target, the clubface travels on an in-to-out swing path, effectively along the line of the feet. Also, adopt a stronger left-hand grip. This encourages a more active release of the hands, and helps impart the necessary spin on the ball.

JOHNNY MILLER – SHAPING SHOTS WITH THE HANDS

Different players adopt different methods to shape their shots. **Johnny Miller** makes a subtle change in his grip to shape the ball in a particular way. For the fade, he grips the club extra tight in the bottom three fingers of his left hand. This delays the release for a crucial fraction of a second. If he wants to hit a draw, Miller holds the club relatively loosely in his left hand to encourage a good release of the club through impact.

Upper body
Align upper body to right of target.

Left hand
Adopt a stronger left-hand grip, showing an 'extra' knuckle.

KEY 2 FOLLOW AN INSIDE TRACK
Everything in the backswing should be geared towards generating the necessary in-to-out swing path. Sense that in the initial stages of the takeaway, the clubhead follows the line of the feet. Remember – this is inside the line in relation to the target.

Clubhead
Aim clubface square to target line.

IDEAL ADDRESS
As with the fade, the clubhead follows the line of the feet in the takeaway. When selecting a club, take into account that a draw usually travels further than a normal shot particularly after it has landed.

Legs
Feel tension in thighs at address.

Feet
Close stance so that everything, except clubface, is pointing to right of target.

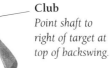

Club
Point shaft to right of target at top of backswing.

KEY **4** STRIKE 4 O'CLOCK
Really attack the ball in the downswing from inside the target line. Remember, it may help to aim for 4 o'clock on the imaginary clockface on the ball (see page 168).

Back
Retain original spine angle through impact.

Head
Only lift head to follow flight of ball.

Shoulders
Fire right shoulder past chin.

Clubhead
Make toe of club pass heel.

KEY **3** AIM RIGHT AT THE TOP

The key position is at the top of the backswing, where the clubshaft should point right of target. How far right it points depends on how far the ball is intended to move. For a big hook it may point as much as 50yd (46m) to the right – with a draw it might only be a matter of 5–6ft (1.5–1.8m).

PRACTICE GROUND
GET THE RIGHT SENSATION

Here are two useful drills to help encourage the correct feelings and sensations of shaping the ball. Bear in mind that these are an exaggeration of the correct technique, and while they help to give the feel of the relevant impact factors, they should not be replicated during an actual round.

1 *To help draw the ball, stand with the right foot drawn back from the target line. This encourages a more inside-the-line takeaway.*

2 *To 'feel' a fade (see pages 168–169), shuffle the left foot away from the target line. This immediately promotes an outside-the-line takeaway.*

KEY **5** RELEASE THE CLUBHEAD THROUGH IMPACT

Feel that the clubhead travels to the right of target through impact and that the toe of the club passes the heel. Also feel that the left forearm rotates anticlockwise as it swings through the hitting zone. The in-to-out swing path starts the ball out to the right while the hook-spin brings it back on line.

LESSON THREE

Playing the low-punch shot

NOTHING, NOT EVEN rain, sends scores soaring quite so dramatically as a strong, gusting wind. Conversely, nothing in golf is more impressive than a good score on a windy day. Avoiding being blown off course is dependent on the ability to shelter the ball from the ravaging effects of the wind. It is all about knowing what works and what does not work. Here we look at the factors involved when playing a mid-iron approach shot into a stiff breeze.

KEY 1 CHOOSE THE RIGHT CLUB

The distance book has little relevance into the wind; club selection is far more reliant on personal feel and experience. One thing is certain, though – more club will be needed. Assess whether it is a one-club, two-club, or three-club wind – even more may be needed on a links course. Adopt a slightly wider stance to provide maximum stability. This also helps to shorten the swing, making it more compact.

Wider stance
Spread feet further apart for maximum stability.

PRACTICE GROUND
LESS LOFT – MORE SHAPE

Always use the longer irons to practise shot-shaping skills. The relatively straight face naturally creates more sidespin and less backspin – in other words, more potential for swerve. Shorter irons produce the opposite effect. It is as well to consider this when sizing up situations and assessing the amount of swerve needed to put on the shot. Remember, to produce a huge amount of shape, use a straight face.

NICK FALDO – THE PUNCHY FADE

Nick Faldo's 5-iron on the 15th at Muirfield during the 1992 British Open is a great example of the perfect wind shot. Staring into a right-to-left headwind he played a brilliant, punchy fade that fought tooth and nail to hold its line, before landing perfectly on the green. Taking an extra club, he committed himself 100 per cent to the shot. Using more club, the last thing he wanted was the ball 'riding' on the wind. But by getting the shape right, he made the ball fight the wind all the way and sit down in just the right spot on the green.

At the top
Set club into position for downswing attack.

KEY 2 TURN TO THE TOP

Once the set-up has been completed, take a normal backswing. Focus on completing the shoulder turn, maintaining a smooth rhythm and transferring your weight in harmony with the swinging motion of the club – just as in any other shot.

Stance for shots into the wind

Normal stance

50%   50%

KEY 3 STAY LOW IN THE HITTING ZONE
It is vital to get the clubhead traveling really low, in the 24in (61cm) hitting zone. Sense that the hands stay ahead of the clubhead, literally driving the ball forwards on a low, penetrating trajectory. Do not be tempted into hitting the ball harder. Even with a stiff gale blowing in your face, you have to concentrate on swinging more smoothly, and a little softer, through the hitting zone. This stops excessive backspin.

Shoulder
Make sure right shoulder is closest point to target.

KEY 4 FINISH WITH THE WEIGHT FORWARDS
Aim to finish with the weight well forwards onto the front foot, and the right shoulder being the closest part of the body to the target. Doing this encourages the body to be more 'over the ball' through impact, rather than behind it.

Balance
Maintain perfect balance through to finish.

20%   80%

Shoulder
Bring right shoulder through.

Hands
Release clubhead through ball, with right hand crossing over left.

SWEEP THE BALL
The move into the downswing is the same as for any other shot. But the key image at impact should be that of the clubhead travelling low to the ground.

Balance
Sense that weight is over ball through hitting area.

PRACTICE GROUND
LAUNCH IT HIGH AND LONG

The tee on a par 4 or par 5 represents the best opportunity to take advantage of a following wind. With the benefit of a tailwind, 40–60yds (37–55m) or more can be added to the length of your shots. To take full advantage, position the ball 1in (2.5cm) further forwards in the stance and settle the weight back on the right side; try to be 'behind the ball'. Really stretch out the backswing – long and wide. Then, in the downswing, feel that your weight 'hangs back' over your right side for a little longer – at least until impact.

40%   60%

CHAPTER FIVE

COURSE MANAGEMENT

Winner of eight major titles, including five British Opens, Tom Watson is a master golf course strategist

SO MUCH OF success in golf is based around damage limitation. It does not matter how well we play for fourteen holes if, on the other four, we inflict so much damage upon our score that it is impossible to recover. The legendary Ben Hogan said, more than once, that in any round of golf he hit perhaps only one or two shots perfectly. Our chances are even slimmer than that. Therefore, we have to make the most of our good shots, and minimize the effect on the overall round of our bad ones. In a word, this can be called strategy or, if you prefer a grander term, course management.

In this chapter, using key moments in major championships as our basis, we look at how sensible thinking and careful planning can help to lower your scores and, conversely, how bad decisions and poor planning can be just as damaging as a poorly struck shot.

Course plan

For top professional players, as here in the 1989 Ryder Cup at The Belfry, dealing with the hazards of a course comes almost as second nature. However, the amateur player must plan his or her strategy very carefully in the bid to avoid wasted strokes.

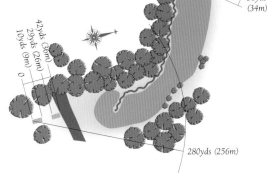

38yds (34m)

42yds (38m)
29yds (26m)
10yds (9m)
0

280yds (256m)

An overhead view of the 13th at the Augusta National where poor strategy has lost many a US Masters

The art of strategic thinking

IT WAS JACK NICKLAUS who took the art of damage limitation on the golf course onto another plane. His powers of concentration, allied to a shrewd golfing brain, have ensured that during his many decades at the top of world golf, Nicklaus rarely hit the wrong shot at the wrong time, or gambled when the odds were too heavily stacked against him. We must learn from that. It is a cliché to say that we should recognize our strengths and play to them, but the element of truth that runs through it is indisputable.

Master strategist
Jack Nicklaus is the perfect role model for anyone trying to improve their course strategy. In his long career, Nicklaus made fewer errors of judgement on what was the right shot to play than probably any other player in the history of the game.

Being a good and consistent striker of the ball is not the sole qualification for success in golfing competition – whether at the highest level of the game or, more importantly, in your regular fourball. There are many players with limited ability as pure ball-strikers who have been highly successful on the course when it matters.

Much of this is because they have had the ability to make the right decision at the right time; they are able to assess correctly what is possible, and stick with the decision. No player, not even a Nicklaus or a Faldo, can play well every time they step onto a course.

FINDING A WAY
One of the main reasons that professional players tend to stand out from the rest of us is that even when they are not on top of their game, they can still score well – because they invariably 'find a way round'. They may not shoot scores low enough to win a tournament but they limit the damage sufficiently to live to fight another day, and avoid recording a confidence-shattering high score. This is something from which we can all learn.

A golf course should be looked upon as an obstacle course, around which there are both easier ways and more difficult routes. Assessing which path should be taken at any given time is one of the keys to better scoring at golf. It has been said many times by golfers, but is just as true now as it was the first time it was uttered: "golf is not about how but how many". For example, three drives that find the out-of-bounds or are lost; two attempts to carry water that just fail; and three putts on four greens in a round all add up to 12 strokes, or potentially the difference between a score of 91 and 79.

AVOIDING DANGER
An immediate and very often dramatic improvement in score will result by avoiding disasters ahead. Every round we play has shots that are critical to the overall outcome, and it is how we assess them and deal with the problems that makes the difference between success and failure. On the following pages, we

Into the green
Nick Faldo, pictured here at the 1992 European Open at Sunningdale, England. is a master player of the percentages. He knows when to attack the pin and when to play safely to the centre of the green.

Weighing up the options
When in doubt carefully weigh up the options as Jarmo Sandelin does here on his way to victory in the 1995 Turespana Open.

examine critical situations that have faced the likes of Ben Hogan, Jack Nicklaus, and Greg Norman in major championships. We look at what the alternatives were, why they took the decisions they did and why, as a result, they ultimately triumphed or, in some cases, failed.

No-one is infallible, and there is just as much to be learned from the bad decisions featured here as there is from the successful ones. It is also worth remembering the high-pressure situations in which these incidents occurred; while we are unlikely to be faced with a putt to win the Ryder Cup or a major Open Championship, it is vital to concentrate the mind on the shot in hand, both strategically and tactically.

After sorting out the fundamentals of the golf swing, the fastest way for a 90-plus player to become one who can break 80 is to learn, as quickly and effectively as the top players, the art of damage limitation.

PLAYING THE HOLES

Each of the holes featured in this chapter illustrates the route followed by a player during a specific championship, together with a path from tee to green that is likely to be taken by an average-handicap amateur, helping to illustrate how and why these strategic decisions were made.

Over the water
Faced with a water hazard, the first essential is to decide whether to lay up or safely play over it. Here, Ian Woosnam makes sure of carrying the water during the 1992 World Cup at La Moraleja in Spain.

KEEPING IT SIMPLE

CARRYING OVER WATER

If you are not certain that you can carry over water with anything other than your career-best shot, then don't think about trying it. Lay up short of the trouble and try for a pitch and putt. You have a chance of pulling it off and at worst should drop only one shot. Failure to carry the water is doubly damaging in that it can seriously affect your morale as well as your score.

PLAYING LONG HOLES

At long par 4s where you know you have little chance of getting up in two shots, decide from where you would ideally like to play your third shot to give the best chance of making par. Don't force your drive in the hope of accomplishing the impossible; keep the ball in play and your temper intact.

Remember, that while a par 4 is always better than a bogey, a five is still two shots better than a seven – and ultimately every shot counts.

APPROACHING THE GREEN

You don't always have to attack the hole with your approach shot. It is much easier to hole out with two putts from the centre of the green, no matter where the hole is, rather than have to get up and down from a greenside bunker because your approach was just a fraction off line.

Safety first
If you are in the rough or are up against any other obstacle, the golden rule is to concentrate solely on getting the ball back onto the fairway (see pages 146–147) as Wayne Grady does here.

Augusta – 13th hole

465yds (425m), Par 5 – Augusta, Georgia, USA

THE 13TH AT *Augusta National is the last of the three holes known collectively as 'Amen Corner'. It is a part of the course where many a Masters title has been won, and lost, and where strategy plays a crucial part. So it was in 1984 when Ben Crenshaw arrived at the par 5, 13th on the final day. He had climbed into the lead with birdies at the 8th and 9th, and then holed a huge putt on the 10th for another. After dropping a shot at the 11th, he got it back at the short and dangerous 12th, but the 13th still lay in wait.*

Driving seat
Sometimes a wayward driver, Crenshaw opted for a straight shot rather than a more unpredictable draw.

0
10yds (9m)
29yds (26m)
42yds (37m)

280yds
(206m)

Rae's Creek

38yds (35m)

Tee shot
The amateur player would drive roughly 220yds (201m).

THE 13TH HOLE
All the holes at Augusta National are named after flowers or shrubs, a legacy of its days as a nursery. The 13th is known as Azalea and is now 10yds (9m) shorter than it used to be, although it still remains a par 5.

2nd shot
From this position, Crenshaw laid up short of Rae's Creek with an iron, leaving a short pitch to the green.

PLAYING THE HOLE

For most players, Azalea is a three-shot hole. There is plenty of room to the right to play away from Rae's Creek although a drive too far right can be stymied by trees. The second shot should be laid-up well short of the creek, to give a full shot to a green that has a saddle in the middle. Big hitters can get home in two, but the tee shot has to be hit with a draw to chase the ball down the slope of the fairway. Some players use two prominent trees on the right side of the dogleg – as Crenshaw did in 1984 – as an aiming point.

Triple hazard
The spectacular backdrop of azaleas and dogwood creates much in the way of false comfort at the 13th. Rae's Creek, four fearsome bunkers, and a small swale all help to protect the green.

Championship tee

Front tee

Tee shot
Crenshaw drove about 250yds (228m) to the right-centre of the fairway.

WHAT YOU CAN LEARN

Ben Crenshaw's decision to lay up short of Rae's Creek and play for a safe par was largely influenced by one remarkable coincidence. As he turned around, considering what to do, he observed Billy Joe Patton, the great amateur player of the 1950s, in the crowd.

Thirty years earlier, Billy Joe had finished one stroke behind Ben Hogan and Sam Snead in the Masters after going for the carry over Rae's Creek on the 13th and failing to make it. His double bogey-seven was a costly price to pay for too cavalier a strategy, and it undoubtedly cost him the chance of winning the coveted green jacket.

After spotting Patton, Ben was determined not to repeat the mistake. He laid up and, although he pitched rather weakly, his par figure was never in danger. It was a crucial factor in his first major victory, as Crenshaw admitted later. It was also a valuable lesson to every golfer. There are times to be bold and there are times when the desire to gamble has to be curbed.

2nd shot
The amateur player would normally lay up around this point on the fairway.

THE ROUTE TO THE HOLE

➤ *Ben Crenshaw, 1984.*

➤ *Amateur player.*

Pitch
Although Crenshaw played a relatively weak pitch, it still landed safely on the green. He then faced a difficult approach putt but he two-putted comfortably.

Holing out
Crenshaw's ability with the putter was crucial to his victory in 1984. However, his putting ability would have counted for little if he had not been able to play his approach shots strategically, to give himself the best possible opportunity to hole putts on such difficult greens.

3rd shot
The amateur player would be faced with a 7- or 8-iron shot to the green from this point.

Rae's Creek
The creek runs down the length of the hole before turning across in front of the green.

Merion – 18th hole

463yds (423m), Par 4 – Merion, Pennsylvania, USA

THE 18TH HOLE at Merion is one of the toughest finishing holes in golf, and the setting for one of the greatest finishes in US Open Championship history. Eighteen months after narrowly escaping death in a car crash, the great Ben Hogan arrived at Merion uncertain as to whether his badly damaged legs would be able to cope with two rounds on the final day of the 1950 Open. Forced to lean on a friend for support, Hogan came to the last hole to be told that he needed a par 4 to tie Lloyd Mangrum and George Fazio, or a birdie to win outright.

Teeing-off
Hogan refused to be intimidated by the line of trees from the tee.

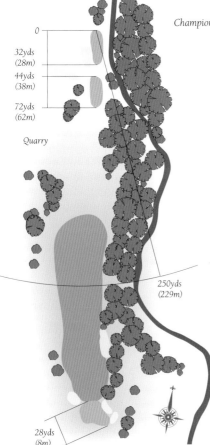

0

32yds
(28m)

44yds
(38m)

72yds
(62m)

Quarry

250yds
(229m)

28yds
(8m)

THE 18TH HOLE
The 18th at Merion is a long and difficult par 4 with the tee set deep in the woods. An old quarry threatens between the tee and the crest of a hill, after which the fairway falls away steeply. The narrow green is well protected by three bunkers with a fairway bunker to the left.

Championship tee

Front tee

Making the carry
Paul Runyon, USPGA champion in 1934 and 1938, once chipped down to the lower tee and then played a fairway wood for his second, because he felt he couldn't make the carry from the back.

Quarry carry
The old quarry has to be carried from the tee.

Long carry
For the amateur player, it is still a long carry over the quarry, even from the forward tee.

PLAYING THE HOLE

The drive is critical on the last at Merion. It has to be flown through a 'tunnel' of trees across the old quarry, and has to be long enough to carry over the crest of the hill to reach the fairway 220yds (201m) away. The second often has to be played from a downhill lie, and is always a long carry up to the narrow green. Hogan hit a perfect drive straight down the middle, but then had to decide whether to attack the pin in the back right of the green with a 4-wood for the birdie he needed for outright victory, or play a safer shot with an iron to the front-left of the green for a safe par and a place in the play-off.

Bunkers with grass

A similar view to the one that Ben Hogan faced with his second shot in 1950. The 1-iron that Hogan used was stolen from his bag while he was marking his card, and was only found years later in a second-hand barrel in a golf shop. It now resides in the USGA museum at Far Hills.

WHAT YOU CAN LEARN

The fate of the 1950 US Open hung on the decision Hogan had to make as he prepared to play his second shot on the 18th. He knew the green ran uphill before falling away towards the back, and that too strong a shot would run through and into the gallery. He had played a 4-iron from a similar spot in the morning, but was tired now and knew that he would need much more club. Hogan studied his lie. He had two options: a 1-iron to the front-left or a more dangerous 4-wood that would need to be cut to get it close to the hole. He opted for his 1-iron and struck the ball perfectly to within 40ft (12m) of the hole. Two putts gave him the safe par he needed to enter a play-off, which he went on to win comfortably. His assessment of the options and the odds on success teaches us all a valuable lesson about the need for patience when the odds are too strongly stacked against the miracle shot.

Hole marker
The wicker hole markers are a unique feature of Merion.

Hogan's drive
Hogan hit a perfect drive straight down the middle to here.

Inspired approach
Hogan's superb 1-iron landed 40ft (12m) from the hole and guaranteed a place in the play-off.

THE ROUTE TO THE HOLE
◀▬▬ *Ben Hogan, 1950.*
◀▭▭ *Amateur player.*

Green hazard
Deep bunkers to the left are a severe hazard.

Best option
For the amateur player, a lay-up shot in front of the green is usually the best option.

Up and down
With a good pitch, the amateur player still has a chance to make par.

Muirfield – 9th hole

495yds (453m), Par 5 – Muirfield, Scotland

THE 9TH HOLE at Muirfield has, over the years, probably caused more destruction to good scores than any other of the many demanding holes on this famous Scottish links. The secret is in knowing when to attack the hole and when to play safe. There are times when boldness is the right strategy, as was the case in the British Open of 1972 when Tony Jacklin and Lee Trevino were locked in their memorable battle with Jack Nicklaus. With the wind from the east at their backs, and the course playing very fast, both Trevino and Jacklin decided to attack the hole.

Medal tee
Championship tee

Ideal spot
This is the perfect placement for the tee shot if the wind is favourable.

Jacklin's drive
Tony Jacklin drove to the light rough.

Trevino's drive
Lee Trevino drove to the light rough on the right.

Bunker threat
The deep fairway bunker which dominates the tee shot strategy.

Long shot
Trevino hit a superb long-iron to the heart of the green.

PLAYING THE HOLE

The tee shot is critical at Muirfield's 9th hole. The wall makes the threat of out-of-bounds on the left a major factor in planning the strategy. The first fairway bunker is also a critical element. From the normal tee, the amateur player needs a carry of more than 200yds (183m) to clear the bunker before facing a second shot that has to be aimed to the left towards the wall, in order to avoid the nest of dangerous bunkers short and right of the green. The safe strategy is to lay up short of the first bunker, and then play short of the right hand bunkers to leave about a 100yd (92m) pitch to the green. Under favourable conditions, however, the green can be reached in two.

0
11yds (10m)
12yds (11m)
28yds (25m)
40yds (36m)
56yds (50m)
73yds (66m)

Wall

257yds (235m)

Out-of-bounds

32yds (30m)

THE 9TH HOLE
A wall, marking out-of-bounds, runs down the entire length of Muirfield's par 5, 9th hole. The fairway runs into a narrow corridor about 240yds (219m) from the championship tee. A fierce bunker protects the entrance to the corridor with another bunker at the exit. A group of bunkers are clustered to the right of the green.

Fairway guard
The nest of bunkers short of the green to the right of the fairway forces the second shot towards the out-of-bounds wall. Consequently, the amateur player must be careful with his lay-up second shot. A ball in any of these five bunkers means an almost certain dropped stroke.

From the rough
Jacklin's long drive downwind finished in the light rough, well clear of the dangerous bunker guarding the fairway corridor on the left. From there he got home comfortably with an iron, and holed the putt for an eagle.

Wall danger
The out-of-bounds wall which threatens the second shot.

Tough rough
The rough on both sides of the fairway can be dangerous.

WHAT YOU CAN LEARN

Tony Jacklin and Lee Trevino attacked the 9th hole from the tee in different ways. Jacklin went for the carry over the left-hand fairway bunker, while Trevino played rather more conservatively down the right. Both finished in the rough, although they remained within iron distance of the green. Two immaculate shots from the rough followed, landing 20yds (18m) short but running onto the surface. Both players then holed their putts to record eagles. It was a perfect example of judging when to attack for the most advantage.

In the 1966 British Open, Arnold Palmer had attacked the hole in a similar fashion with a driver from the tee, when a safe lay up seemed the discretionary shot. He took a six, severely denting his chances of winning a third British Open title.

Safety first
The amateur player would lay up to here.

On guard
This group of bunkers forces the second shot towards the wall.

Open green
The hole depends on fairway defences. There are no greenside bunkers.

Eagle putts
Trevino and Jacklin both sank putts for eagles.

Eagle putt
Lee Trevino's long-iron from the right-hand rough set up a putt for an eagle-three, which he duly made.

THE ROUTE TO THE HOLE
← *Lee Trevino, 1972.*
← *Tony Jacklin, 1972.*
← *Amateur player.*

Pebble Beach – 18th hole

548yds (501m), Par 5 – Pebble Beach, California, USA

TEXAN TOM KITE had won more money than anyone in the history of golf. Yet when he came to the last hole at Pebble Beach in the final round of the 1992 US Open, he had still to win a major championship. In deteriorating weather, Kite knew he could achieve his long-time ambition if he could make a par on the treacherous 18th hole alongside the Pacific Ocean. It is a difficult hole in normal conditions, but on that memorable day the wind was whipping off the sea, the small greens were lightning fast, and it was difficult to stand still over any putt. Kite had to control five strokes for victory.

30yds (27m)
0
275yds (251m)
29yds (26m)

THE 18TH HOLE
One of the world's classic finishing holes, the 18th skirts Monterey Bay and has two trees in the centre of the fairway at driving distance. A huge bunker protects the green on the right.

Pitch for victory
Kite pitched safely to the green for his first major victory.

Lay up
Kite played a perfect lay-up shot with an iron short of the green.

Circle of sand
Bunkers surround the 18th green close against the ocean.

Safety zone
The amateur player should aim for this safety zone, short of the green.

Victory at last
Jubilation for Tom Kite as he holes out at the 18th to end his long wait for a first major championship win.

PLAYING THE HOLE

The tee shot has to be hit across the corner of Monterey Bay. How much the player bites off depends on how well he or she is playing and how brave they are prepared to be. Two trees in the fairway, the first at 270yds (247m) from the tee, have to be avoided, because they can easily block the next shot. The second shot must be carefully placed in the fairway to allow a short pitch to a green well-defended by bunkers. Trees line the right side of the fairway from tee to green and can seriously impede progress, particularly when the wind is from the ocean and blowing the second shot that way.

Under control

Tom Kite played a conservative drive, allowing the wind to carry the ball well to the right past the obstructing fairway trees. The ball finished in the rough but he knew he could safely reach the green in two shots from there. It was a perfect example of making the conditions work to his benefit.

THE ROUTE TO THE HOLE

➤ *Tom Kite, 1992.*

➤ *Amateur player.*

Tree trouble
Two trees in the fairway can easily block out the second shot.

Tree line
Trees line the fairway from tee to green.

Tactical drive
Kite's drive was played to finish far right of the fairway trees.

Championship tee

Front tee

Bolder line
In better conditions, the amateur player can play a much bolder line.

Monterey Bay
The Bay is very much in play from the tee.

WHAT YOU CAN LEARN

Tom Kite's problem as he stood on the 18th tee at Pebble Beach was at once both simple and complex. All he needed was a par 5 – in normal circumstances for a player of his standing, a relatively easy proposition. But with a fierce wind blowing off the ocean and the US Open title at stake, par was far from simple.

The wind ensured that he had no need to be concerned with biting off any of the dogleg across Monterey Bay. He knew he had to play a conservative drive, making use of the wind to swing the ball away from the ocean, but he also had to avoid the fairway trees which could make his lay-up second shot extremely difficult.

The drive was perfect in the circumstances. It was wide of the trees, leaving him a clear shot from the light rough. His second was a safe iron shot that held into the wind to finish on the fairway. A beautifully controlled pitch to the green followed, and Kite was left with two putts to win his first major championship. Cool planning and controlled shot-making in difficult conditions had won him the title. Kite's example of finding the best solution to a difficult problem, and then playing carefully to a plan to overcome it, is a valuable lesson for us all.

Victory march
Tom Kite begins his march down the 18th into US Open history. His carefully controlled tee shot allowed him the opportunity to lay up safely, leaving a short pitch to the green.

Royal Liverpool – 16th hole

560yds (512m), Par 5 – Hoylake, England

THE GREAT ARGENTINIAN player, Roberto de Vicenzo, arrived on the 16th tee in the final round of the 1967 British Open, leading Jack Nicklaus by three strokes. Nicklaus, playing in front, had just birdied the hole and De Vicenzo was faced with the decision of whether to play this dangerous par 5 safely, or try for a birdie to maintain his lead. It is by such narrow decisions that major championships are won and lost. The Argentinian opted for the attacking approach, knowing that he would have to flirt with the out-of-bounds to give himself any chance.

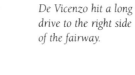

THE ROUTE TO THE HOLE

⬅ *Roberto de Vicenzo, 1967.*

⬅ *Amateur player.*

Bunker danger
Deep bunkers threaten the drive down the left side.

Safe line
The amateur player should play safely to this area.

Championship tee

0
14yds (12m)

Medal tee

84yds (77m)
103yds (94m)
119yds (109m)
143yds (131m)

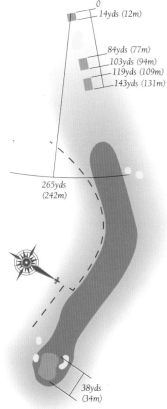

265yds (242m)

38yds (34m)

THE 16TH HOLE
The long 16th at Hoylake, officially known as Royal Liverpool, is dominated by the practice ground, one corner of which protrudes into the fairway. Two bunkers on the left also threaten the drive, with three others guarding the green.

De Vicenzo's line
De Vicenzo hit a long drive to the right side of the fairway.

Practice ground
Lying the other side of a small wall is the practice ground, which runs along most of the length of the 16th.

Boundary wall
The low wall that marks the practice ground and out-of-bounds. De Vicenzo hit his drive close to this spot.

PLAYING THE HOLE
The strategic decision on whether to play boldly across the out-of-bounds – the only way to reach the green in two – or safely to the left, has to be taken on the tee. Only a long drive down the right will put the green in range. The safe line is to play right of the fairway bunker, and lay up the second shot far left of the practice ground to leave a pitch to the green. Two deep bunkers to the right of the green threaten any attempt to play the second shot across the practice ground, which in any case, even in calm weather, involves a considerable carry.

Popular champion
Roberto de Vicenzo was a prodigious hitter of a golf ball, a shrewd strategist, and a modest and likable individual. The combination of these qualities made him one of the most popular winners of the British Open in modern times.

WHAT YOU CAN LEARN

Knowing that Jack Nicklaus had birdied the hole before him to reduce his lead, Roberto de Vicenzo's strategy was to play the 16th boldly in an attempt to reach the green in two, and preserve his slim advantage with a birdie of his own. The Argentinian had always been a prodigious hitter and he knew that reaching the green was well within his capabilities. However. he started badly, pushing his drive a little too close to the low wall that marked out the course's practice area and out-of-bounds.. But his second with a 3-wood was perfectly struck. It flew over the wall, carrying all the trouble, and settled in the heart of the green. Two putts gave him a birdie that effectively snuffed out the Nicklaus challenge and ensured Roberto's first and only major championship victory.

De Vicenzo's strategy was a classic example of playing the bold shot in a tight situation, while being safe in the knowledge that the shot was well within the limits of his ability. The danger for the amateur player, however, is playing the bold shot when the chances of success are marginal.

Lay-up zone
The amateur player should aim the second shot to this area short of the green.

Tight opening
In addition to carrying the out-of-bounds, De Vicenzo had to find a way clear of the deep bunkers which protect the 16th green from shots hit from the right-hand side of the fairway.

Greenside trap
A deep bunker guards the green on the left side.

Long carry
De Vicenzo carried his second shot all the way to the green.

Royal Lytham – 18th hole

412yds (377m), Par 4 – Lytham St Annes, England

When Tony Jacklin arrived on the final tee at Royal Lytham in the 1969 British Open, he led by two strokes. On his shoulders rested the possibility of breaking 18 years' domination of the championship by overseas players. But first he had to negotiate the hole with perhaps the toughest final tee shot in Open Championship golf. His lead was slim and he was only too aware that the hole had destroyed the hopes of great players before him, including Jack Nicklaus five years earlier.

Top drive
Jacklin hit a superb drive to here, avoiding all the potential hazards.

Winning approach
Using a favourite club, a 7-iron, Jacklin played a controlled shot to here.

Bunker menace
A circle of greenside bunkers gather any approach shot off-line.

Green line
The amateur player has a long but clear second shot to the green from here.

Carry
Jacklin was confident he could carry the first line of bunkers.

Clubhouse

45yds (40m)

250yds (228m)

124yds (115m)

91yds (83m)

50yds (45m)

0

THE 18TH HOLE
Two rows of bunkers, seven in all, run diagonally across the fairway in the driving area. The three to the left, at the 250yd (229m) mark, are the most dangerous for the professional. Heavy brush and scrub on the right also intimidate the drive.
A further eight bunkers are sited around the green.

PLAYING THE HOLE
The key to playing the 18th at Lytham is the tee shot. Except in a following wind, the landing area with a driver is extremely small, both for the professional from the championship tee and the amateur from the medal tee a little further forwards. The fairway must be found from the tee, either by playing left and short of the bunkers on that side, or carrying the bunkers to the right into the narrow neck between the rough and the left-hand bunkers. The safer drive to the left leaves a much longer and more difficult approach to the well-guarded green.

Taking the applause

When Tony Jacklin holed out on the last green at Royal Lytham in 1969 it broke an 18-year domination of the Championship by overseas players. British fans had been unable to cheer a home winner since Max Faulkner triumphed at Royal Portrush in 1954. Jacklin's bold and courageous drive at the last hole left him with only a quiet 7-iron to the green. He found the green comfortably, and stood back to enjoy the acclaim of the crowds.

WHAT YOU CAN LEARN

Standing on the 18th tee, with only a slim lead, Tony Jacklin had a big decision to make. Should he attempt a safe tee shot short of the left-hand bunkers, or attack the hole with a driver – taking on the threat of the bunkers to the left and the thick bushes to the right?

As he prepared to play, the Englishman recalled the host of good players who had lost British Open championships by taking a six at this testing final hole. But Jacklin did not hesitate.

With his swing under control he was confident he could reach the safety of the fairway with a driver. He aimed his drive over the left-hand bunkers and watched the ball gently fade back into the centre of the fairway. Jacklin had produced his best drive of the day, 260yds (238m) into the breeze. It was a stroke worthy of a great champion, and the subsequent 7-iron to the green and two putts for victory were little more than a formality.

Jacklin's calmness under pressure was a fine example to the rest of us to trust our swing when the bold shot is called for. The key is to concentrate on a smooth swing, pick out the landing area, aim for it, and shut out any thoughts of the danger zones that may lie in front of you.

THE ROUTE TO THE HOLE

⬅ *Tony Jacklin, 1969.*

⬅ *Amateur player.*

Minefield

The combined dangers of bunkers and thick bushes are evident in this aerial shot of the 'minefield' 18th hole.

Bushes
Thick bushes to the right of the fairway often force the drive towards the left-hand bunkers.

Thick rough
Finding the rough on either side of the fairway means an almost certain dropped shot.

Medal tee

Championship tee

Safe drive
The amateur player aims safely on this line to find the centre of the fairway.

Tee thought
On the tee, Jacklin remembered the great players who had taken six. He would not be cautious.

Vital drive
Tony Jacklin simply trusted his swing for the most important drive of his career – it paid off.

Royal Troon – 18th hole

452yds (413m), Par 4 – Troon, Scotland

WHEN GREG NORMAN went into the final round of the 1989 British Open, he forecast that he would need a 63 to win. He was correct, but he shot 64 instead, and finished in the first four-hole play-off in Open history with Mark Calcavecchia and Wayne Grady. Despite winning the Open in 1986, Norman seemed fated never to win another major after heartbreaking losses in the US Masters and USPGA. He stood on the 18th tee in the play-off in good shape, but fate and doubtful strategy were to thwart him once again.

Path danger
The path in front of the clubhouse is out-of-bounds.

Safe route
The safest route for an amateur would be to lay up to here.

Clubhouse

Out-of-bounds

38yds (34m)

Safety first
The amateur player should play for the safe side of the green, away from the right-hand bunkers.

Rough trouble
Accuracy is important – the rough can be thick on both sides of the fairway.

262yds (240m)

37yds (33m)
30yds (27m)
6yds (5m)
0

Bunkered still
Norman's bid for Open glory ended in this bunker. With Calcavecchia safely on the green in two, and close to the hole, Norman knew he had to hole this shot to have any chance.

Bunker threat
At just over 200yds (183m) from the medal tee, this bunker is a serious threat to the amateur player.

THE 18TH HOLE
Three bunkers on the left side of the fairway threaten the drive on the 18th. A fourth, on the right side, is normally out of range during the British Open. The green is guarded by a nest of bunkers.

PLAYING THE HOLE
The drive is the critical shot on the 18th, because of the variety of tees available. The fairway bunkers are as much of a threat for the amateur player from the medal tee as they are for the tournament professional from the championship tee further back. It is vital to hit the fairway, even though it will still leave a long approach shot to carry the bunkers guarding the green. A drive down the right presents the shortest approach. The close proximity of the clubhouse windows to the green can be another inhibiting factor for those rather too bold of spirit.

Having to gamble

Norman's drive was aimed at this bunker 320yds (293m) from the tee. He did not think he could reach it but when he did, he had no choice but to gamble with his second. The odds were stacked against him – his attempt to reach the green from the bunker failed and landed him in more sand, still well short of the green.

WHAT YOU CAN LEARN

When Greg Norman unleashed a huge drive in the 1989 British Open play-off, he was aiming to fade his drive down the right side of the fairway, away from the deep bunkers on the left. Despite being a renowned big hitter, even Norman considered the right hand fairway bunker at 320yds (293m) from the tee to be out of range, particularly with a fading shot.

But the Australian was disastrously wrong. His phenomenal tee shot flew down the fairway and ran straight into the bunker. His massive underestimation of his tee shot, which killed off his challenge for the British Open title, carries a useful lesson for us all.

Few of us, if any, are ever likely to reproduce the kind of drive that Norman launched that day, but if you are playing for safety, make absolutely certain of being safe. A 'safe' shot that is played as intended, but then ends up in trouble is effectively worse than a gamble that might come off – just ask Greg Norman.

THE ROUTE TO THE HOLE

⬅ *Greg Norman, 1989.*

⬛ *Amateur player.*

Aerial View

This aerial view of the 18th at Royal Troon clearly shows how vital it is to get the strategy right from the tee. Greg Norman's flawed tactics contributed to him missing out on the British Open title.

Mark perfect

Mark Calcavecchia safely drove to this area, from where he went on to make a birdie and win the play-off.

False hope

Initially, Norman's tee shot appeared to be perfect as it flew into the distance.

Championship tee

Safe area

The amateur player should aim for this point well away from the left-hand fairway bunkers.

Medal tee

St Andrews – 17th hole

461yds (422m), Par 4 – Old Course, St Andrews, Scotland

THE 17TH ON the Old Course at St Andrews – the Road Hole – is probably the most famous hole in world golf. It strikes fear into the hearts of even the bravest, and has been at the centre of countless dramas throughout its long history. There was none more dramatic than in the final round of the 1984 British Open Championship. Tied for the lead with Seve Ballesteros, who was heading down the last, the holder and five-times champion, Tom Watson, launched his drive over the 'railway sheds' into the perfect position. But, he followed it with an error of judgement that would cost him the chance of equalling Harry Vardon's record of six British Open titles.

Up against the wall
After his disastrous second shot, Watson played a marvellous recovery shot back onto the green from hard up against the wall. But it was not good enough to secure the par 4 he needed to stay in touch with the eventual winner, Seve Ballesteros.

PLAYING THE HOLE
The tee shot has to be played across the replica of the old railway sheds in the grounds of the Old Course Hotel. Only the perfect tee shot across the corner of the out-of-bounds makes it possible to attack the green with the approach shot, and again only the perfect shot will avoid disaster. In 1984 Watson had to choose whether to attack the green to make a two-putt par, or play safely to the front edge of the green, and rely on a chip and putt for par.

Diagram labels:
0
37yds (33m)
Railway sheds
Cheape's bunker
220yds (201m)
Hotel
Out-of-bounds
65yds (59m)
Road

THE ROAD HOLE
The 17th on the Old Course is a long, dogleg par 4 of 461yds (422m). The back tee is set hard against the boundary wall that once separated the course from the railway line. On the right is the Old Course Hotel Country Club and Spa. Deep rough separates the 17th fairway from the 2nd fairway, and from this thick rough it is almost impossible to reach the green.

Road
The road and pathway which give the famous Road Hole its name.

Chip shot
Watson played his recovery shot from here.

Road Bunker
The deep Road Bunker which eats into the green.

WHAT YOU CAN LEARN

Tom Watson chose to attack the Road Hole rather than lay up to the front edge of the green. He was undecided which club to play, and may have been influenced by the fact that his 2-iron was a vital key in his first British Open victory at Carnoustie in 1975, and again on the final hole at Royal Birkdale in 1983.

In difficult situations, trusting to what you know is usually a sound strategy to follow. But with 210yds (192m) to go and with adrenaline flowing freely, he either struck the ball much harder than intended, or it ran much further than he anticipated. It is easy to be wise with hindsight, but this was one occasion when 'safety first' with a shorter iron might have given Watson his sixth title.

It is a good example of the need to assess the odds carefully when playing a demanding shot in difficult circumstances. In this case Watson's judgement was, for once, wrong.

Driving off
Everything looked rosy for Watson after he launched his drive into the perfect position.

Old Course Hotel
The hotel has specially toughened glass in some windows as a precaution against wayward drives.

Watson's drive
Tom Watson hit his drive to the perfect position on the right-hand side of the fairway.

Championship tee

Medal tee

Railway sheds
Railway sheds were once a feature of the drive at the 17th. The hotel built replicas to recreate the original view after the closure of the railway.

Safe line
The safe line for the amateur player is to this area.

Rough
The rough between the 2nd and 17th fairways has been allowed to grow, making it very treacherous.

Lay up
The amateur should lay up safely in front of the green in this area.

Tee shot
Across the corner of the dyke and over the 'railway sheds' is the best but also most demanding line from the tee. To the left is safer, but deep rough makes the approach much more difficult.

THE ROUTE TO THE HOLE

◄━━ Tom Watson, 1984.

◄▦▦ Amateur player.

Turnberry – 18th hole

431yds (394m), Par 4 – Ailsa Course, Turnberry, Scotland

IT BECAME KNOWN as the duel in the sun; the now legendary battle between Jack Nicklaus and Tom Watson for the 1977 British Open, over the famous Ailsa Course at Turnberry on the west coast of Scotland. Coming to the last hole, these two great champions were locked together with the rest of the field strung out far behind. Watson led by one, but knew that Nicklaus had not given up the fight. Nicklaus had to find a way to make a birdie and Watson had to hold on to win. The result was pure theatre and a fitting finale to Turnberry's first Open Championship.

Dramatic finish
Open Championship crowds surround the 18th green, scene of perhaps the most dramatic finish in British Open history.

0

16yds (14m)

257yds
(235m)

29yds
(26m)

PLAYING THE HOLE

There is a vast difference in the approach to playing the 18th for the amateur and the professional. The championship tee increases the angle of the dogleg and lengthens the hole. The shot from this tee has to be played further to the right towards a jungle of gorse. Once on the fairway, the approach to the green is relatively straightforward. Because he was behind, Nicklaus had to gamble with his tee shot; he went for maximum distance with a driver to get as close as possible, while Watson played a 1-iron to the centre of the fairway.

Under bush
Jack Nicklaus drove under a gorse bush here.

Miracle shot
Nicklaus forced an 8-iron to here from the gorse.

THE 18TH HOLE
The championship tee of the 18th on the Ailsa Course makes the hole longer and much more of a dogleg. Two dangerous bunkers in the corner of the dogleg 250yds (229m) from the tee, force the drive to the right towards thick gorse. Rough surrounds the green and eats into the front on the left, but there are no greenside bunkers.

Winning approach
Watson hit the perfect 7-iron approach to within 3ft (1m) of the hole.

WHAT YOU CAN LEARN

The closing hole of the 1977 British Open was a classic example of safety against risk. Jack Nicklaus' gamble with the driver ended up with his ball under a gorse bush to the right of the fairway. Tom Watson was in perfect position and, playing first, he rifled a 7-iron to within 3ft (1m) of the pin.

It should have been all over, but Nicklaus, in classic style, demonstrated why we should never give up. He gambled again, using an 8-iron from under the gorse to force the ball onto the front right of the green. He then rolled in the huge putt to force Watson to hole his putt for victory, which he duly did for a famous victory. Watson's strategy was faultless; Nicklaus, the past-master of playing the percentages, had no choice but to try a gamble that might just have paid off. Watson sensed that Nicklaus would go all out for a birdie, and had to ensure that he made one of his own.

Mixed emotions
Nicklaus, gambling with his driver, follows the flight of his ball towards the gorse on the right. Watson, already in the centre of the fairway with an iron shot, looks on.

Easier drive
The amateur player has a much easier drive from this tee.

Hunch
On the tee, Tom Watson had a hunch that Nicklaus would somehow make a birdie.

Medal tee

Championship tee

Safety first
Tom Watson hit a perfect 1-iron to safety here.

In the dogleg
The bunkers in the corner of the dogleg are more in play from the championship tee.

Amateur line
The amateur should aim for a safe drive to this area to leave a straightforward approach to the green.

THE ROUTE TO THE HOLE

◄ *Tom Watson, 1977.*

◄ *Jack Nicklaus, 1977.*

◄ *Amateur player.*

On course
Despite hitting by far the better tee shot, Watson knew that the only way to shut Nicklaus out was to score a birdie. His magnificent 7-iron approach helped him do just that, with the ball finishing within 3ft (1m) of the hole.

Spreading rough
Rough surrounds the green and eats into the left side.

CHAPTER SIX

PLAYING
within the
RULES

Distinctive names and
markings can be a great
aid to ball identification

TO BE A GOLFER *rather than just a
hitter of golf balls, is to understand
and respect the values that set the
game of golf apart from all others.
To play golf is to honour traditions
and conventions echoed over five centuries, and to
guard the spirit of fair and honest competition.*

*Through the generations, golf has transcended
simple sport and become a way of life; a code which
binds like-minded people together in a universal
bond of friendship and respect for the heritage of
the game. No other sport demands so much of its
participants in terms of integrity. Its complex rules
present endless opportunity for abuse, yet such
abuses are rare indeed. In this chapter we look at
the rules and etiquette which turn hitters of golf
balls into golfers.*

Free drop
*Japan's Nobuo Serizawa, (left)
under guidance from an official,
works out where to take relief
from television cables.*

Keeping the score
*Golf is the only sport where
official scores are recorded by
fellow competitors (right).*

The rule makers

IT WAS NOT until the middle of the 18th century that golf needed a stipulated set of rules. Originally there were 13; now there are 34 with countless sub-sections and appendices. In a troubled world, the Rules of Golf remain perhaps the only code for which there is universal and voluntary acceptance.

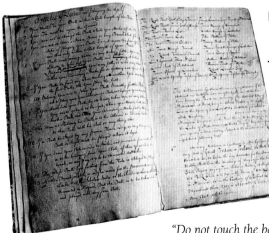

The first code
The 13 original rules of golf as laid out by the Gentlemen Golfers of Leith in 1744. It now lies on display in the British Golf Museum at St Andrews, Scotland.

"Do not touch the ball from the time you tee it up to the time you take it out of the hole. When you are in rough, never bend down. When you are in trees, keep clapping your hands."

Charlie Price

In the three sentences above, the great American golf writer Charlie Price perhaps best summed up the principles that are basic to the Rules of Golf. Every player of the game is his or her own referee. To transgress in the rules and the etiquette of the game is to abuse no-one but oneself. Golf is the searching test of the individual, the seeker out of weaknesses of character and spirit, as well as weaknesses of technique. It is how we handle these three elements that we inwardly judge ourselves, and are outwardly judged by others. Golf survived

without a written set of rules for three centuries until 1744 when the Gentlemen Golfers of Leith, later to become the Honourable Company of Edinburgh Golfers, drew up 13 Articles and Laws in Playing at Golf. The rules were formulated after the Gentlemen were presented with a silver golf club to be used as a competition prize, thus necessitating a common agreement on how the game should be played.

JOINT DECISIONS

As new clubs were formed, they each established their own interpretations of the rules until, in 1897, the Royal & Ancient Golf Club of St Andrews (R & A) – which had steadily gained in influence during the 19th century – was invited by the leading clubs of the day to compile a uniform code. Meanwhile, responsibility for rules in the United States, where the game had been developing rapidly during the 1890s, was assumed by the United States Golf Association (USGA), founded in December 1894 by the country's five leading clubs. The R & A (for everywhere except the United States and Mexico) and the USGA became the recognized rule makers of golf – applying the same basic rules but making separate interpretations on decisions.

A conference in 1951, which also included representatives from Australia and Canada, resolved most of the differences between the R & A and USGA. It also agreed upon the

American home
The United States Golf Association (USGA) headquarters at Far Hills, New Jersey. Together with the R &A, the USGA help to administer golf throughout the world.

formation of a joint Decisions Committee to unify future rule changes, apart from one notable exception – agreement on a common ball size – which wasn't resolved until the R & A finally ratified the use of the 1.68in (42.67mm) diameter ball throughout the world in 1974.

EQUIPMENT CHECK

Every four years the R & A and the USGA review the Rules of Golf and make any amendments that may be necessitated by changes in equipment or clarification and re-evaluation of existing rules. Thousands of unusual or controversial incidents are reported each year by golf secretaries, and rulings are made and recorded in *Decisions on the Rules of Golf*, published by the USGA in the United States and Mexico, and by the R & A throughout the rest of the world.

With advances in technology and materials, new golf equipment is constantly coming onto the market. But before any 'new' style of equipment can be used, it has to be approved by the game's governing bodies. The rules on equipment are complex and, to ensure that any new equipment conforms to all the requirements, the USGA set up a testing complex in 1984.

The USGA's Research and Test Center at their headquarters in Far Hills, New Jersey, tests equipment under impact conditions similar to those experienced in normal play. In conjunction with the R & A, it is the sole arbiter for sanctioning the use of clubs and balls throughout the world. At the core of the centre's testing programme is a machine named 'Iron Byron'. The machine has been programmed to reproduce the classical swing of the great US professional Byron Nelson in order that all designs and brands of golf ball can be tested under standard conditions.

The Research and Test Center also has laboratories for weighing and sizing equipment, testing the initial velocity of balls, assessing impact performance, and conducting aerodynamic tests; considerable proof that new technology has its part to play in the royal and ancient game of golf.

Royal & Ancient
The clubhouse of the Royal and Ancient Golf Club of St Andrews (R & A), situated beside the 18th green of the Old Course, regarded the world over as the spiritual home of golf.

BALL SPECIFICATIONS

The R & A's decision to allow the use of the American 'bigger ball' in the 1974 British Open (it had been allowed in other R & A organized competitions since 1968) meant that there was a single standard for golf balls. All brands are tested by the USGA before they are sanctioned and must meet certain guidelines:

Weight – The maximum permissible weight of a golf ball is 1.62oz (45.93g). There is no minimum.
Size – The minimum permissible diameter for a golf ball is 1.68in (42.67mm). There is no maximum.
Initial Velocity – The speed at which a ball leaves the clubhead after impact (initial velocity) must not be greater than 250ft (76m) per second.

This represents an equivalent speed of 174 miles (280km) per hour.
Overall Distance Standard – Any brand of golf ball tested by 'Iron Byron' on the outdoor range at the USGA Research and Test Center under controlled conditions must not travel further than 280yds (256m) in carry and roll. The tolerance is 6%, above which the ball is rejected.

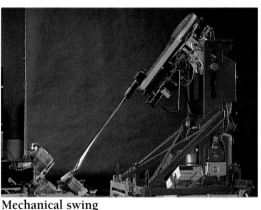

Mechanical swing
The USGA testing machine, 'Iron Byron', is named after Byron Nelson, who won five major titles and 54 US Tour events between 1935 and 1946. To many, his swing is considered to be one of the best ever seen.

Understanding the code

To many professionals, one of the most complex parts of golf is the interpretation of the rules. Even today, experienced tour players fall foul of the official Rules of Golf – and for any of us the addition of penalty strokes can turn a decent round of golf into a nightmare.

Bad advice
During the Tournament of Champions in 1980, Tom Watson was penalized two strokes for advising his playing partner Lee Trevino about a slight flaw in his swing which he had happened to spot.

The official book of the Rules of Golf, including the Rules of Amateur Status, published by the R & A and the USGA, is divided into three sections: Etiquette, Definitions, and The Rules of Play. In the 1995 Code there were 34 rules subdivided into more than 120 clauses – many of which also have subdivisions. Golf's rule book is therefore a comprehensive and complex publication, and it is not within the scope of this book to publish the Rules of Golf in full.

However, ignorance or lack of understanding of the rules can lead to penalty strokes ruining even the hottest round of golf, and there are certain areas that seem to repeatedly confuse even the game's top performers. It is to these that we address ourselves in this section. It is every player's responsibility to know and understand the rules and procedures of the game. Copies of the Rules of Golf are generally available to all golfers free of charge through club secretaries and other sources – and every player is well advised to carry a copy whenever out on the course.

Where disputes cannot be settled by the Rules, rulings on incidents should be called for from the organizing committee in the case of a competition, or from the R & A or USGA. However, all requests for rulings must be officially submitted through a golf-club secretary.

There have been many instances where the Rules have played a major part in the outcome of a professional tournament, and several of the most celebrated are outlined here. By their illustration we learn about the rule in question but also the one fundamental rule in golf not contained in the rule book – the need for constant vigilance in understanding and complying with the laws of the game. As in other walks of life, ignorance of the law cannot be offered as an excuse for its contravention.

PLAYER'S RESPONSIBILITIES

A player has several responsibilities when he or she plays in either matchplay or strokeplay competition. The player has the responsibility for knowing the conditions under which the competition is being held, and for declaring the handicap under which he or she will play.

In strokeplay, the player is entirely responsible for making sure that his or her correct handicap is recorded on the card before it is handed in. Furthermore, a player must not offer advice to another player, except when he is a fellow team member. The player has full responsibility for the correctness of his or her score on every hole. Disqualification will result for returning a card with a score marked lower than was taken, for any hole.

Flawed master
Roberto de Vicenzo suffered despair at the 1968 US Masters when he signed for a last round 66, even though he had gone round in 65. The meant that de Vicenzo missed out on a possible play-off for the title by one stroke.

Pitch repair
The constant pounding of balls pitching onto greens means it is essential to repair pitch marks, as Payne Stewart is doing here, at every opportunity.

If the card has a score higher than taken, the score marked down will stand – as the Argentinian Roberto de Vicenzo found to his cost in the US Masters in 1968. A player must also play without undue delay, and bad weather is not necessarily a reason for discontinuing play. However, at the first sign of lightning, players are strongly advised to put their clubs away and seek safe shelter.

THE ESSENTIALS OF ETIQUETTE

On every score-sheet distributed to spectators at the US Masters at the Augusta National, there is a message from its founder, the great Bobby Jones: "In golf, customs of etiquette and decorum are just as important as rules governing play."

COURSE CARE

- Replace divots carefully.
- Always rake bunkers after use.
- Repair your own pitch mark and at least one other every time you are on a green. Pitch marks which are repaired immediately heal within a few hours – those which are not take weeks to recover.
- Be aware of where you leave your bag or cart. Always leave them off the green.
- Be careful taking the flag from the hole and putting it back. Careless use can damage the hole.
- Avoid any scuffing of spikes on the green.
- Keep quiet when your partners are playing. It seems like obvious advice but there are still many players who rustle or jingle coins when others are about to play.
- Mark the scorecard after leaving the green. Don't hold up the game behind by standing on the green and counting up the strokes.

Golf has always been revered for its insistence on the highest standards of behaviour, despite the fact that the vast array of accepted conventions have never actually been set down in the same way as the rules. How we behave and treat other golfers – simply etiquette – is as important as how we play. It is the application of good manners and courtesy to others on the course.

The Rules of Golf do not spell out penalties for breaches of etiquette; there is no two-shot penalty for those who digress. Etiquette is a voluntary code. It has evolved over the years into an essential element in making golf different from other sports that rely on a referee or umpire to enforce rules and behaviour.

SETTING STANDARDS

The following are the essentials of the etiquette of golf; a basic code that helps preserve the reputation for the high standards of sporting behaviour and honest competition that golf retains today.

- After you agree a tee-time with partners, make sure you get there in good time.
- As soon as you tee off it is important to show courtesy to the players with whom you are playing, and to those who are playing in other games.
- Never play until players in front have moved to a safe distance.
- Be ready to play when it's your turn; keep up with the players in front without harassing them.
- Be aware of the pace at which you play and show a good example to others.
- Always invite following players through if you have to spend time looking for a ball.

KEEP CONTROL

Remember, if you are having a bad or unlucky day on the course, you must always keep control of yourself, and accord due respect to fellow players. Your bad form is not their fault, and an angry golfer is likely to become a poor golfer. Remaining calm and considerate is not only good manners – it may also save you from wasting strokes.

"The golfer is very soon made to realize that his most immediate and perhaps most potent adversary is himself."

BOBBY JONES

Keeping the score
Arnold Palmer keeps a check on the scorecard.

Staying on course

THE LARGEST SECTION of the Rules of Golf covers the procedures to follow when a player has strayed from the straight and narrow of the fairway and ended up in a less than favourable position – a familiar situation to all of us. Here we look at finding your ball, what to do if you lose it, when and where you are entitled to take relief (and whether it carries a penalty), and how to avoid the wrath of the rule book when your shots stray away from their intended target.

Informal address
By never grounding his club, the great Jack Nicklaus is deemed not to have officially addressed the ball – thus avoiding potential penalties should the ball be moved or disturbed.

With personalized markings, a ball on the fairway should be easily identified, but it is not so easy when a ball is, for example, in deep rough or partly buried in a bunker. There are provisions for properly identifying a ball which many players do not realize, and which are a vital safeguard against the penalties for playing a wrong ball.

Players are entitled to lift, without penalty, a ball they believe to be their own for the purposes of identification. But before lifting the ball, they must announce their intention to opponents, markers, or fellow-competitors, and allow them to observe the lifting, placing, and marking of the position of the ball. The ball can be cleaned, but only to the extent necessary to identify it. In a bunker where a ball is covered or partially covered with sand, the sand may be brushed away to allow identification of the ball.

The penalties for playing the wrong ball can be harsh. In matchplay, a player playing the wrong ball loses the hole; in strokeplay the penalty is two shots – provided the error is discovered and rectified before the player tees off on the next hole.

It is a mistakenly held view by many players that, if they play a shot or shots with a wrong ball before discovering the error, the shots played with the wrong ball count in addition to the statutory two-shot penalty. Strokes played with a wrong ball do not count in a player's

Finding the right ball
No stranger to the rougher areas of a golf course, Seve Ballesteros realizes, more than most, the need to identify his ball clearly.

Name your ball
Golfers have all kinds of ways of identifying their ball, be it by distinctive names, or simply by marking with a pen.

Seve Ballesteros
1

score. If the wrong ball belongs to another competitor, its owner should place a ball on the spot from which the wrong ball was first played. In a sand or water hazard there are many difficulties involved in establishing ownership, therefore there is no penalty for playing the wrong ball.

BALL-AT-REST MOVED

One of the reasons Jack Nicklaus does not ground his club when addressing the ball is to reduce the possibility of incurring a penalty through moving a 'ball-at-rest' (Rule 18). Under the rules a player has 'addressed the ball' as soon as he takes his stance and grounds his club. If the ball moves from its position after the club is grounded at address, a penalty stroke is incurred.

By not grounding the club, Nicklaus is not considered to have formally addressed the ball. As a result, he would escape penalty if, for instance, the ball was moved by the wind as he prepared to make his stroke. (The one exception is in a hazard, when a player is considered to have addressed the ball as soon as he has taken his stance.)

Players are often confused about procedure when a ball is moved and a penalty has been incurred as a result.

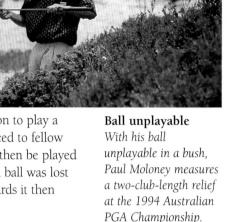

Ball unplayable
With his ball unplayable in a bush, Paul Moloney measures a two-club-length relief at the 1994 Australian PGA Championship.

If a player suspects he or she will have difficulty finding his or her ball, a provisional ball can be played from a point as near as possible to where the original ball was struck. However, the intention to play a provisional ball must be announced to fellow players. The provisional ball can then be played until the point where the original ball was lost is reached. From that point onwards it then becomes the ball in play.

BALL IN PLAY

There is also confusion when a player who, having hit a wayward tee-shot, cannot find his or her ball and then walks back to the tee to put another ball into play, only to discover that his or her playing partner, or a fellow competitor, has found the original ball. However, the rules are quite clear here.

Provided that the player has not put another ball into play, and the original ball has been located within five minutes of the start of the search, the player must return to the original ball and continue play with it. It is still the ball in play and must be played until the hole is completed (unless it is subsequently lost or struck out-of-bounds).

Frantic search
Watched by his caddie, Mark McNulty delves into the reeds in a search for his ball during the 1994 Peugeot French Open.

If a ball at rest is moved for any reason – other than by wind or water – it should be replaced. A lost ball or a ball out-of-bounds are among the most common problem areas. However, there is considerable confusion about what exactly constitutes a lost ball; the procedure for searching for it; the playing of the provisional ball; and what should happen when a ball is out-of-bounds.

AN 'OFFICIAL' LOST BALL

It is a misapprehension, and a common one, that a player can simply declare a ball 'lost'. A ball is only officially lost if:
1 It is not found or identified by the player after five minutes of searching for it.
2 The player has put another ball into play under the Rules, whether he or she has searched for the original ball or not.
3 The player has played a stroke with a provisional ball at the point (or nearer to the hole) where the ball is likely to be.

HOW TO DROP

In situations where the rules require the ball to be dropped, the player must stand upright, holding the ball both at shoulder-height and arm's-length, before dropping it. If the ball touches the player, fellow competitors, their caddies, or any of their equipment, it must be redropped without penalty. The ball must not be dropped nearer to the hole and must strike a part of the course where the applicable rule requires it to be dropped.

For example, for relief from interference (free drop) this is within one club-length of where it finished. For a ball that is unplayable, or has, for instance, landed in a water hazard (incurring a one-stroke penalty), the designated distance is two club-lengths. If the ball comes to rest outside the specified area, it must be redropped. But if, after a second attempt, the ball still rests outside the permitted distance, it should be placed as near as possible to the spot on which it struck the course when it was dropped for the second time.

Working it out
Sandy Lyle demonstrates the correct procedure for taking a drop.

Getting at the ball
Watched by an official during the 1994 Dunhill British Masters at Woburn, Miguel Martin tries to assess whether his ball is playable from the foot of a tree.

The player is the sole judge of when a ball is unplayable, and he or she can declare it unplayable anywhere on the course, except when it is in, or touching, a water hazard. Some players are unsure of the procedure after declaring a ball unplayable, but essentially there are three basic options:
1 The player can play a ball as near as possible to the spot from which the ball was last played.
2 The player can drop a ball within two club-lengths of the spot where the unplayable ball lay, but not nearer the hole.
3 The player can drop a ball behind the point where the unplayable ball lay, keeping that point directly between the hole and the spot on which the ball is dropped (there is no

limitation as to how far behind that point the ball may be dropped). The only variations occur when a ball is declared unplayable in a bunker. The second and third options can still be applied as long as the ball is dropped in the bunker. The penalty for dropping a ball in these circumstances is one stroke.

A ball suspected of being out-of-bounds is treated in the same way as a lost ball: if there is any doubt about whether the ball is out-of-bounds or not, then a provisional ball should always be played. Once again, the provisional ball can be played until the point where the original ball finished is reached. If the original ball is then discovered to be out-of-bounds, the provisional ball becomes the ball in play. If the original ball is still in bounds it remains the ball in play and must be played.

TAKING RELIEF
There are some situations in which a player is entitled to take relief from interference without incurring any penalty (dealt with under Rule 25). These situations include casual water (water that is not an integral part of the course, such as puddles), ground under repair, and certain damage to the course, such as holes or runways made by burrowing animals or birds.

Also included under this heading are any cuttings and clippings that may have been left around the course by the greenkeeping staff, television towers, power cables, and temporary grandstands. In any of these situations the player may drop the ball, without penalty, within one club-length of the nearest point of relief from the interference.

Another situation where relief without penalty can be taken involves loose impediments. These are defined under Rule 23 as "natural objects such as stones, leaves, twigs, branches and the like, dung, worms and insects and casts or heaps made by them,

IF IN DOUBT

Unlike professional tournaments, the amateur rarely has the opportunity to call upon a course official for an instant ruling. When a player is not sure how to proceed in a certain situation there is provision (Rule 3–3), though in strokeplay only, to play a second ball without penalty.

The player must, of course, inform his or her marker or fellow-competitor of what is intended, and with which ball he or she will be scoring. The facts must then be reported to the organizing committee as soon as possible before the card is officially returned.

This is a valuable rule to prevent undue delay on the course, and should always be encouraged and invoked whenever there is any doubt or disagreement about rights and procedure.

Working it out
Seve Ballesteros and an official discuss whether the Spaniard should have a free drop during the 1994 Volvo Masters at Valderrama.

provided they are not fixed or growing, are not solidly embedded and do not adhere to the ball." These can be removed without penalty, but if the ball moves as a result of touching a loose impediment, the player incurs a two-stroke penalty.

The most frequent transgression of this rule happens just off the putting green when a player decides to putt and removes sand or loose soil from his or her line. Sand and loose soil are only classed as loose impediments when they are lying on the putting green; if they are moved anywhere else on the course then the player is penalized two strokes.

ON THE GREEN

In the Rules of Golf, the putting green is defined as "all ground of the hole being played which is specifically prepared for putting or otherwise by the Committee". This is because there are rules which apply specifically to play on the green. For instance, a player is allowed to mark, lift, and clean a ball once it is on the green, although he or she must be careful to follow the correct procedures regarding marking and interfering with another player's line (see the box below). Unlike other areas of the course, certain types of damage to the surface can be repaired; pitch marks and old hole plugs are included here, but not any damage or scuffing made by players' shoe spikes.

A part of the green that sometimes causes confusion is the flagstick that marks the hole. A player, if playing on the green, can have the flag removed or held up, but if the ball touches the stick after a stroke has been played, a two-stroke penalty (strokeplay) or loss of hole (matchplay) is incurred. This does not apply to shots played from off the green.

Another area which can lead to some degree of confusion is when a ball stops on the lip of the hole, only to drop in sometime later. Under the rules, a player is allowed a "reasonable amount of time" to reach the ball, followed by a further 10 seconds. If the ball has still not dropped, the player must then play the ball. This particular misfortune befell Scottish Ryder Cup player Sam Torrance during the 1991 English Open. Torrance saw his putt drop, eventually, only to be penalized a stroke for not playing the ball within the required time.

Cloud burst
Seve Ballesteros takes relief from a puddle without penalty following a downpour at the appropriately named Saint Cloud course, the setting for the 1985 Paris Open.

LOCKE OFF HIS MARK

On his way to a fourth victory in the 1957 British Open at St Andrews, Bobby Locke of South Africa committed a famous, if inadvertent, breach of the Rules of Golf on the last green of the final round.

Locke had played a wonderful approach shot to the Home Green which ended up within 4ft (1.2m) of the hole. His playing partner, Bruce Crampton, requested that Locke mark the ball a putterhead-length away from his line in order to allow him a clear putt to the hole. The South African duly obliged but when he replaced the ball, he forgot to move the marker back to the original position of the ball. Locke then proceeded to hole his putt from the wrong point and accepted the applause which greeted his victory. It was not until an official recalled the incident later in the day that Locke's mistake was realized.

There was considerable discussion between officials over what should be done, but as Locke had won by three strokes and the famous Claret Jug had already been presented, they decided to take no action.

Newsreel film confirmed the breach of Rule 20 (Lifting, Dropping and Placing; Playing from Wrong Place). Strictly speaking, Locke should have been penalized two strokes for this breach of the rules, but as he would still have won, commonsense prevailed. This is a salutary lesson that the greatest care is required when a ball is marked and replaced. Locke's mistake was all too easy to make.

Bad mark
Bobby Locke prepares to hole out for the 1957 British Open title – albeit from the wrong place.

Dealing with water

LIKE THE REST of us, the top professionals are no strangers to water hazards, particularly in the United States where there is an abundance of water around many courses. However, the pros are very careful when it comes to procedure after finding water, and that is an example every golfer would do well to follow.

Dry lie
The red markers clearly indicate that Jose Maria Olazabal is playing the ball from a lateral water hazard. The fact that there is no trace of water in the hazard is irrelevant.

Consultation
New Zealander Greg Turner discusses his point of relief with an official after landing in the water at the 18th hole during the 1993 Italian Open.

Most golfers view water on, or beside, the course with fear and trepidation. This is hardly surprising; water hazards probably account for most penalty shots a golfer collects in his or her career. But water hazards, dealt with under Rule 26, are often a source of controversy when it comes to actually interpreting the rule.

Many players become confused in the belief that there are two types of water hazard, when this is not the case. The Rules of Golf define a water hazard as "any sea, lake, pond, river, ditch, surface draining ditch or other open water course (whether or not containing water) and anything of a similar nature." Water hazards are marked out on a course by yellow stakes and lines. But in addition, and this is where the confusion arises, the Rules make provision for a part of a water hazard to be defined as a "lateral water hazard" – a part of a water hazard "so situated that it is not possible or is deemed to be by the Committee to be impracticable to drop a ball behind the water hazard in accordance with Rule 26-1b." In effect, this means a water hazard that doesn't lie between the player and the green. A lateral water hazard should be clearly defined by red stakes or lines. It is simply a type of water hazard, yet it often causes breaches of Rule 26.

The basic procedure for dealing with a ball immersed in, lost in, or touching a water hazard is fairly simple. The options are:
1 A ball can be played from as near as possible to the spot from which the original ball was played.

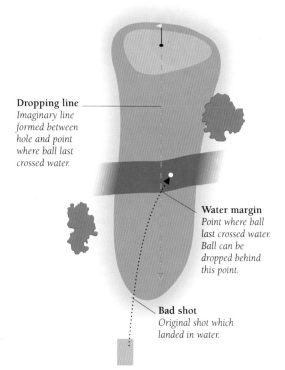

Dropping line
Imaginary line formed between hole and point where ball last crossed water.

Water margin
Point where ball last crossed water. Ball can be dropped behind this point.

Bad shot
Original shot which landed in water.

Where to drop from a water hazard
This diagram indicates where to drop the ball if you have landed in a water hazard.

2 A ball can be dropped behind the hazard, keeping the point at which the original ball last crossed the edge of the water hazard directly between the hole and the spot where the ball is dropped. There is no limit to how far back from the water hazard the ball may be dropped, provided the point of crossing the margin is kept in a line between the dropping point and the hole.
3 The player also has the option – though only rarely exercised – of playing the ball as it lies within the water hazard.

However, if the ball lands in a lateral water hazard, a player has a further option:

Out of the water
Payne Stewart opted to play the ball from the water rather than take a drop on the final hole of his 1989 Ryder Cup match with Jose Maria Olazabal. The gamble failed, and he lost the hole and the match.

Where to drop from a lateral water hazard
The additional dropping option from a lateral water hazard means that the ball can be dropped either side of the hazard, provided that it is within a two-club-length radius of the hazard margin and not nearer the hole.

Dropping line
Imaginary line formed between hole and point where ball last crossed water.

Drop zone 1
Ball can be dropped within this area.

Drop zone 2
Ball can be dropped within this area.

Drop zone 3
Ball can be dropped along this line as long as it is behind water hazard.

Bad shot
Original shot which landed in water.

4   A ball in a lateral water hazard may be dropped away from the hazard within two club-lengths of the point where the ball last crossed the water (Drop zone 1 on the illustration, right); or a point on the opposite margin of the water hazard equidistant from the hole (Drop zone 2). However, the dropped ball must not come to rest nearer the hole than the point where it last crossed the water on the original shot.

The most common breach of Rule 26 is in the correct establishment of where the ball last crossed the margin of the water hazard, particularly in the case of the lateral water hazard. The ball must be dropped in relation to where the ball *last crossed* the margin of the hazard. not where it *landed* in the hazard. This is particularly relevant if a ball pitches on dry land, before rolling or spinning back into the water.

The best way to deal with these situations is to go to the point where the ball was last on, or over, dry land before it crossed into the water. Also establish whether that point is within an area of yellow or red lines or stakes. From there, you can then work out the best course of action.

OTHER HAZARDS

The only other official 'hazard' to contend with on the golf course is a bunker, defined in the rules as "a prepared area of ground, often a hollow, from which turf or soil has been removed and replaced with sand or the like. Grass-covered ground bordering, or within, a bunker is not a part of the bunker. The margin of the bunker extends vertically downwards, but not upwards."

In a bunker, or indeed a water hazard, the rules do not permit a player to ground his or her club at any stage during address (see page 202). This means that the player must not touch the sand or the water before playing the ball. A common breach of this rule occurs when a player correctly addresses the ball in a bunker with the club well above the sand, but then accidentally brushes the sand while taking the club away on the backswing (see page 140).

This may be entirely unintentional, but it is in breach of the Rules of Golf. It is subject to a two-stroke penalty in strokeplay, and loss of the hole in matchplay. So take care – playing out of a bunker can be difficult enough without adding to your score before you have even hit the ball.

Getting out of sand safely
Nick Faldo shows how to play safely out of a bunker. His club does not make contact with the sand until just prior to impact.

Scoring the games of golf

THERE ARE ESSENTIALLY only two forms of scoring in the game of golf – matchplay, in which the number of holes won or lost decides the match, and strokeplay (medal) in which the number of strokes taken for a stipulated round is the deciding factor. However, within these two methods there are many variations designed to match players of differing abilities, and to add even greater interest to the game.

Although it is much more common in the professional game, strokeplay still plays a crucial part in the amateur game. Amateur clubs will normally hold 'monthly medal' contests as well as a number of other strokeplay competitions during the course of the season, and it is through playing in these events that a player's handicap is assessed (see page 209). Handicaps can be used in both strokeplay and matchplay as well as in play under the Stableford System (see below) where the player competes both against other competitors, and against the par of the course.

STROKE INDEX

The Stroke Index of a golf course is a rating system which assesses the degree of difficulty of a hole, and is vital for implementing a handicap during play. The No. 1 Stroke Index hole is therefore the most difficult while No. 18 is the least difficult. Players allocated strokes take them at the Stroke Index holes,

Conceding a putt
In matchplay, a player may concede a putt to his opponent rather than forcing him to hole out. One of the most famous and 'sporting' concessions came during the 1969 Ryder Cup when Jack Nicklaus conceded a 3ft (90cm) putt to Tony Jacklin, thereby ensuring the entire match was dramatically halved.

Versatile genius
Equally at home with strokeplay or matchplay, the great Walter Hagen won five British Opens. He was also a five-times winner of the USPGA when it was a matchplay championship.

up to and including the number equal to their handicap. For example, a player with a handicap of seven would receive strokes at the holes one to seven on the Index.

In 1983 the USGA developed a variant of stroke indexing, the Slope System. It is designed to provide a realistic assessment of a golf course's degree of difficulty. The system rates courses for the average player, as well as for the expert, and makes handicaps equitable and transferable to other clubs. It adjusts the strokes players receive when they are playing away from their home club. On a more difficult course, the higher Slope rating results

THE STABLEFORD SYSTEM

Stableford is a system of scoring first invented in 1932 by Sir Frank Stableford of the Wallesey Golf Club in England. Individual players compete against the par of the course under handicap and award themselves points as follows:

- Holing out in one stroke over the par for the hole – 1 point.
- Holing out in a score equal to the par for the hole – 2 points.
- Holing out in one stroke under the par for the hole – 3 points.
- Holing out in two strokes under the par for the hole – 4 points.
- Holing out in three strokes under the par for the hole – 5 points.

The player with the the highest number of points is the winner. When a player cannot score a point on a hole, he or she lifts the ball and moves on to the next hole. Stableford, and its various offshoots, is therefore a much quicker form of the game than strokeplay and, as such, is now a very popular form of the game with large groups and golfing societies.

in players receiving more strokes than usual. Conversely, players receive fewer strokes when they play at a course with a lower rating.

Since it was introduced, more than 12,000 courses in the United States have been re-rated. It is now used throughout Canada, and is gradually becoming accepted in the United Kingdom and the rest of the world.

MATCHPLAY

The most popular form of golf at club level by far is matchplay, not least because it is considerably quicker than strokeplay. In matchplay, a hole is won by the player, or a team of two, taking the least number of strokes for the hole; it is shared or 'halved' if both teams take the same number of strokes.

A match is decided over a stipulated round or number of holes, with the winning side being the side which is winning by more holes up than there are holes left to play. Where the allotted holes have been played and the sides are still level, the match may continue over stipulated holes until a conclusion has been reached.

The two most common forms of matchplay are fourball and foursomes contested between two teams of two players. In a fourball, the hole is simply won by the best scoring ball of the four played. In foursomes, only two balls are played (one by each team), with players taking it in turns to play their team's ball. Both these formats are used, along with singles matches, in contests such as the Ryder Cup.

Matchplay
Nick Faldo lines up a putt during the 1989 Ryder Cup. Despite being popular among club players, this is one of the rare occasions on which matchplay is played professionally.

FILLING IN YOUR SCORECARD

The scorecard is not only a record of your score but also a source of valuable information about the course, including distances and local rules. Your score is always recorded by a fellow player, therefore it is always worth taking some time at the end of a round to make sure that your marker hasn't filled in or added up your score incorrectly.

Tee lengths
Most courses have a selection of tees from which to play.

Hole length
Lengths of the holes measured from various tees.

Stroke Index
Holes at which allocated strokes have to be taken.

Score record
Column for recording strokes taken at each hole.

Points record
Column for recording points recorded at each hole (if playing under a points system).

Signatures
No card is valid without the signatures of player and marker.

HANDICAPPING

As handicapping is not covered in the Rules of Golf, there is no universal handicapping system; different countries employ their own schemes. However, all are based broadly along the lines of a golf course having a basic, or scratch, score. This is the score a top-class amateur player might expect to return under normal conditions.

A club player's handicap is calculated on the basis of their performance, over a certain number of rounds, compared to that standard score. The player will then receive strokes according to the stipulated Stroke Index of any course played.

In the United Kingdom, only scores returned in medal competitions are usually accepted for assessing handicaps, while in the United States the system allows for continuous reassessment of a player's handicap each time a round is completed. The USGA first developed a national handicapping system in the early 1920s, and now has a Handicap Research Team dedicated to updating and improving methods of assessment – such as the introduction of the Slope System. In the United Kingdom, the Council of National Golf Unions (CONGU) is the governing body in charge of all matters relating to handicapping.

Handicaps can also be taken into account under matchplay conditions. In these circumstances, the amount of strokes received by a player is three-quarters of the difference between the handicaps. For example if Player A had a handicap of 26 and Player B had a handicap of 13, then Player A would receive 10 strokes – the exact difference of 9.75 is rounded upwards.

GLOSSARY

A

Albatross Term used in Britain for a score of three under the **par** for a **hole**. In the United States this score is known as a **double-eagle**.

Approach Shot played to the **green** from the **fairway** or **rough**.

B

Back nine Second set of nine holes on an 18-hole golf course.

Balata Natural or synthetic compound used to make the cover for top-standard golf balls. Its soft, elastic qualities produce a high spin rate and it is favoured by tournament players.

Bent grass Type of fine-leafed grass that produces an ideal surface for putting greens. It is, however, difficult to maintain in hot climates.

Birdie Term used for a score of one under the **par** for a **hole**.

Bogey Term used for a score of one over the **par** for a **hole**.

Borrow British term for the amount a putt will deviate from a straight line due to the slope of the putting **green**.

Break American term for the amount that a putt will deviate from a straight line due to the slope of the putting **green**.

C

Carry Distance between the point from which a ball is played to the point where it lands. When the ball is hit over water or a bunker, it is said to 'carry' the hazard.

Cavity-back Iron clubhead designed with the weight on the periphery of the head to create a larger **sweet spot**.

Chip Low running shot normally played from near the edge of the **green** towards the **hole**.

Cross bunker Bunker lying across the line of the **fairway**.

Cut To miss the cut is to fail to score low enough, usually over the first 36 holes of a 72-hole tournament, to qualify for the final two rounds.

Cut shot Shot that makes the ball spin in a clockwise direction, resulting in a left-to-right bending flight. It can either be deliberate or a mistake.

D

Divot Piece of turf removed by the clubhead when a shot is played.

Dogleg Hole that sharply changes direction midway through, normally in the landing area for the tee-shot. It can either be a turn to the left or the right.

Dormie Term used in **matchplay** for the situation in which a player or team is leading by as many holes as there are left to play and therefore cannot be beaten.

Double-eagle Term used in the United States for three under the par for a **hole**. In Britain this score is known as an **albatross**.

Draw Method that decides who plays against whom in a matchplay competition, or a group of fellow competitors playing a strokeplay competition. Whoever is drawn first has the honour of playing first on the opening tee.

Draw (as a stroke) A stroke deliberately played with right-to-left spin (for a right-handed player) which causes the ball to curve from right to left in its flight.

Driver Club with a long shaft and little **loft** used for driving the ball the maximum distance from the **tee**.

E

Eagle Term that denotes a score of two under the **par** for a **hole**.

F

Fade Stroke deliberately played with left-to-right spin (for a right-handed player) that causes the ball to curve from left-to-right in its flight. An uncontrolled fade becomes a **slice**.

Fairway Area of closely mown turf between **tee** and **green**, which has as its boundary either longer grass known as semi-rough or completely uncut grass called **rough**.

Feathery Early type of golf ball made by filling a leather pouch with boiled feathers. It was highly susceptible to damage and began to go out of use in the mid-1880s after the introduction of the cheaper **guttie** ball.

Fourball Match involving four players in teams of two, in which each player plays their own ball.

Foursome Match involving four players in teams of two, in which each team plays one ball by alternate strokes. At the start of play each team decides which player will play the first tee-shot, after which they alternate the tee-shot on each hole.

Free drop Ball that is dropped without penalty away from an immovable obstruction, or in other circumstances, in accordance with the Rules of Golf.

Front nine First nine holes on an 18-hole golf course.

G

Graphite (carbon fibre) Carbon-based substance that, when bonded in layers, produces an exceptionally strong but very light material ideal for golf-club shafts. It is increasingly used also in the manufacture of clubheads.

Great Triumvirate Name given collectively to the three outstanding British professionals who dominated the game before the First World War: James Braid, J.H. Taylor, and Harry Vardon.

Green Area of closely mown grass specially prepared for putting, into which is cut the **hole**. It is separated from the fairway by the 'apron', a fringe of grass longer than the green but shorter than the fairway. Originally the term 'green' was used for a whole course, and hence a 'three-green' tournament was one played over three courses.

Guttie Ball introduced in 1848, made of gutta percha, a rubber-like substance obtained from the latex of a Malaysian tree species.

H

Handicap System that subtracts strokes from the scores of weaker players to enable people of varying abilities to play against each other on theoretically equal terms. The handicap is usually based on the average scores of a player set against a standard for a course.

Hanging lie Situation in which the ball rests on a slope running away from the player.

Haskell ball Name of the first **rubber-core ball** that revolutionized the game, invented by American, Coburn Haskell.

Hole General term for the whole region between **tee** and **green**, but also means the specific target in the ground. It has a standard diameter of 4¼in (10.8cm).

Hook Stroke that bends sharply to the left, caused by the application of anti-clockwise spin, either deliberately or unintentionally.

Hosel Socket on an iron-headed club that serves to connect the iron clubhead to the shaft.

I

Interlocking grip Method of gripping the handle of the club in which the little finger of the right hand intertwines with the forefinger of the left hand (the opposite applies for a left-handed player). It is usually favoured by players with small hands or short fingers to maintain a firm grip.

L

Lie   Situation in which a ball finishes after completion of a stroke. The lie can vary from good to bad, depending on how far the ball has settled down in the grass or, in the case of a bunker, in the sand.

Links   Stretch of ground beside the sea upon which golf is played. Linksland is usually low-lying, with sand dunes supporting fine, salt-resistant grasses. The word probably derives from the fact that linksland *links* the foreshore and agricultural land farther from the sea.

Loft   Angle of slope of a face of a club away from the vertical. The loft increases with the number of the iron, giving a higher flight trajectory and less distance.

LPGA   Acronym for Ladies' Professional Golf Association.

M

Matchplay   Form of competition in which the number of holes won or lost, rather than the number of strokes taken, determines the winner. The alternative and more common in the professional game is **strokeplay**.

Medal play   Alternative name for **strokeplay.**

Monthly Medal   Monthly **strokeplay** competition.

O

Off the pace   American expression to describe the number of strokes or the position of a player behind the leader of a tournament – for instance, 'two strokes off the pace'.

Overlapping grip   Another name for the **Vardon grip**.

P

Par   Estimated standard score for a hole, based on the length of the hole and on the number of strokes a first-class player would expect to take to complete it in normal conditions.

PGA   Acronym for the Professional Golfers' Association.

Perched lie   Situation in which the ball finishes suspended in rough grass slightly above the ground.

Pin high   A ball is said to be 'pin high' on the green when it has been played as far as the placement of the hole and any distance either side. It is also known as hole high.

Pitch   Lofted shot to a **green** with little run at the end of its flight.

Pitch-and-run   Stroke in which the ball is pitched onto the green making allowance for the run of the ball up to the hole. It is the opposite of a **pitch** shot.

Plugged lie   Situation in which a ball remains in the indentation or plug mark it makes when it lands. Except under a Local Rule which permits a plugged ball to be lifted and moved not nearer the hole without penalty, a plugged ball must be played as it lies.

Plus handicap   A handicap less than the scratch score of the course. Plus handicap players have strokes added to their score because they regularly beat the standard scratch score in medal play.

Pot bunker   Small, round, and deep bunker commonly found on traditional British links courses, such as the Old Course at St Andrews.

R

R & A   Acronym for the Royal & Ancient Golf Club of St Andrews – the governing body of golf in all countries except for the United States and Mexico.

Rough   Area of unmown grass alongside the **fairway** that punishes an off-line shot.

Rubber-core ball   The golf ball invented by Coburn Haskell that revolutionized the game at the turn of the century. Also known as the **Haskell ball**, it was composed of a solid rubber centre around which was wound many yards of elastic thread under tension. It was then covered in gutta percha. The rubber-core ball superseded the **guttie**.

S

Sand wedge   Extremely lofted club, also known as a 'sand iron', with a wide flange designed for playing from bunkers. The wide flange 'bounces' the clubhead through the sand. The American player Gene Sarazen is credited with its invention.

Scratch   Description of a golfer whose **handicap** equals that of the scratch score of the course. The scratch player gives strokes to all players with a higher handicap and receives strokes from players who have plus handicaps.

Shank   Badly mis-hit stroke in which the ball is usually struck with the hosel or socket of an iron-headed club.

Slice   Shot carrying considerable clockwise spin that consequently curves violently to the right.

Slot   Ideal position at the top of the backswing in which the club is set ready for the downswing.

Splash   Stroke from a bunker in which the sand wedge enters the sand before the ball and carries it out of the bunker on a cushion of sand.

Strokeplay   Form of competition in which the number of strokes a player takes to complete a round is compared with the other players' scores for a round. Strokeplay has largely supplanted the traditional **matchplay form** in professional tournament golf.

Stymie   Situation in which one player's ball blocked another player's ball's route to the hole. The stymied player was required to play over the top of the offending ball. The stymie was outlawed in 1951 by the **USGA** and the **R & A**.

Surlyn®   Trademark of a thermo-plastic resin similar to natural balata, used in ball manufacture. It is an extremely resilient material and virtually indestructible by clubs.

Sweet spot   Precise point on the face of a golf club, usually in the centre, that will deliver the maximum possible mass behind the ball. A ball struck at this point will travel farther than one struck on any other part of the face.

T

Tee   Closely mown area from which the first stroke on a hole is played. The term is also used to refer to the tee peg.

Topped   Stroke in which the club strikes the top of the ball, causing it to run along the ground.

U

Up and down   Approach shot and a single putt from anywhere off the green. Usually refers to holing out in two shots from a bunker or from just off the green.

USGA   Acronym for the United States Golf Association – the governing body for golf in the United States and Mexico.

USPGA   Acronym for the United States Professional Golfers' Association.

V

Vardon grip   Method of holding the handle of the club in which the little finger of the right hand overlaps the forefinger of the left (the opposite applies for left-handed players). Popularized, but not invented, by Harry Vardon. It is also known as the **overlapping grip**.

W

Whipping   Waxed thread used to bind the area on a club where the shaft meets the clubhead. Modern production techniques have made this practice redundant.

Y

Yips   Nervous disorder that can destroy a player's ability to putt, turning the stroke into a twitching or jerking movement.

INDEX

ACKNOWLEDGMENTS

Author's acknowledgments

It is of course in the very nature of things that there are many people to whom I owe an immense debt of gratitude for their help and support during the production of this volume.

I am very grateful to David Lamb of Dorling Kindersley for his encouragement in the development of this project and to James Harrison who worked so diligently and contributed so much to the early stages. To David Preston, who has been a hard-pressed and stoical editor in the face of his author's peripateticism for much of the project, I extend my warmest thanks. I am particularly grateful to Arthur Brown of Cooling Brown who has been not only a major contributor to the development of this project but a valued friend throughout. Alistair Plumb has done valiant work on the design side for which I am also very grateful.

I have been fortunate indeed to have had the technical assistance of Steve Newell. He has brought a wealth of knowledge and support to the project for which I am extremely grateful.

I am indebted to Mr Jamie Patino and all his staff for his kindness in making his wonderful club at Valderrama available for some of the photographic work, to Charlotta Sorenstam who so charmingly modelled for it, and to Dave Cannon of Allsport who captured it all on film. A special word of thanks to Steve Gorton and his photographic team for their invaluable contribution in the photographic studio, and to Ted Pollard and Mike Wood for their expert help.

Finally, I owe a very special debt of gratitude to Jane McCandlish, without whose unfailing support, encouragement, and cajolery this book would never have been completed. And to my very good friends Dr Ian Wallace and Dr Charlie Croll who without their early and recuperative summer morning challenges over the links of the Lundin Golf Club, the book might well have been completed in half the time!

Publisher's acknowledgments

Dorling Kindersley would like to thank the following for the kind loan of golfing equipment: The David Leadbetter Academy, Chart Hills; Footjoy; Proquip; Harold and Alma Swash of Align Engineering Ltd; Roy Stirling at Silvermere Golf Club; Titleist; and Wilson Sporting Goods.

Thanks also to the following golf clubs for providing valuable reference and information: Augusta National Golf Club, The Belfry, Pebble Beach Golf Links (Pebble Beach and Pebble Beach Golf Links are trademarks and trade dress of Pebble Beach Company), Royal Liverpool Golf Club, and Turnberry Hotel and Golf Courses; and to the following people and organizations for their help during the creation of this book: Biovision; Bernard Cooke for the kind loan of his teaching films; the PGA European Tour; all the staff at the USPGA; Matthew Farrand and Andrea Sadler for editorial assistance; The Maltings Partnership for illustrations; Arthur Phillips for computer artworks; and Libby Pepper and Strokesaver for artwork references. The design and editorial input of Roger Tritton, Tracy Hambleton-Marsh, and Bob Gordon was also greatly appreciated.

Picture credits

(Abbreviations: b=below, c=centre l=left, r=right t=top)
Allsport, 28l, 28tr, 45br, 46tl, 69tl, 76bc, 94l, 147tr, 177c, 183t, 183b, 195t, 195b, 199t, 202b, 203tl, 203tr, 203b, 209t. Allsport/ Hulton Deutsch, 15tl, 16tl, 16tr, 16bl, 17tl, 17tr, 17br, 19t, 20l, 22b, 26t, 26b, 45bl, 47tl, 47tr, 135tr, 205bl. Allsport/MSI, 188l, 189r. Howard Boylan/Allsport, 21r, 76bl, 107br, 201b. Simon Bruty/Allsport, 35tl, 45tl, 46bl, 78tr, 143bl. Dave Cannon/Allsport, 6, 23tr, 29tr, 30–31, 32tl, 38tl, 40tl, 46tr, 47bl, 47bctr, 58–59, 59tr, 68tl, 68tr, 68b, 69l, 69br, 69tr, 71bl, 73bl sequence, 78–79 sequence, 79tl, 80tl sequence, 80bl sequence, 83tr sequence, 84tr sequence, 87bl sequence, 88tr, 90–91-sequence, 91tl, 99tr, 99tc, 101br sequence, 104tr, 104–105 sequence, 105tl, 109br-sequence, 114–115 sequence, 117r sequence, 119tr sequence, 120b, 122tl, 124tr, 124–125-sequence, 126tr, 128tr, 129tr sequence, 130br, 133tr, 139 sequence, 141tr sequence, 142c, 142tl, 143tl, 144tr, 148tr, 153tr, 156–157 sequence, 157tr, 158bl, 159tr, 162bl, 163tr, 164bl, 165tl, 166–167 sequence, 167tl, 168tr, 170tr, 172tr, 176b, 178t, 179c, 184, 185t, 190b, 201t, 204t, 207t. Russell Cheyne/Allsport, 97tl. Phil Cole/ Allsport, 39tr. Mike Cooper/Allsport, 84tr. John Gishigi/ Allsport, 177t, 206b. Michael Hobbs/ Allsport, 186b. Phil Inglis/ Allsport, 136-sequence. Rusty Jarrett/ Allsport, 114tr. Trevor Jones/Allsport, 161tr, 175, 192t, 193t. Joe Mann/Allsport, 177b. James Meehan/ Allsport, 190/l. Steve Munday/ Allsport, 23tl, 36br, 44bl, 90tr, 103tr, 106l sequence, 113tr, 115tl, 151tr, 155tr, 176t, 200t, 205t, 206t, 207b. Adrian Murrell/ Allsport, 47br. Jon Nicholson/ Allsport, 44tl. Gary Newkirk/ Allsport, 156tr, 166tr. Gary Prior/Allsport, 142bl. Dave Rogers/ Allsport, 174–175. Pascal Rondeau/Allsport, 42–43, 142br. Dan Smith/Allsport, 143tr. Anton Watt/ Allsport, 44tr, 69tc, 99tl. Sarah Baddiel, 14t, 14b, 15l, 15tr, 21b, 24tl, 24r, 25br. Colorsport, 23bl, 187t. Frank Gardner, 208b. Golf World, 18t, 24b. Imperial Tobacco, 25t. Jollands Editions, 18l. Lawrence Levy, 121tr-sequence. London News Agency, 20r. G. Low, 93bl. Brian Morgan, 181tl, 182b, 187r, 189l. Popperfoto, 21t, 22t, 48tr, 180t, 208t. Phil Sheldon, 46br, 62–63 all sequences, 89tr, 178b, 185b, 191, 193b, 194t, 196–197, 198tl, 200b, 204b, Sothebys, 15br, 31t. USGA, 19b, 181tr, 198b, 199b.

40–687